My Brother's Keeper

To Paul + Lori —

I hope you enjoy this take on McGovern +
his career.

all The Best,

Mark A. Lempke

My Brother's Keeper

GEORGE McGOVERN AND PROGRESSIVE CHRISTIANITY

Mark A. Lempke

University of Massachusetts Press
Amherst & Boston

Copyright © 2017 by University of Massachusetts Press
All rights reserved
Printed in the United States of America

ISBN 978-1-62534-277-5 (paper); 276-8 (hardcover)

Designed by Jack Harrison
Set in Adobe Garamond Pro
Printed and bound by The Maple-Vail Book Manufacturing Group

Cover design by Jack Harrison
Cover photograph: Democratic Presidential candidate George S. McGovern
speaking at an Operation Breadbasket rally held in his honor, August 26, 1968.
(Photo by Declan Haun/The LIFE Picture Collection/Getty Images).

Library of Congress Cataloging-in-Publication Data
A catalog record for this book is available from the Library of Congress.

British Library Cataloguing-in-Publication Data
A catalog record for this book is available from the British Library.

This book is dedicated with love to my parents,
Charles and Carol Lempke.

Contents

Preface

As the plane began its descent into Singapore, where I was about to start a new job, I watched bolts of lightning hurtle to earth outside my window. A nervous traveler even in the best of circumstances, I fully believed the plane's destruction was imminent. Yet my seatmate, seemingly oblivious to our peril, chose this moment of our eleven-hour flight to share his opinions about the state of the world: "All the world's problems—right now and back long ago—come down to religion." As he counted examples on his fingers—the Crusades, Islamic radicalism, Northern Ireland—I realized that he saw religion as little more than a smokescreen for territorial violence and greed. "Don't you think so?" he inquired. I did not think so at all. But doubly apprehensive about starting a new job on a new continent if I was spared, and a fiery crash if I was not, I muttered a noncommittal answer and betrayed no disagreement. I think of this book as the answer I wish I had given if I'd had my wits about me on that flight.

Replaying the exchange in my head, I've recalled the long tradition of progressive, reform-minded Christianity in the United States. Frequently, traces of humanitarianism and social reform have surfaced even in very theologically conservative corners of American Christianity—such as my alma mater, Houghton College. Sponsored by the Wesleyan Church, the college banned alcohol, smoking, and dancing on campus. Well into the 1980s, even playing card games was forbidden. The Wesleyans were steadfast in their cultivation of personal holiness and in earlier times had also taken a firm stance against slavery and hosted the famous gathering in Seneca Falls, New York, that began the women's suffrage movement. That progressive legacy survived in unexpected ways, as I learned when I was a junior at Houghton. Fascinated by presidents and presidential elections since childhood, I came across a tidbit that intrigued me while researching a term paper: I learned that George McGovern's father, Reverend Joseph McGovern, had been one of Houghton Seminary's first generation of students. To me, this seemed deeply paradoxical. Despite the Wesleyans' reformist past, almost everyone on campus believed that conservatism was the appropriate political philosophy for the Christian life. It strained my imagination to accept that one of the most iconic liberals of the past fifty years had come from an austere Bible-believing background.

In time, curiosity gave way to research, and the rich vein of material I found demonstrated that the story of George McGovern's life and his 1972 campaign could serve as a useful narrative arc in a study of the fortunes of progressive Christianity in postwar America. At the start of McGovern's public career, progressive, social justice–oriented Protestant Christianity was a cornerstone of respectable civic life. Although often establishmentarian in character, it also carried a strong prophetic element that challenged the powerful and supported marginalized communities. In the 1960s and early 1970s, liberal churchmen and liberal politicians such as McGovern worked together against war and hunger and in favor of a robust, inclusive Christian humanism. Even a band of radical evangelicals, suspicious of conventional liberalism but devoted to social justice, was attracted to the politics of conscience espoused by McGovern during these years. These "McGovern Evangelicals" became the unlikely torchbearers for progressive Christianity during the Reagan years and beyond, as mainline attendance declined and liberals such as McGovern lost their offices. In recent years, American progressive religious history has enjoyed new vitality, and it is likely that the singular candidacy of Bernie Sanders may inspire a deeper study of social and participatory democracy in America. In the United States, the histories of liberal religion and social justice are entwined and need to be told in tandem. As my seatmate on the plane might have been surprised to learn, progressive Protestants such as McGovern were often the most prominent voices in support of alleviating suffering and want in a hurting world.

As I uncovered McGovern's role in this story, I accrued many debts of gratitude—among them, to the archivists and librarians who climbed ladders, retrieved boxes, and gave me sound advice. I thank Laurie Langland and Danelle Orange, caretakers of the McGovern Collection at Dakota Wesleyan University. Laurie, in particular, was indispensable in tracking down many of the photographs reprinted in this book. I also thank Marc

Gordon at Drew University, Regine Heberlein at Princeton University's Mudd Library, and Wayne Weber and Bob Schuster at Wheaton College's Billy Graham Center Archives in Illinois. In addition, I am grateful to the many McGovernites who consented to interviews. Nearly everyone I approached graciously agreed to share their insights into their work in the 1972 election and as well as their understanding of faith and politics. I particularly appreciate the contributions of George McGovern and James Armstrong. During what turned out to be the final years of his life, Senator McGovern twice took time out of his busy schedule to talk with me. I was struck by his candid tone, his precise memory, and his ongoing commitment to ending hunger. Dr. Armstrong, for his part, kindly invited me to his home, participated in a long and frank interview, and gave me access to many of his personal files.

The team at the University of Massachusetts Press helped this rookie book author navigate the road to publication. In particular, I commend my editor Matt Becker for his patience and aplomb, especially given that large sections of this book were composed far away from him in Singapore, where I teach for most of the year at SUNY Buffalo's overseas campus. Many others, including Dawn Potter, Carol Betsch, and Mary Bellino, contributed their expertise in preparing the book for publication. My students in Singapore also deserve a share of credit; they have given me a fresh interpretation on American life from an Asian perspective and have forced me to answer complicated and sometimes uncomfortable questions about where my country has been and where it is headed. My supervisors, Patricia Shyhalla and Kevin McKelvey, have fostered a great working environment that lets me balance time for writing with the teaching that I love. I am grateful to everyone who has read parts of the manuscript or helped me wrestle with its more difficult questions. Gail Radford has probably seen more of this project than anyone else and has always been a sharp critic, a helpful mentor, and a living example of progressivism in action. I also thank Rick Mikulski, David Swartz, Christopher Evans, Claude Welch, David Gerber, Michael Frisch, Jon Lauck, David Herzberg, Jim Stanley, Jay Learned, Jennifer Willford, Bruce Miroff, Rebekah Ramsay, and Zachary Van Tassel. Of course, my wife has been my most steadfast supporter. Thank you, Heather, for your affection and encouragement throughout and beyond the writing process. I know that I have found my perfect running mate.

This book is lovingly dedicated to my parents. Their patience, love, and generosity of spirit have always been an example that I hold close to my heart. So this book goes out to my mom, who turned eighteen the year McGovern ran for president, when she cast her very first vote for him. It also goes out to my dad, who insists that he doesn't remember whom he voted for that year (or if he voted at all), thus manifesting a strand of amnesia common among Nixon voters.

My Brother's Keeper

Introduction

There is a grim adage in Washington that a statesman is merely what one calls a politician after rigor mortis sets in. When George McGovern died on October 21, 2012, at the age of ninety, the word *statesman* was uncharacteristically used in earnest and not as a euphemism. Most of the headlines and tributes described him as a stalwart liberal, a voice of peace, and an unlikely war hero. The *Washington Post*'s headline praised him as a "Patriot and Hero." CNN eulogized him as "a politician who cared more about being on the right side of an issue than on the popular side." President Barack Obama called him "a statesman of great conscience."[1] Vice-President Joe Biden, McGovern's colleague in the Senate for eight years, spoke at the memorial service, spinning yarns about how McGovern's opposition to the war in Vietnam had inspired him to enter politics.[2] McGovern's friend and occasional adversary Senator Bob Dole mourned his death and recalled their mutual work to provide school lunches in classrooms throughout the developing world. Grasping at straws on a morning news program, Newt Gingrich, a former speaker of the House, recalled McGovern's sense of humor. Gingrich remembered the senator's rueful frustration with bureaucratic red tape—in particular, as he was running a guesthouse in Connecticut and wading through the regulations he had once voted for.[3]

Most of the eulogizers tactfully waited two or three sentences before mentioning what most Americans knew about McGovern. Despite all of his work in defining and defending liberalism, he was, to put it indelicately, a loser. As the Democratic candidate, he had lost the 1972 presidential race by a landslide, winning only Massachusetts and the District of Columbia and failing to earn even 40 percent of the popular vote. One of the most striking elements of his defeat had been his poor performance with historically

Democratic groups. Blue-collar workers and Catholics had voted against him in unprecedented numbers, and he was the first nominee in his party's history who had failed to carry a single southern state.[4]

The reasons for the loss were manifold. Richard Nixon's incumbency and accomplishments such as his historic trip to China had made him a formidable opponent. The president had also outplayed McGovern's strongest suit, the American public's antipathy toward the war in Vietnam. Nixon's team had expertly timed public promises of disengagement, releasing them at key moments in the campaign and even declaring, shortly before the election, that "peace is at hand."[5] Among those who longed for the troops to come home but craved a strong and proud America, Nixon was making a compelling case. In contrast, McGovern's call for a rapid peace in Vietnam contributed to his public image as a radical with rabid supporters, and many in his own party fought mightily against his nomination, uniting under the aegis of Anybody but McGovern. Other voters' shaky confidence in McGovern collapsed when he chose Missouri senator Tom Eagleton as his running mate, only to accept Eagleton's resignation eighteen days later, after his history of mental illness became public knowledge.

For years, the term *McGovernism* has been a catchword for leftwing enthusiasm and countercultural indiscipline run amok. In most political discourse, to be compared to George McGovern has not been a compliment. Rather, it suggests an un-American radicalism, a dangerous naïveté, and the cardinal sin of American politics: unelectability. At various points in the 1980s, Republican provocateurs even invited McGovern to their opponents' rallies, offering to pay his airfare because they believed that any Democratic candidate would be tarnished by association with him.[6] On the cartoon sitcom *Futurama,* where the cryogenic head of Richard Nixon serves as President of Earth in the year 3000 A.D., Nixon laments a foolish action by sighing, "What a McGovern I've been."[7] Scholars of history and political science have put forward variations of this view, seeing McGovern's campaign as a rupture in the history of liberalism and a crisis point for the Democratic Party, which went on to struggle throughout the late 1970s and into the Reagan, Bush, and Clinton years.[8] At the turn of the millennium, few saw leftwing liberalism as a selling point, and most observers believed that any successful Democrat would need to reclaim the vital center.

Within the past few years, however, a new political calculus has called this interpretation into question. Only two weeks after the senator's death, Barack Obama, running on a peace and social justice platform, was reelected as president. Though Obama's commitment to these ideals was not always perfect, the coalition that gave him a solid victory (just shy of four percentage points over Mitt Romney) bore a striking resemblance to the coalition that had carried McGovern to his ignoble defeat in 1972. In 2012, Obama won with even fewer working-class white and urban ethnic voters than he had in 2008, thus shedding the last vestiges of the New Deal coalition in the Democratic Party. Instead, the voters courted by McGovern's campaign—single women, African Americans, Latinos, young people, and gay and lesbian citizens—showed up in numbers significant enough to tip the scales. These groups, which were just beginning to organize in McGovern's day, had become political veterans with a cogent sense of identity and a proven capacity to get out the vote. They took notice when Tea Party members focused on idealizing a time in the nation's history when marginalized voices had been stifled. The pundits John B. Judis and Ruy Teixeira, explicitly took note of this demographic sea change, calling it "George McGovern's revenge."[9] Conservatives are fond of saying that Barry Goldwater had actually won in 1964; it just took sixteen years—Reagan's election—to count all the votes. Likewise, Obama's reelection in 2012 was, in some ways, McGovern's victory, arriving forty years behind schedule.

Other 2012 events also demonstrated the declining influence of Christian conservatism, which had swept McGovern from the Senate in 1980 and given Republicans a reliable voting bloc for the next thirty years. In the Republican presidential primaries, the Christian conservative candidates, Michelle Bachmann and Rick Santorum, were both soundly rejected in favor of Mitt Romney, who favored fiscal discipline and managerial competence over culture wars. For the first time, voters rejected a signature religious Right objective: the prohibition of same sex marriage. Even other conservatives began to see the faction as more of a hindrance than a help. During the Great Recession that began in 2008, Mitch Daniels, the governor of Indiana, suggested reaching a "truce" on social issues so that Republicans could focus on free-market messages.[10] The conservative columnist Ross Douthat condemned the Christian nationalism of Bachmann, Sarah Palin, and Mike Huckabee, as having "embodied evangelical politics at its worst" and noted that "the tendency toward purely sectarian appeals [and] the reliance on the language of outrage and resentment" might mobilize religious voters but would leave scorched earth in its wake.[11]

Now the religious Right seemed to be serving everyone badly, including its own foot soldiers, who were supplying the votes and the grassroots activity but rarely seeing any satisfactory gains. As the twentieth century drew to a close, Cal Thomas and Ed Dobson, two lieutenants of the Moral Majority during the 1980s, lamented that the movement was a failure because "real change must come from the bottom up" and its leaders had become transfixed by political power at the expense of personal faith.[12] In a study of young evangelicals under the age of thirty, researchers found that 50 percent of respondents believed that the Church was engaging in politics badly, 80 percent believed that it was antigay, and 47 percent thought it was hypocritical.[13] Even worse for the movement, the percentage of Americans who identified as evangelicals was beginning to dwindle, from a Reagan-era high of more than a third of the population to perhaps a quarter of the population today.[14]

Accordingly, fewer and fewer see politicking as a priority. One pastor in his early thirties has written, "Like most young evangelical ministers, I am less concerned with politics than with the exodus of my generation from the church."[15] Yet the scorched-earth tactics of the culture wars continue, even as aging veterans of the religious Right approach demographic midnight. We are all the poorer for these wars, and the American public is left with the bitterness, distrust, and suspicion that arose from a long struggle between the forces of so-called Christian patriotism and secular humanism. Francis Schaeffer Jr., whose father was a key architect of this dichotomy, has since repented of his role in the affair. Evangelicals, he believes, were misled by their leaders into voting for a program of giveaways for the wealthy, thus becoming "cannon fodder in a larger political battle."[16]

Growing numbers of younger religious voters agree that, in the words of the social activist Shane Claiborne, "when we [look] at the Moral Majority, we [see] the inconsistency of the Church."[17] From their point of view, conservative Christians have neglected the Bible's clear teachings about caring for the poor, showing compassion to immigrants and sojourners, and practicing a wise stewardship of the earth's resources. At the same time, the Democratic Party has hardly seemed to be a welcoming alternative for voters of faith. The journalist Amy Sullivan notes that John Kerry's 2004 campaign hired only two employees to cover religious outreach. As one of his advisers blithely said, "we don't do white churches," thereby effectively conceding most voters of faith to the candidate's opponent.[18] The subtitle of *God's Politics,* written by the well-known progressive evangelical Jim Wallis, directly underscores their dilemma: "why the Right is wrong and the Left doesn't get it."[19]

Many of the faithful who dislike choosing between callous conservatism and irreligious liberalism have wondered if there is another way for Christians to engage in politics. I believe that George McGovern's career and his 1972 campaign offer an overlooked example of the possibilities for a prophetic and politically progressive form of Christianity. This religious ethos made significant inroads into national politics, even as it ran counter to the nationalism and militarism that ruled in mainstream culture during the Cold War. As McGovern called for a politics based on compassion, inclusion, and uplift for the most vulnerable, he showed how Judeo-Christian and humanist ethics could reinforce rather than short-circuit one another. One of the great foundations of McGovern's worldview was his devotion to social Christianity and his belief that religious faith was best put to use by transforming the world. His presidential campaign was rooted in the reform-minded Protestantism that was dominant earlier in the twentieth century, particularly in the social gospel and the ecumenical movements. The political stances for which he was best known—improving access to nutritious foods and limiting American militarism—came from this philosophy. He was a godfather of modern progressive Christianity, and many of its current leaders have direct ties to his 1972 campaign.

In McGovern's progressive Christianity, people were called to transcend self-interest and live as though their salvation depended on others' well-being. According to this vision, no one could enjoy comfort while another suffered from want, and peace was the highest form of patriotism. The epistemic truth of Christ's resurrection or the concept of eternal life were beside the point to McGovern; the value of faith lay in how it guided relationships among the living. On the campaign trail he trumpeted these ideas with missionary zeal. He saw his campaign as an opportunity to convince Americans to abandon the unneighborly insularity and self-interest that he associated with Nixon and his "Silent Majority" of Americans weary of subaltern protest.[20]

Just as Reagan's background as a lifeguard and an actor defined his approach to politics, McGovern's time as a preacher's son, a student pastor, and a historian at odds with the Cold War consensus helped to shape his moralizing and schoolmasterly tone. His vision drew heavily from the theologians of the social gospel, an early twentieth-century movement that urged American Christians to view sin as structural and communal. Its leaders nudged the movement's largely middle-class followers into transforming slums and other forgotten places, though adherents often confused the Christian life with middle-class respectability. In the 1950s and 1960s, such activism was common among leaders of mainline Protestantism—the period's more theologically liberal, liturgical, socially conscious, and culturally prominent denominations, which were in easy conversation with one another. In an institutional sense, the mainline churches can be described as the seven sisters: the American Baptist Churches, the Disciples of Christ, the Episcopal Church, the Lutheran Church, the Presbyterian Church USA, the United Churches of Christ, and the United Methodist Church.[21] But more important than the individual denominations were the common prestige they gave, the trust they generated, and the moral authority they bestowed.

In a 2011 address to the Organization of American Historians, David Hollinger noted, "If you were in charge of something big before 1960, chances are that you grew up in a white Protestant milieu."[22] During the Eisenhower era's historically high church membership, mainline leaders used this influence and prestige to exert a voice in public affairs and secure access to the halls of power. The National Council of Churches (NCC), founded in 1950, was the chief ecumenical means through which mainline churchmen engaged with one another. The organization had an enviable influence on public affairs, for its churches were traditional pillars of American society, and most political leaders belonged to one of them. Yet times changed. Even though NCC leaders exerted their influence successfully during the civil rights movement, their protest of the Vietnam War and other left-of-mainstream causes generated acrimony in their congregations.

The same worldview that guided the mainline churches contributed to McGovern's conviction that the Vietnam War was not just mistaken policy but a grave moral error. As a lay representative of Methodism and an engaged parishioner, he attended Sunday services, corresponded with church leaders, and joined in many ecumenical functions. One of his closest friends from the late 1960s onward was James Armstrong, a prominent Methodist bishop, war critic, and ecumenist. Together, the two fashioned a working relationship between clergyman and statesman, attempting to give war protest a greater air of moral respectability during a time when most Americans associated dissent with unkempt longhairs and dangerous radicals such as Abbie Hoffman.

Believing they had a pastoral obligation to hasten the war's end, many of these churchmen openly endorsed McGovern's candidacy, secure in the knowledge that the senator was similar to themselves. Their organization,

Religious Leaders for McGovern, attracted support from the highest echelons of American Protestantism. Yet its effectiveness was hindered by the same problems that were besieging the mainline as a whole during these years. It was bureaucratic and top-heavy, and its leaders absurdly expected that prominent names on a letterhead would influence how the laity perceived the key issues of their time. The organization typified the concerns of many churchgoers, who believed that their pastors and bishops were getting too political and too critical of their country and were neglecting the local duties of pastoral care. This discord between the pulpit and the pews anticipated a rising double crisis for the mainline churches: a distrust of church leadership and a marked decline in absolute numbers.

At the same time, McGovern's reputation for bold condemnations of the war attracted attention from a group that was new to American politics: young evangelicals committed to social justice. Some are still active leaders today—among them, Ron Sider of Evangelicals for Social Action, Jim Wallis of Sojourners, and Richard Mouw of Fuller Seminary. Theologically, they held the Bible in a higher and more literal regard than the mainliners did, and they took the cross and the resurrection as historical truths upon which any political activity must be premised. Socially, these young men and women had grown up in the evangelical subculture of the 1950s, sometimes called the neo-evangelical movement, and had thus been active conscripts in the Cold War. Even the most open-minded of these evangelicals viewed mainline perspectives as apostasy. Many alternately begrudged the mainliners' prestige and disdained their liberal theology, which often took the Bible as example and metaphor rather than revealed truth. Among this group, Billy Graham was the exception who proved the rule.[23] Although he was well respected and enjoyed close relationships with every president from Eisenhower onward, most evangelicals were on the outside looking in.

These young men and women heard their neo-evangelical elders calling for increased attention to social problems but also saw that they were doing little to implement that vision, having largely sat out both the civil rights movement and the War on Poverty. Like more secular activists of their generation, the neo-evangelical progeny published journals, taught classes, and toiled in the cities, urging others to recognize that a serious belief in the Bible meant a serious commitment to social justice. Their understanding of political activism often involved personal discipleship rather than direct government action. To some, it meant living modestly among the poor. For others, it meant withholding taxes that funded the military and accepting the consequences. Some were veterans of the New Left and cherished its ideals of participatory democracy; others were Calvinists who wished to turn the state toward holy purposes. Still others came from historic peace churches and advocated a life of holier and simpler living. Eventually these diverse factions were brought together under the banner of a group called Evangelicals for McGovern, founded by Ronald J. Sider, a teacher at an inner-city Philadelphia campus.

Even as McGovern's career was shaped by the progressive Christian tradition, his campaign was a crucial moment that altered the tradition's trajectory. Politically, his campaign "drove out the old guard" in the Democratic Party, as one political scientist put it, in ways even he did not fully anticipate.[24] Likewise, his inclusive campaign engaged the young, socially conscious evangelicals who would ultimately wrest the mantle of progressive Christianity from the old-guard Protestants. At the beginning of the Kennedy era, progressive Christianity was a strong, confident, cultural force dominated by the mainline churches. Over the course of the 1970s, it became a smaller but no less conscientious movement whose energy and dynamism resided in young evangelicals. By virtue of his long alliance with the mainline and because his campaign welcomed evangelicals in ways that few liberal enterprises did, McGovern played an understated (and somewhat unwitting) role in shifting progressive Christianity's center of gravity.

Examining this transformation highlights a problem in definition: just what is progressive Christianity? By "progressive" I do not mean theologically liberal (the McGovern evangelicals would certainly have objected to that). Instead, I mean a program of political and spiritual reform built around four precepts that bridge the devotion to social justice shared among the diverse strands of American Christianity.

1. *An affinity for the marginalized.* Progressive Christians, whether mainline or evangelical, Catholic or Orthodox, see an inequitable access to power (including the power that comes from wealth) as a deep social and moral problem. Their activism engages people who have historically been voiceless, a group that may include the poor, racial minorities, women, immigrants, the disabled, criminals, the hungry, and, depending on the branch, the unborn or sexual minorities. Crucially, they do not view *themselves* as marginalized, a decision that differentiates them from both liberation theology as practiced in the global South and the resentment-fueled politics of the religious Right in the United States.

2. *A prophetic approach.* When addressing major problems in society, many progressive Christians find a model in the prophet Amos, who in his short book in the unfashionable section of the Old Testament cries out against empty ritual, senseless war, and the hoarding of extravagant wealth. Instead, he speaks for the widow, the orphan, and the stranger. Whereas the religious Right assumes that it is a natural majority under attack from a small corps of political and media elites, progressive Christians usually acknowledge that they are a natural "moral minority," in the words of the historian David Swartz.[25] This means that they self-consciously voice perspectives that cut against the grain of the wider Christian community, viewing themselves as a faithful but countercultural force trying to point the way back to holiness.

3. *A political program of peace and social justice.* Generally, progressive Christians do not glory in violent solutions to conflict, preferring negotiations, diplomacy, and active peacemaking. In the 1970s, this approach was tantamount to a rejection of Kissinger-era realism, which saw ethical concerns as distractions. "Prophetic politics," writes Jim Wallis, "finds its center in fundamental moral issues like children, diversity, family, community, citizenship, and ethics."[26] Among progressive Christians, the prevailing philosophy is that human hurt and human need should not be ignored and that good people usually make things better in partnership. Unlike some members of the modern Left, who are libertarian on social issues, progressive Christians tend to insist on holy interconnection and mutual responsibility. Many believe that sick systems contribute to poverty, violence, exploitation, and discrimination, perhaps through poor education or because of laws that reflexively punish rather than rehabilitate. Today, however, religious progressives seriously disagree about what social justice might look like, particularly with respect to abortion, same-sex marriage, and the contraceptive mandates raised by the Supreme Court's 2014 Hobby Lobby decision. They also disagree about the best way to address human need. Some prefer a robust social democracy with greater opportunities for state-guaranteed food, housing, education, and security. Others desire a more hands-on approach, choosing to identify with and live among people at the margins of society, where they work to balance advocacy with relationships.

4. *Meaningful ecumenism.* As I will discuss later in this book, McGovern sought aid from evangelical Christians at a time when the ecumenical movement itself—comprised largely of mainline Protestant ministers

with assistance from Catholics and Jews—did not. Ecumenism, as Jill K. Gill, one of the movement's preeminent historians, defines it, "transcends cultural biases through listening to others; creating a church witness that speaks truth to power." She argues that it remains "separate from government, political parties, and cultural bandwagons in order to preserve its voice and identity as the church."[27] In fact, however, McGovern's base of support was broadly ecumenical; he received explicit support from mainline, evangelical, and other religious figures who committed themselves to a conscientious partisanship in order to stymie the war machine.

In this book, I focus almost entirely on the Protestant branch of progressive Christianity, though I recognize that like-minded Catholics were plentiful during these years. The brothers Philip and Daniel Berrigan fiercely opposed the Vietnam War, Sister Mary Luke Tobin had a long history of activism against nuclear proliferation, and Dorothy Day championed a robust agenda of working-class rights and an equitable distribution of wealth. Nonetheless, the bulk of McGovern's religious support came from Protestants, and his revivalist language alienated a large number of Catholics, as Chapter 5 will show.

Much of the tension in my narrative is linked to a long-running family feud within American Protestantism: the inability of mainliners and evangelicals to play nicely with one another. Their contrasting theological cultures and years of shared mistrust challenged any attempt at a true partnership for social justice. An even greater challenge was the fact that most Americans did not agree with the progressive Christian view that they were complicit in the nation's misdirection during the Cold War. Many citizens saw critiques by McGovern and his supporters as unpatriotic and fault-finding. His colleague in the Senate, Herman Talmadge of Georgia, spoke for many when he declared that McGovern spoke as though "he was mad at the country . . . [and] people aren't going to support a candidate like that. This is a great country. It makes mistakes, but by God if you get up there and preach day and night against America, you're not going to get elected."[28] Recent scholarly studies of conservatism in the 1960s and 1970s demonstrate why McGovern and his message did not resonate with the electorate.[29] His focus on empathic social concern clashed with the public's desire to cap property taxes, end integrationist busing, and keep their neighborhoods homogenous. They had become disgusted with leftwing protest. Like Don Quixote, McGovern believed that he was slaying giants, but most Americans thought he was tilting at windmills.

To explain the McGovern campaign's links to progressive Christianity, I've kept the content of this book selective and focused. Chapters 1 and 2 explore McGovern's development as a thinker and a believer, looking at how he came to adopt the social gospel as his moral code and how he refracted that code through his experiences as a seminarian and a historian. Chapter 3 looks at his entrance into politics, showing how he carefully established a relationship with the mainline churches and the global ecumenical movement. Chapter 4 details his friendship with James Armstrong and their work to reframe America's involvement in Vietnam as an act of sin.

Chapter 5 asserts that McGovern's 1972 presidential campaign was not only beholden to his progressive Christianity but an attempt to communicate that vision to the wider American public. The remaining chapters explore organizations that were receptive to McGovern's vision. Chapter 6 looks at how Armstrong built up Religious Leaders for McGovern (RLFM) and brought the ecumenical movement into electoral politics. Chapter 7 traces the development of an evangelical Left and how its first collective act manifested as Evangelicals for McGovern (EFM). Chapter 8 contemplates the difficulties of bringing together progressive evangelicals and mainliners by exploring McGovern's speech at evangelical Wheaton College during the middle of the 1972 campaign season. Finally, Chapter 9 looks at how progressive Christianity has weathered the populist outrage and burgeoning conservative energy of the 1980s.

For a group that began in relative obscurity, progressive evangelicals are presently the beneficiaries of a great deal of scholarly attention. David R. Swartz's acclaimed *Moral Minority* traces the disparate branches of the evangelical Left's history, while Brantley W. Gasaway's *Progressive Evangelicals and the Pursuit of Social Justice* shows that evangelicals concerned with social justice have often been divided on controversies such as environmentalism, LGBTQ rights, and abortion.[30] Jill K. Gill's *Embattled Ecumenism* has revitalized the history of the mainline with a sharp exploration of the churches' protest against the Vietnam War, and David Hollinger's *After Cloven Tongues of Fire* is an erudite survey of liberal Protestantism in recent American history.[31] As one historian has sardonically remarked, "it's heartening that dead, white, powerful Protestants are getting another look."[32]

For the most part, this book focuses on events that led up to or surrounded the 1972 presidential campaign, although most of my narrative's major characters continued to make substantive contributions to American public life for many years thereafter. By then, however, they exerted only a fraction of the influence they had once enjoyed. They had become outsiders—some by choice, some by compulsion—and that was where they would stay. During the 1980s, McGovern and Armstrong became vocal defenders of the liberal order at a time when freewheeling corporatist economic policies and social conservatism dominated American electoral politics. Sider and Wallis became dual leaders of a persistent, and often more radical, faction of evangelicalism that insisted that the powerful religious Right had gotten its approach to politics disastrously wrong. As an alternative, they advocated social justice through a position framed as "completely pro-life," whose more traditional tenets on sexuality and abortion often put them at loggerheads with the wider, generally more secular Left.[33]

During these wilderness years, mainliners and evangelicals who were committed to social justice slowly, awkwardly, learned to work together after resisting such an accord throughout the 1970s. In a way, the strength of organizational conservatism drove them to work in tandem. This new spirit of cooperation was most noticeable in the nuclear freeze movement of the 1980s and, more recently, in opposition to an avalanche of budget cuts in programs for the poor, immigrants, and women. The issue of same-sex relationships, which divided progressive evangelicals and mainliners in the 1990s and the early 2000s, no longer seems so divisive to millennials. Even many young evangelicals are now at peace with the idea, and a few are even fervently supporting it. In 2008, the organization Equality Rides was founded as way to help LGBTQ activists develop a dialogue with students at Christian colleges, while a growing number of apologetics on same-sex relationships have entered evangelical print culture.[34]

From emergent theology to the Moral Monday protests in North Carolina, from the biblical feminism of Rachel Held Evans and Sarah Bessey to a revived evangelical interest in the liturgy, many current developments have roots in what happened when McGovern called out to men and women of good faith. A liberal in the 1960s and 1970s was not the militantly secular creature who lurked in Jerry Falwell's imagination. The inclusive liberalism McGovern inaugurated did not reject Christianity. In fact, it scarcely could have existed without such belief.

Today, when many Americans are growing more anti-establishment in their political beliefs, as suspicious of overregulation and bureaucracies as they are of faith in the voting booth, the question prompted by McGovern's campaign is still a worthwhile one to consider: What does a person of conscience owe society? McGovern never viewed the American government as "them" or "those people." He rarely used "Washington" as a pejorative term. Instead, he saw the government as a commonwealth of its people, a way of pooling talents and energies in order to do great things that no individual could do on his or her own. Throughout the 1960s and 1970s, many of his generation, including Republicans and independents, also obeyed that call of responsibility. As Ira Shapiro chronicles in *The Last Great Senate,* the era's legislators demolished Jim Crow, established landmark environmental and consumer protection laws, made sure that millions of hungry people across the world received food, helped cut America's poverty rate in half, forced a culpable Nixon to choose between resignation and impeachment, and gave the Panama Canal back to its rightful owners. Could a politics built chiefly on personal liberty and abrogating a sense of mutual concern have done the same?

As I researched and wrote this book, I wrestled with many questions; and perhaps you, too, will find yourself pondering them as you read. What does it mean to be prophetic? Is it a specific calling or a common, shared responsibility? How does a person of faith effectively dissent in a democratic but persistently imperfect society? More broadly, how can a person engage fruitfully in the rough world of politics without compromising the imperatives of his or her conscience? Perhaps an answer lies in one of McGovern's favorite quotations from his King James Bible. (For all of his liberalism, he never cared for any of the modern translations.) "What doth the Lord require of thee, but to do justly, and to love mercy, and to walk humbly with thy God?"[35]

1

George McGovern's Soul

George McGovern's religious journey began on the American prairie, a place that our national mythology often ties to an ethic of tradition, conservatism, and self-reliance. Yet as a region where the bonds of community are often necessary for survival, the Dakotas also harbor an iconoclastic streak predicated on a greater voice for ordinary people in affairs of government. The prairie settlements have a long history of efforts to ward off the forces of what the plains progressive George W. Norris of Nebraska often called "wrong and evil." From Bleeding Kansas, to the agrarian populism of the Peoples' Party, to the arson of Carrie Nation, radicalism and religious fervor have long had a symbiotic relationship in the Great Plains. McGovern touted a peaceful and humanitarian, but no less radical, gospel with the same kind of holy fervor. Throughout his life, he prided himself on his nondescript South Dakota upbringing and his evangelical childhood. Much of this ordinariness, however, was only surface deep. Many of the elements that defined McGovern's public life and made him such an unconventional politician stemmed from his youth: his earnest, revivalist speaking style, his embrace of the social gospel, and his belief that Christianity was a call of service to mankind.

"My father gave me a conscience"

The first and perhaps most indelible figure behind George McGovern's fervor was his father, Reverend Joseph C. McGovern, the pastor of the local Wesleyan Church in Mitchell, South Dakota. Much of what has been recorded about Reverend McGovern is shrouded by fuzzy theology. Most have characterized him as a fundamentalist Christian, and certainly a number of outward signs have created this impression. The elder McGovern had a reputation as a stern father, the patriarch of a household in which the corrupting influences of motion pictures and cosmetics were forbidden, to say nothing of swearing, smoking, sex, and alcohol. Yet to label him a fundamentalist is mistaken, because it misconstrues both the man and fundamentalism. George Marsden, the great scholar of American fundamentalism, has conceptualized this idea as theologically committed to the idea of the world as a lost cause in declension.[1] In the late 1800s, fundamentalism was forged in the doctrinal furnaces of Princeton Theological Seminary as an intellectual counter-reformation against liberal and modernist movements that privileged inquiry and undermined orthodox certainties. By the 1920s, the fundamentalists were teaching about the utter depravity of mankind and retreating from mainstream society. In contrast, Reverend McGovern was rooted in the Holiness tradition of American Methodism, which stressed personal righteousness and resourcefulness. While fundamentalism, by the time of Senator McGovern's birth, often meant shunning the world, the Holiness movement called on men and women to transform it. Well into the twentieth century, the Holiness movement stressed that Christianity was a regenerative experience, one that would free the body and soul of baser instincts on its journey toward sanctification; and it emphasized that upright individuals would in turn transform the world around them.[2] Much of the reverend's strictness came not from hating the world or from fighting modernity but from carefully cultivating the holy.

Joseph McGovern's path to the ministry paralleled that of Billy Sunday, the most renowned evangelist of the early twentieth century. It is staggering to think that George McGovern, a presidential candidate in 1972, had a father born near Philadelphia more than a century earlier in 1868, merely three years after the Civil War had ended. Like Sunday's, his boyhood was difficult. Before his tenth birthday, Joseph was working as a breaker boy in the coal mines of Pennsylvania and Illinois. Rarely easy, life was made worse by his father, Thomas, who began to drink heavily after the untimely death of his wife, Mary, in 1881, at the age of only thirty-five. Thomas's alcoholism was a harbinger for a recurring struggle with drink in later generations: while the senator rarely drank to excess, his younger brother Lawrence and two of his own children battled alcoholism throughout their lives.[3]

In another parallel to Billy Sunday's life, Joseph McGovern's first salvation was baseball, which allowed him to escape the drudgery and danger of the mines.[4] By 1880, he was playing second base on a Des Moines, Iowa, team in the minor leagues. Still, the life of a baseball player was often more sordid than glamorous. During Joseph's years on the circuit, prostitutes, games of chance, and drink readily tempted the lonely young men who were passing through unfamiliar bush-league towns.[5] Perhaps fearing he would fall prey to the same vices that had afflicted his father, he decided before his mid-twenties to leave the sport and pursue a career in the ministry. In later days he rarely talked about his time as a professional athlete. George was nearly a teenager before he knew that his father had once been a baseball player.

Joseph pursued the equivalent of a high school diploma at Houghton Seminary, a Wesleyan Methodist secondary school located in the sparsely populated region of New York State known as the Southern Tier. Even today, Houghton remains so remote that its students joke that the school is thirty miles from the nearest sin. Despite its isolation, however, the region brimmed with religious dynamism, attracting utopian communities, health spas, and bold Christian experiments to improve human life.[6] Here, the embers of the Second Great Awakening, which had sparked a religious conflagration in the 1830s and 1840s, continued to flicker well after the turn of the twentieth century. The worldview of many of those who had settled in the region was very much in keeping with that of the earlier abolitionists, humanitarians, and reformers of the Awakening, who had posited that virtuous human action, as prescribed by the Bible, might improve a fallen society. These men and women were not retreating from modernity or awaiting the end of time. Rather, they were endeavoring by way of their faith to forge a more perfect humanity.[7]

Such a worldview aligned with the Wesleyan Methodist Church's heritage of biblically guided social improvement, although over the years many of its members had forgotten or eschewed this heritage. The denomination had formed in 1843 when its members broke off from the Methodist Church so that they could more openly voice their objections to slavery. The 1848 Seneca Falls Convention, one of the earliest manifestations of the women's suffrage movement, was held in a Wesleyan church. At first, Wesleyans labored in the belief that they could, through religious guidance and inspiration, create a more just society; but in the decades after the Civil War, they departed from their activist roots and turned inward, although they never became world-denying. They continued to believe that, once regenerated by faith, a soul could cultivate holy habits, become sanctified, and thus strive to make the world more perfect by emanating and living out one's personal virtue. While fundamentalists often viewed the world as a realm of declension and depravity, Wesleyans held fast to a belief system that allowed room for improvement and rectification when guided by God's grace. Nonetheless, they were not liberals and remained squarely evangelical.

By 1895, Joseph McGovern had become an ordained Wesleyan minister and had married a fellow Houghton graduate, Anne Faulds. Soon the church sent the couple to the new state of South Dakota, where many congregations were in need of pastoral leadership. McGovern's carpentry skills may have influenced his assignment to the desolate prairie towns, for he often took part in physically constructing his churches.[8] After Anne died in 1919, he quickly remarried, this time to Frances Myrtle McLean, a shy and introspective immigrant from Calgary who often sang at his church services.[9]

Reverend McGovern imposed a sense of order on the often chaotic Wesleyan administrative structures that were common in the western states, and his ministry was characterized by a stubborn, proactive zeal. His eldest child, Olive, recalled in 1972 that "when my father built a big church campground for a central conference of Methodist ministers in Aberdeen, people said it couldn't be done, but he just went out and raised the finances and built the whole thing himself—a giant tabernacle and dining room and dormitory."[10] Church records describe an active church builder and a man devoted to furthering the gospel in an unforgiving environment. "J. C. McGovern of Mitchell, South Dakota is a man that God has used mightily in past years throughout this western country in the furtherance of scriptural salvation," reads one Wesleyan communiqué, acknowledging Joseph's role in establishing six churches in the state.[11] Writing in the short, clipped sentences typical of many South Dakotans of that era, a colleague recalled, "He was God's man for the hour. He was a good executive. He had a deep appreciation for youth. He was a good preacher. He manifested the spirit of the Good Samaritan. He was my friend. Sometimes I wonder what would have happened if he had not crossed my path."[12]

George McGovern's father was a methodological man, and his son would later follow his habit of rising early to make time for writing and contemplation. In a small study in his bedroom, the pastor typed out his carefully organized sermons verbatim, leaving little to chance or spontaneity. "He didn't like what he called emotionalists, he didn't think the pulpit was a place you pounded, he thought it was a place from which you reasoned," his son explained.[13] His sermons often told stories with flecks of humor, where the protagonist faithfully prays to God but also works, sometimes deviously and mischievously, to achieve what he or she has prayed for. The message in these sermons is always clear: Christians should not merely pray while leaving the results to God; they need to take the initiative themselves. For Reverend McGovern, the importance of actively participating in the world was paramount.

George McGovern was born on July 19, 1922, at his father's parsonage in tiny Avon, South Dakota, a desolate prairie town with a population of six hundred and a Wesleyan congregation of twenty to thirty families. The McGoverns did not remain in Avon for long. After a brief sojourn to Calgary, where Frances cared for her ailing mother, the family finally settled in Mitchell, South Dakota, a town that was still small by eastern standards but was considerably larger than Avon. Bounded by the Chicago, Milwaukee, St. Paul, and Pacific railway at one end and the Chicago, St. Paul, Minneapolis, and Omaha line on the other, the town had ample access to other cities in the Midwest. In Mitchell in the 1920s, there were thirteen beauty parlors, eleven confectionaries, and three taxi companies. Although virtually everyone's fortune was directly or indirectly tied to agriculture, the regional commercial center bore only a superficial resemblance to the hardscrabble Dakota so famously described in Ole Rolvaag's novel *Giants in the Earth* (1924–1925).

Mitchell was, in many respects, an ideal town for a young boy to grow up in. It boasted a Boy Scout troop, movie theaters, and a roller rink. Residents could fish and swim in nearby Lake Mitchell, and there was remarkably little crime.[14] Even so, the Wesleyans remained suspicious of even simple pleasures. Church leaders had long viewed roller rinks and movie houses as portals to temptation, places where darkness and the close proximity of flesh could lead people astray. But the McGovern parents tended to focus on guidance and wisdom rather than dogma. According to McGovern's younger sister Mildred, "they didn't pressure us on decisions, they let us use our own conscience. I always had a feeling that they were more broad-minded than other people in our church. Dad always felt that there was good in every religion."[15] The lives of ministers' children usually involve heightened scrutiny, and Holiness thinking created even greater expectations for sanctity. McGovern's older sister Olive described their childhood as "not quite the same as [that of] other children. We were expected to be a standard for the community. Everything that other Christians did, we had to do double."[16]

"My dad," added George many years later, "would never let us go to school without reading a chapter from the Bible. My classmates would peer through the window, and you'd hear a certain amount of giggling."[17]

There were also prohibitions: the cinema, cosmetics, and alcohol were all forbidden. The McGovern household functioned like a tiny Christian commonwealth, constructing a stern set of rules with the goal of raising young people who would project holiness outward. For the family, the Christian faith was more than just a list of sinful acts to avoid; it implied a commission to do good as well. George believed that the example of John Wesley, who had admonished his followers to be mindful of the most vulnerable in society, was a source of the "empathic nature" of both of his parents. The Wesleyan tradition privileged "basic human compassion," and McGovern never forgot that important value.[18]

Yet a barrier of age always stood between Reverend McGovern and his children. When George, the second of four children, was born, his father was already fifty-four years old. With an aging, cerebral, and at times emotionally distant father, George naturally developed a quiet and reserved temperament. Church functions dominated his meager social life. He recalled, "There was never any question that Sunday was devoted to the church. The day began with Sunday school at nine-thirty, followed by the morning worship service at eleven, which was conducted by my father. At four o'clock in the afternoon, we return[ed] for . . . Young Missionary Workers Band . . . , for the Young People's meeting at seven. Then came the evening worship service at eight, when my father preached again in a more evangelical style."[19]

Each summer these habits of holiness were punctuated by a series of revival meetings, which young George dreaded. His family would pitch a tent at the Mitchell Holiness Campground, and fellow believers from miles around would gather around them. Even as a boy, McGovern chafed at the fervent revivalism on display at these meetings, so different from the temperate, reasoned delivery of his father's Sunday sermons. In an interview with *Life* magazine during his presidential campaign, he vividly recalled being "terrified as a small child of some of these hellfire sermons by visiting evangelists." He remembered one gruesome tale of an unbeliever who, after stubbornly resisting an altar call at a camp meeting, was struck by a train on the way home and consigned to eternal torment. "I think that gave me a fear of emotionalism, almost a hatred of it," McGovern said.[20]

This use of religion to invoke fear left young McGovern with a lifelong aversion to hellfire preaching. These revivals probably marked the beginning of his enduring unhappiness with evangelical Christianity, which he perceived as manipulating the conscience and forfeiting good sense. For the boy, the act of salvation seemed to demand showmanship and artifice. This soured his feelings about evangelicalism; afterward, he rarely expressed his faith in evangelical terms such as "being saved," "finding Jesus," or having "a personal savior." To him, these words would always suggest a kind of hucksterism and bald inauthenticity. Yet in his later career, McGovern never entirely rejected the timbre of the 1930s Wesleyan Methodist Church, even if he had qualms about its doctrine. He continued to recognize evil as an absolute, and he clung to the understanding that men and women might be spiritually transformed in character. As much as McGovern hated the revivalist language of death and destruction, much of it seeped into his campaign speeches. When he ran for president, he vividly described the effects of napalm and other weapons in an attempt to turn conscientious souls against the Vietnam War. He put his childhood Bible lessons to use rhetorically, retaining a cache of memorable quotations, an invaluable asset for a prairie politician.[21]

As young George was enduring those summer revivals, the Great Depression was enveloping the nation, descending onto the prairie states with a special, almost biblical wrath. Everywhere, the desperation of the times stoked deep-seated unrest, whether in the anti-Semitism inherent in Father Coughlin's popular radio programs or the marked rise in Communist Party membership. In South Dakota, it manifested itself in what became euphemistically known as the Farm Holiday protests, held in the summer of 1932. These protests revealed the subterranean radicalism that endured in the state.[22] As the prices of grain and livestock plummeted and mortgages became imperiled, a consortium of farmers' unions proposed a moratorium on sales until farm prices began to exceed the cost of production. The movement was particularly strong in the eastern section of the state, where Mitchell was situated: the strikers blocked off roads, demanded redress, and threatened to bring South Dakota's economy to a standstill. Although the unrest soon dissipated, it demonstrated that the state harbored a dormant holy anger.

Thanks to the Depression, Franklin Roosevelt carried South Dakota twice in the presidential elections, though there was not much enthusiasm for the New Deal in the McGovern household. Still, just as Reverend

McGovern believed that all religions contained grains of truth, his sense of Christian charity gave the president the benefit of the doubt. George recollected,

> When a parishioner would start railing about Franklin Roosevelt, my dad would always say, "Now, Brother Smith, the man is doing the best he knows how. You and I might disagree, but he wants to be a great president and he's doing what he thinks is right. You have to remember that when you disagree with a president. They're doing the best they know how." Somebody would come in and rail against the income tax, and my dad would say, "Well, now, Sister Jones, if you're paying a high income tax, that means you're making a lot of money. Praise the Lord." He was an unusual Republican.[23]

In general, Reverend McGovern leaned toward reform-minded Republicans. He admired South Dakota's somewhat progressive Republican senator and governor Peter Norbeck, and in 1924 he had voted for Robert LaFollette in his third-party presidential bid.[24]

The Depression offered McGovern's father the opportunity to display the decency that his son later saw as crucial to public and private life. "I always admired my dad for really living his religious beliefs," McGovern recalled on the campaign trail. "I remember so many times the whole family would be sitting down to a meal and here some hobo would come along, knock on the door, begging for food. My dad would always invite him in. And though we were never hungry, we were often short of food."[25] He concluded later in life that "my father gave me a conscience and my education gave me a social conscience."[26] Reverend McGovern was the first among many to teach George that religion is lived, practiced, and projected outward, not merely accepted and believed.

College and Wartime

The intellectual freedom that Reverend McGovern made available to his children extended to versions of Christianity that differed sharply from his own. He did not prevent them from listening to religious voices that contrasted with his own conservative background. For instance, they were free to listen to the radio programs of Harry Emerson Fosdick, George's first exposure to the social gospel. Huddled by the radio (made available by the New Deal's Rural Electrification Act), the family sat transfixed by Fosdick's broadcast, despite the elder McGovern's reservations about such a "modernist."[27] Although Reverend McGovern used the term as a pejorative, it was nonetheless an apt descriptor: Fosdick not only preached liberal Christianity but vociferously defended it against fundamentalist critics. From his post at Riverside Church in New York City, he released dozens of books, broadcasts, and pamphlets, all of them promoting a strong, strikingly masculine Christianity that sought intellectual respectability. During the 1920s, as he noted the shift toward fundamentalism, he began speaking out against what he called "the timid literalisms which bound men by a text instead of liberating them by a truth." He expressed dismay at how fundamentalists had marginalized Christianity, which in his view ought to be the most progressive force in society. "Multitudes of churches," he wrote, were "swamped by theological obscurantism, fanatical premillennialists, anti-evolutionary propaganda, or any other kind of reactionary movement in religious thinking."[28] Fosdick argued that fundamentalism's bellicose and anti-intellectual attitude was gravely injuring Christianity, damaging it in the eyes of the learned, the curious, and the young. "Liberal Christianity," he said, "will never win the day merely because it is intelligent but because, being intelligent, it proves able in this new generation to inspire ardent faith in God." Reconciling Christianity with modernity would not dilute the faith but strengthen it with a new vibrancy. Fosdick predicted that liberal Christianity would "subordinate the details of ritual, creed and church to the major objects of Christianity—the creation of personal character and social righteousness," ending it as a form of superstition and turning it into an engine of transformative progress.[29] George's early, if limited, exposure to Fosdick gave him a viable form of Christianity that eschewed the histrionics of revivalist evangelism and made a case for the faith on the grounds of reason and humanitarian concern. For McGovern, Fosdick's belief that humanity could achieve an upward trajectory if Christians would reject superstition and embrace progress and mutual concern was profoundly influential.

At the same time, the boy was learning to articulate these ideas through debate, thanks to an instructor at his high school, J. Robert Pearson.[30] As a child, McGovern had been painfully shy, so reluctant to read aloud in class that his teachers had considered holding him back a grade. Even as he grew, he chose hobbies that could be pursued in isolation, such as collecting stamps and playing the piano, rather than taking part in the typical local pastimes of baseball, hunting, and fishing. Pearson, however, recognized that the boy's reticence hid a perceptive and methodical mind.

Using McGovern's fierce introversion and stubborn idealism as an advantage, Pearson encouraged him to studiously gather facts and quotations for debate, slowly coaching him to present his arguments cogently and eloquently. This began McGovern's lifelong habit of collecting memorable quotes that he could use as necessary in speeches, debates, or editorials. His archives at Dakota Wesleyan University and Princeton University brim with sheaves of sayings collected over the decades, and he often credited the study of forensics with building his confidence, sharpening his reasoning, and drawing him out of his childhood insularity.[31]

William Wendt, a boyhood acquaintance who went on to become an Episcopal priest, recalled that "George was a keen thinker, studious rather than attractive as a person, neat, well-mannered, an outstanding student, respected, terribly cautious, inquisitive, sharp."[32] His boundaries had largely been set by a biblical theology, a pious and stable family life, and a regional wariness about New Deal liberalism. But just as many stolid South Dakotans had subterranean impulses toward iconoclasm, McGovern's safe evangelical childhood contained the seeds of a righteous discontent.

Having spent his own youth in the coal mines, Reverend McGovern desired to see his children receive good educations that would promote the cultivation of holiness. He had hoped to send his promising eldest son to Wheaton College, the most highly regarded evangelical school in the country.[33] However, the family could not afford the Illinois school's costly tuition and boarding fees, so George elected to attend Dakota Wesleyan University, a small Methodist-affiliated college of six hundred students located in Mitchell itself. The university had offered him a scholarship based on his forensics performances.

The social environment of Dakota Wesleyan University was, at least on paper, little different from the strictures of his childhood. Campus rules permitted neither alcohol nor card playing on campus and required mandatory chapel services.[34] Because dancing was considered too sensual an amusement for its student body, the university arranged for an orchestra to play the latest hits as couples strolled chastely across the gymnasium floor. In this pious atmosphere, George struggled to reconcile the heavy expectations of "P.K.s" or "preacher's kids" with his lifelong dislike of being thought prudish. He relished chances to tell a salty joke or swear a bit, if only to assure himself and those around him that he wasn't a moralizing milquetoast. He needn't have worried: he was astonishingly popular, a young man who, for all his boyhood shyness, was coming into his own and growing more confident through his debating. During his junior year, Dakota Wesleyan's yearbook even named him the school's "Glamour Boy."[35]

Off campus, George was occasionally able to escape the stern Wesleyan gaze, and near Lake Mitchell he had his first sexual encounter—a fleeting, almost spontaneous experience with Laura, the girlfriend of his friend Arthur.[36] To his horror and regret, she became pregnant. McGovern was, in the words of his biographer and confidant Thomas Knock, "wracked with guilt" and "paralyzing anxiety" for having so seriously troubled her life and jeopardized his own prospects and reputation.[37] At a time when illegitimate children were an unwelcome mark against one's character, the young woman chose to move to Indiana, apparently without consulting McGovern, and in or near September 1941, she gave birth to a daughter. The mother, whose full name remains a secret, discouraged McGovern from establishing a relationship with his child, with whom he had only indirect contact.

Convincing himself that the unfortunate situation had worked out as well as it could have, George moved on with his life, a privilege his lover did not enjoy, and continued to hone his intellect on the debating team. During a debating contest, he first met his true partner, Eleanor Stegeberg, who was debating with her twin sister; they were among the few who could best the Mitchell team. When George and Eleanor reconnected as Dakota Wesleyan undergraduates, he found her to be a sharp, original thinker, gifted with confidence and inquisitiveness. He also took a liking to her father, who had bucked South Dakota orthodoxy twice over by being both a Democrat and an atheist, one of the first of either species that McGovern had ever met. While the thoughtful and polite McGovern made a good impression on Mr. Stegeberg, Eleanor did not immediately charm her future father-in-law. She remembered that Reverend McGovern "was kind to me, even though according to his beliefs, I was neither saved [nor] sanctified."[38] The mere fact that she wore makeup made her a dubious influence to his Wesleyan parents.

McGovern's collegiate successes were interrupted by the Japanese attack on Pearl Harbor. Like so many others of his generation, he put his studies on hiatus and committed himself to the struggle against the Axis. Having taken pilot lessons before the attack (as a way to conquer his fear of flying), he now chose to join a force in sore need of pilots. Quickly he and Eleanor married. They spent their first night together in the spare room of his parents' house, and then he shipped out to San Antonio, Texas, to train as a bomber pilot. McGovern's experiences in World War II further loosened him from the religious institutions that had monitored and circumscribed his behavior. On every American military base, the forbidden pleasures of his youth were readily available: drinking, dancing, women, and cursing. As he told his friend Bob Pennington (who was also the boyfriend of Eleanor's twin sister), "My father's pious teachings have had to go since I entered the so-called Sack [the San Antonio Aviation Cadet Center]."[39]

During his tour in Europe, McGovern's weighty responsibilities and the war's physical dangers broadened his understanding of the depth and reality of structural sin.[40] He also began to comprehend the effects of poverty and hunger. For instance, while en route to a base near Naples, he was a passenger on a large troop carrier. As they approached the harbor, the troops were warned not to throw candy to the shore, where a crowd of children had gathered. They were told that, on an earlier occasion, famished children had drowned after jumping into the sea to get the sweets.[41] At night he could hear the sound of mothers foraging through the camp's refuse, hoping to find discarded morsels of food. At other times, he saw women, desperate for sustenance, selling their bodies to American G.I.s. These heartbreaking scenes taught the young pilot that the deprivations of war were creating systems of sin; hunger and war were intricately knitted together.

Despite his humanitarian impulses, McGovern was still no liberal Democrat. Politically, he aligned with the small vestiges of progressivism within the Republican Party. Looking ahead to the 1944 presidential election, the first in which he would be able to vote, he told Pennington, "I like the vigor and efficiency that [Thomas Dewey] has shown in the past, and even the way he is conducting his campaign." He predicted that Dewey would "give business a confidence in the government that they haven't had for quite a while now" and complained about the nebulous character of Roosevelt's New Deal programs.[42] He kept abreast of current events, as he had during his debating seasons, and began looking forward to a peacetime career as a professor. In a letter to Pennington, he noted how much he had enjoyed college and mentioned plans to seek a master's degree, probably in history, after returning to graduate from Dakota Wesleyan.[43]

For now, however, successful bombing runs rather than the intricacies of American presidential elections were commanding his immediate attention. During World War II, serving on a B-24 was among the most dangerous of military missions; nearly half of all B-24 crewmembers did not live to see the end of the war. The planes were cumbersome and had difficulty avoiding enemy fire, and their missions were dangerous to Europe's civilian population as well. During one of his final bombing runs, a member of McGovern's crew released a live bomb on the trip back to base, accidentally hitting a farmhouse precisely at noon, when its family would have been inside eating lunch. "That thing stayed with me for years and years," he said. "If I thought about the war almost invariably I would think about that farm." For a young man from agricultural South Dakota, the notion of destroying a farm family had a profound resonance, and his memory of the incident made him reluctant to view his war service as glamorous or praiseworthy. McGovern never regretted his participation in the war; but the knowledge that, as the pilot of the Dakota Queen, he had been involved in such collateral damage, coupled with the death of many of his fellow pilots and his own frequent peril, made his transition to civilian life painful.[44] Eleanor later recounted the symptoms of post-traumatic stress disorder he endured after returning home, when he would wake suddenly, crying out warnings about heavy flak and tailspins as he relived the war's most terrifying moments.[45]

"And my education gave me a social conscience"

The war changed McGovern profoundly. As he later said, "I came back from World War II and the atomic bomb really wondering if civilization would survive, and would be wiped out by the unleashing of the atom."[46] By now, his familiarity with the social gospel had changed from a passing fancy to a devout passion, and during his final year at Dakota Wesleyan he had an opportunity to articulate his hopes for a peaceful postwar order. Once again, McGovern showed his knack for finding the right mentor at the right time when he began taking philosophy and history classes with a new professor, Reverend Donald McAninch. A pacifist Methodist minister, McAninch was the first in a series of educators who would gradually introduce McGovern to intellectual traditions that cut against Dakotan conservatism.

McAninch himself had studied at Boston University with the celebrated theologian Edgar S. Brightman, renowned as a leading proponent of higher criticism of the Old Testament.[47] By using literary and historical theory to identify the Old Testament's multiple authors and layered construction, this approach gave readers the opportunity to view the scriptures as the work of many people over many centuries and thus inspired by God only indirectly. Brightman aligned himself with the Christian philosophic school of personalism, which understood Christ as the supreme moral being and saw his teachings as an exemplar for reordering human social relationships in a radically egalitarian manner. Yet his most original contribution to liberal theology, and one that inspired McGovern's social action, was the idea of finitistic theism. This concept posited that God could not be both fully good and fully powerful at the same time. Because evil clearly existed, finitistic theists argued for a self-limiting God who was technically able to intervene in the world but chose not to do so to preserve free will. As a result, personalists placed little hope in providence or the supernatural but believed that humankind bore the burden of improving the world.[48]

In his first class with McGovern, McAninch assigned students to read John Herman Randall's seminal text, *The Making of the Modern Mind* (1926), which had an abiding effect on McGovern's worldview.[49] Tracing the development of Western thought, Randall began with the development of Judaism, including a lengthy treatment of the Old Testament prophets. He saw Elijah and Elisha as voices of reform within a staid, ritualistic, and uncaring social order, "rais[ing] a bitter cry against the new vices of a richer community, the greed of land and wealth, the selfish luxury of the rich [and] the harsh oppression of the poor." This tendency toward reform continued with the minor prophets Amos and Hosea, two of the biblical figures that McGovern quoted most often in his political career. In Randall's view, these revolutionaries shifted the heart of Judaism from the covenantal minutiae of Mosaic Law to the universal ideals of social justice. He connected their ancient message to the contemporary idea of the social gospel. Citing the German theologian Albrecht Ritsch and the German-American theologian Walter Rauschenbusch as two modern examples, he wrote that "ethical religion is found at its best among those Protestants and Jews in whom the prophetic Puritan and Hebraic strain is prominent."[50]

As the title of his text suggests, Randall's view of history had a teleology wherein reason and science were increasingly applied in service to humanity. His interpretation of Judeo-Christian history as a progressive force corroborated the progressive Christianity that McGovern had first encountered in Fosdick's radio broadcasts. Writing at length in his autobiography, he recollected:

> This effort to find in the New Testament and the Hebrew prophets an ethical imperative for a just social order strongly appealed to me. To know that long years of familiarity with the Bible and the idealism nurtured

in my public-school years were resources that I could direct to humane political and economic ends was a satisfying discovery. Religion was more than a search for personal salvation, more than an instantaneous expression of God's grace; it could be the essential moral underpinning for a life devoted to the service of one's time. Indeed, one's own salvation depended upon service to others.[51]

McGovern ravenously worked through the Rauschenbusch canon, focusing on his two most well-known works, the companion volumes *Christianity and the Social Crisis* (1907) and *Christianity and the Social Order* (1912). One of the preeminent figures in the social gospel movement, Rauschenbusch sought to apply the moral lessons of the Old Testament prophets to society's treatment of the urban poor.[52] Revisiting the minor prophets and the historical books of the Old Testament, he encountered a Hebraic people who both sinned and sought repentance collectively as a society, not as discrete individuals. "The prophets," Rauschenbusch concluded, "were religious reformers demanding social action. They were not discussing holiness in the abstract, but dealt with concrete, present-day situations in the life of people which were sometimes due to the faults of the people themselves, but usually to the sins of the ruling classes."[53] Informed by his ministry in the Hell's Kitchen section of New York City, he came to understand that evil was often systematic and institutionalized, and not always strictly the product of individuals' sinful choices. His theories, derived from firsthand experience in urban slums, helped other proponents of the social gospel to observe the intricate connections between vice and environment. "The community," he wrote, "is *particeps criminis* with the individual in almost every sin committed. [This includes] the girl who drifts into shame because no happy marriage is open to her; the boy who runs into youthful criminality because he has no outlet for his energies except the street."[54] Improve and enrich the environment, he argued, and its sinfulness will be curbed. Rauschenbusch's prodigious study of modern German theology led him to believe that, even in a fallen world, men can overcome their sinful nature and sinful environs and improve society; in fact, they have an obligation to do so.[55]

Rauschenbusch's ideas about reform and restructure influenced McGovern's own vision of what a Christian commonwealth could look like and seemed to point a way forward from the horrors he had seen during the war. His lifelong idealism and his vigor in spreading it had a theological foundation in these writings. In a 2004 interview with the ecumenical magazine *Zion's Herald,* he declared,

[Rauschenbusch's] books on the social crisis in Christianity changed my life and my outlook. For the first time, Christianity appeared to me as a very practical code for dealing with social, political and international questions. Rauschenbusch expressed contempt for ritual, for public prayer, and that kind of thing. He sounded more like an Old Testament prophet addressing the moral and ethical responsibilities we have to deal with the problems of the poor, with minorities, with women, the neglect of their rights, world peace. So I became a Social Gospel Christian from that day to this. I still think it's the best formula for dealing both with the religious life and the secular problems that we have.[56]

Moreover, Rauschenbusch's conception of the kingdom of God had ramifications in the kingdom of politics, an idea that McGovern would also appropriate in time. Rauschenbusch prescribed using the government as a holy instrument to promote material improvement in society. He wrote, "Against the doctrine that the best state governs least, I set the assertion that the finest public life will exist in a community which has learned to combine its citizens in the largest number of cooperative functions for the common good." He believed these citizens would, in turn, create networks of libraries, hospitals, and vocational centers for those who needed them.[57] Thus, the mechanics of government could be channeled by properly guided men as a means to correct the malignant features of society. The government was not the solution in itself but a tool that Christians might use. McGovern later recollected that Rauschenbusch's books came "very close to describing my philosophy of government and what government should be doing."[58]

Inspired, McGovern took strongly to the work that McAninch assigned him. "I think," he reflected, that the social gospel "emphasized an idealistic leaning in my heart, a philosophy of idealism to apply to our social and economic problems . . . [and] it fortified my tendencies toward liberalism and humanism."[59] Under the suasion of these ideas, he privately left the Wesleyan Church while finishing his undergraduate education. He instead joined its near relative (and the denominational sponsor of Dakota Wesleyan), the Methodist Episcopal Church. In 1972, when a group of evangelical theologians asked him why he had switched denominations, McGovern explained, "The Wesleyan Methodists were a little light on the social gospel. . . . Their prophetic zeal against slavery had not been translated into a zeal against poverty or those chained to the slums."[60] Since boyhood, he had fought against the emotionalism and the strict rules of the Wesleyans, and

Methodism, with strong institutional ties to the social gospel, offered him a compelling alternative.

When McGovern moved from the Wesleyan Methodist Church to the Methodist Episcopal Church, he crossed a spiritual chasm that divided American Protestantism in the 1940s. As hair splitting as the difference may seem today, his switch marked his transition from the evangelical, theologically conservative tradition into the theologically liberal one. He shed his father's high view of scripture; now, rather than valuing it for its inspired nature, he admired its elegant language and its transcendent truth. "When I thought of it that way," he told Princeton chaplain Charles P. Henderson in 1972, "then it began to become more meaningful."[61] His cosmology did not require a saving experience or substitutionary atonement; society, not the individual soul, was what needed saving.

Convinced by these ideas, McGovern joined the collegiate oratory circuit, a natural progression from his love for debate. He no longer focused on winning points and outmaneuvering opponents but on turning hearts. His speech "My Brother's Keeper," which won a state prize for oratory, proffered an ethos of fraternal responsibility in line with Rauschenbusch's ideas. Another speech reflecting his postwar frame of mind, "From Cave to Cave," demonstrated a new urgency. The title referred to McGovern's belief that nuclear weaponry might annihilate civilization, returning humankind to a primitive state of nature. In a way, its concentration on imminent danger and its call to reform hearkens back to the grim jeremiads of the summer revivals of his childhood. Yet for all its apocalyptic overtones, the speech struck a hopeful tone, arguing for a new era of human cooperation that was consonant with the teleology of liberal Christianity. McGovern argued, "It has been said that what we most need is not to realize the ideal but to idealize the real. In other words, we can't expect a Providential dispensation transforming the world into Utopia over night. Nor can we expect man to change his moral character instantaneously. We can, however, intensify our efforts to make the real world more ideal by applying the Christianity which thus far we have only been talking about."[62] The passage encapsulates young McGovern's beliefs, and many of his intellectual forebears are present in his words. Like Brightman, the speaker perceived that God's work in the world is limited and that humanity must harness its understanding of ethics to improve society. Like Rauschenbusch, he favored the "applied idealism" of Christianity.[63] Like his father, he had a self-reliant understanding of the Christian life, hopeful about prayer but trusting legwork.

Remarkably, the war and its aftermath had strengthened rather than desensitized McGovern's idealism. While many Europeans and some Americans (for instance, Reinhold Niebuhr) believed that the war had revealed humanity's utter depravity, McGovern had new hope that brotherhood might prevail.[64] McGovern propagated this hope with a singleminded commitment similar to the conviction that had driven his father to build Wesleyan churches across the Dakotas. He must have been persuasive, since "From Cave to Cave" won first prize at the national Peace Oratory competition in 1946.

By the age of twenty-four, George McGovern had been victorious in war and peace and had earned a sense of confidence. As he graduated from Dakota Wesleyan University in 1946, he knew that he could be more than a mere student of the social gospel. He was convinced that he could help to realize its lofty ideals. The only question was where and how. Given his introversion and his love of study, most expected him to enter academia, and eventually he would. But for now he would surprise many of those who knew him best. Like his father, McGovern intended to become a minister, and he would preach the good news.

2

For-Prophet Education

Despite the years he had spent chafing against the high expectations for preachers' children, McGovern's impulse to join the ministry was partly a posthumous act of filial piety: his seventy-six-year-old father had suffered a fatal heart attack in December 1944. This sense of obligation commingled in the young man's mind with the lessons of the social gospel thinkers he had come to admire. Thus, although Reverend McGovern might have been pleased that his eldest son had chosen to follow in his footsteps, he probably would not have approved of the school in which George enrolled. Located in Evanston, Illinois, Garrett Theological Seminary was one of the most theologically liberal and socially engaged of the Methodist seminaries. In 1943, while Americans were focusing intently on winning the war, Garrett stubbornly held a series of peace lectures.[1] Many of its students, party to the pacifism that liberal Methodism had defended during the 1920s and 1930s, had sought conscientious objector status; and a 1945 seminary poll showed that a clear majority of them opposed peacetime military training.[2] In short, the seminary was a respected, though controversial, locus of the social gospel and peace activism in the American Midwest. It was an ideal place for McGovern.

The Seminarian

In addition to its connection to the social gospel, Garrett was institutionally tied to the mainline churches. In contrast to Dakota Wesleyan, which was seen as a competent but provincial school, Garrett attracted faculty members who were powerful forces in both the Methodist denomination and the wider ecumenical movement. McGovern's time as a seminary student overlapped with the postwar fear of communist infiltration, and the civil libertarian stances of activist mainliners often attracted charges of being soft on communism. Today, McCarthyite inquisitions into the State Department, the army, and Hollywood remain as familiar Cold War narratives, but many forget that America's liberal mainline churches also attracted suspicion. In 1953, the House Un-American Activities Committee summoned one of the nation's most controversial Methodist churchmen, Bishop G. Bromley Oxnam, to a hearing. One congressman, Donald L. Jackson of California, charged that Oxnam, a familiar and admired figure among Garrett's faculty, "served God on Sunday and the communist front the balance of the week."[3] This and other largely baseless hearings fueled suspicion that the mainline churches, particularly Methodism, harbored a "pink fringe" of naïve communist sympathizers.[4] At Garrett, both the sociologist Rockwell Smith and the resident Bible scholar Murray Leiffer were harassed by anticommunist critics who were suspicious of their involvement in the Methodist Federation for Social Services and their activism for leftwing causes.

In this uneasy atmosphere, the seminary's strongest voice for the social gospel was Ernest Fremont Tittle. When McGovern arrived at Garrett, Tittle was reaching the end of a long career at Evanston's venerable First Methodist Episcopal Church. From this prestigious pulpit, he eschewed the eloquent but cautious solutions of Rauschenbusch's generation in order to challenge and, at times, condemn middle-class acquiescence to unjust social systems.[5] This transition was important in the history of the social gospel. Tittle and other radical Methodists created networks between the denomination's church boards, which were among the surest strongholds of the social gospel, to strengthen the church's commitment to improving race relations and engaging in peacemaking. This gave likeminded clergy respectable posts from which they could critique rather than collaborate with those in positions of power.

Like Donald McAninch, McGovern's mentor at Dakota Wesleyan, Tittle was heavily influenced by the Boston personalist school and the idea of a self-limiting God who left the responsibility for improving the world to people of good will. "God in history works through men," he wrote in the *Christian Century.* "When it comes to the achievement of a historic justice and peace, God is necessarily dependent on human cooperation. In history, there are things which even God cannot do until men can set to work with him, not against him."[6] These initiatives included a responsibility to prevent war, although Tittle did not share the absolute pacifism of some of his colleagues at Garrett. Nonetheless, having served as a chaplain in World War I, he had witnessed the horrors of battle firsthand and had subsequently become an ardent supporter of limiting American military escalation and intervention. During the buildup to World War II, he had opposed the Lend-Lease Act of 1941, arguing that it compromised American neutrality and was leading the country headlong toward war. Instead, he supported the Ludlow Amendment, which stipulated that a declaration of war required a national referendum in lieu of congressional approval. Yet even in the midst of World War II, Tittle retained his belief that society could be rendered into the kingdom of heaven, declaring in 1940 that God was "slowly but surely drawing mankind to Himself."[7] By the time McGovern arrived at Garrett, Tittle had become a nuclear pacifist, arguing that the destructive capabilities of these new weapons was unconscionable under any circumstance, a sentiment that McGovern had already expressed in his "From Cave to Cave" speech.

Although he was active on Methodist church boards, Tittle considered himself primarily a pastor and a pulpit orator rather than a social activist or a theologian. In this capacity, he frequently stirred controversy among his affluent flock at the First Methodist Church. Tittle conceptualized his ministry as a prophetic pulpit and called on his well-to-do congregants to remember their responsibilities to their less fortunate brothers and sisters. In sermons on race relations and slum clearance he argued that empathy and social improvement were the most faithful expressions of the gospel. As he told his seminarians, "The prophet is not a man before a microphone saying: 'I predict'; he is a man declaring: 'thus saith the Lord.'"[8] He practiced a form of prophetic civil religion, urging his fellow citizens to return to an earlier state of grace and accept humanitarian responsibilities, themes that McGovern would put to use years later.[9]

Throughout Tittle's career, his use of the pulpit to spur social action drew a great deal of criticism from both his congregants and other Christian intellectuals. Unlike his neo-orthodox foil Reinhold Niebuhr, Tittle held fast to the progressive ideal of a more perfect humankind whose advances could stem the tide of sin. Meanwhile, Niebuhr spent the postwar period vehemently refuting this idea, notably in his landmark book *Moral Man and Immoral Society*.[10] Niebuhr and many like-minded Protestants believed that while individual persons could aspire to goodness, societies as a whole could not, as the recent world war had demonstrated. With this renewed emphasis on the historical doctrine of original sin, Niebuhr was wary about social reforms, viewing such efforts as an unrealistically optimistic, even dangerously naïve, view of the human condition. In one missive, Tittle satirized the morose character of Niebuhr's philosophy, writing, "God, I thank Thee that I am not as the rest of men—stupid optimists, would-be reformers, social gospelers—or even as this pacifist. Twice in the week, I wrote an article proving that there is no hope in the world."[11] Yet despite such differences within mainline Protestantism, realists such as Niebuhr and pacifists such as Tittle shared a common hatred of racism and a skepticism about nationalism and economic inequality.[12]

Tittle's impact on the impressionable George McGovern may be among his most enduring, if least acknowledged, legacies. Every Sunday McGovern spent in Evanston, he listened raptly to Tittle's sermons. He found the pastor's activism and pulpit oratory appealing, grounded as they were in the familiar trappings of personalist philosophy. What was different was Tittle's straightforward delivery, which often involved criticizing the listeners. Tittle was the first genuinely prophetic preacher with whom McGovern would have regular contact as well as the first to point out the Christian commonwealth's collective neglect of the marginalized. In contrast to the sometimes ponderous Rauschenbusch, Tittle directly confronted racism, warmongering, and public indifference. But he could cajole as well as confront; he easily toggled between prophetic and pastoral responsibilities. In later years McGovern warmly recalled the didactic qualities of his sermons, his fluid incorporation of storytelling, and his skill at weaving social teachings into his sermons. Importantly, Tittle taught him that personal salvation "doesn't always lead to the redemption of a suffering world."[13]

Like McGovern, the students who enrolled in Garrett in 1946 were members of a postwar cohort whose outlook differed sharply from that of the upperclassmen. Thanks to the G.I. Bill, a wave of recently discharged soldiers had enrolled in school, and at Garrett their presence created a contentious dynamic in a seminary known for supporting pacifism and conscientious objection. One G.I. said that he felt "constant conflict within me between the idealism which is rampant at Garrett and the practical life as found both in the service and the outside world in general. Most of us in the service who are here are basically idealistic, yet we have been able to make this idealism practical, and maybe more useful."[14]

Despite their differing experiences, Garrett's students, whether they were veterans or not, had a common affinity for applied idealism and recognized that their social activism cut against the tendency of their times.

Fundamentalist and evangelical Christians often saw the mounting international tension between the United States and the Soviet Union as a bellwether of the end times, not least because the line between good and evil was so resolutely drawn. Fundamentalist Baptist and Presbyterian ministers such as Carl McIntire and Edgar Bundy (and, to a lesser extent, young Billy Graham) drew apocalyptic visions of the Cold War from passages in Daniel and Revelation.[15] In contrast, the community at Garrett argued that scouring the scriptures for eschatological clues during the nuclear age misconstrued the nature of prophecy. As Tittle exhorted, prophets do not predict the unfolding of history but deliver important, uncomfortable truths to those who need to hear them. One alumnus wrote in the seminary's newspaper, the *Garrett Tower*, "It is utterly fantastic to read into [such predictions] the names and places and dates of current history. The great value of the prophets lies in the moral ideals and the spiritual faith they had. . . . The Prophecies then are not so much crystal balls, giving previews of the future, as they are clarion calls, summoning men and nations to belief in a righteous God and conduct consistent with such belief."[16]

It is no surprise that one student described the seminary as, above all else, a "prophet's school," for a Garrett education emphasized the art of prophetic preaching.[17] Yet as another student explained, "The call for dynamic, stimulating preaching is not a call for tent-revival delivery. But it is a call for preaching that is instilled with positive, deep conviction, and sincere, heartstirring enthusiasm."[18] Some faculty members such as Charles F. Kraft, who specialized in the prophetic books of the Old Testament, believed that this radical style dated back to the exhortations of Amos and Ezekiel. Others, such as McGovern's favorite professor, William Warren Sweet, focused on the history of Christianity in America and its role in actualizing social reform.

The Garrett staff was strikingly inclusive by the standards of the day, and the institution was one of the first co-ed seminaries to have a woman on its faculty: the celebrated theologian Georgia Harkness. Both students and professors were closely tied to important organizations in the vast network of ecumenical progressivism, particularly the Fellowship of Reconciliation, the Methodist Federation for Social Action, and the Religion and Labor Foundation.[19] Thus, during his time in Evanston, McGovern was drawn into a large, established circle of Methodists whose politics ranged between mainstream liberalism and deep structural critiques in the vein of the perennial socialist candidate Norman Thomas. His associates were theologically liberal Christians whose understanding of the scriptures gave them an impetus for social action. Throughout his career, McGovern would continue to turn to like-minded Methodists for advice, companionship and spiritual counsel, for they understood his mind and his aspirations in ways that few conventional politicians did.

While he took classes in Evanston, McGovern also served as a student pastor in Diamond Lake, a small town thirty miles away from the school. The congregation at Diamond Lake was too small to sustain a permanent pastor, so it participated in an arrangement with Garrett known as "accepted supply," which allowed a seminary student, with the approval of Methodist officials, to conduct all rites of the church, even if he was years away from ordination.[20] Thus empowered, McGovern presided for eighteen months, from July 1946 until January 1948, over a tiny congregation of 130 souls. On a meager annual salary of $1,600, he and his family, which by now included two daughters, moved into the parsonage. With little but his father's example, his familiarity with the social gospel, and his entry-level classes at Garrett to guide him, he found himself responsible for the spiritual well-being of a parish.

As a town populated chiefly by retirees and vacationers, Diamond Lake was an unreceptive place to preach the social gospel. Like Tittle's in Evanston, his congregants were not especially eager to hear a Sunday sermon about remote social problems in the wider world. Nonetheless, they were nothing if not hospitable. When the McGoverns arrived, the church's women's club feted them with a buffet dinner and gave them dishes, lamps, and vases so that they could furnish their small parsonage in the best midwestern tradition. Such pleasant moments reinforced Diamond Lake's idyllic reputation. Its rows of vacation houses seemed designed to ignore rather than confront the urban grime and malaise of nearby Chicago. Members of the congregation expected McGovern to visit the sick, counsel the doubtful, and, most importantly, preside over weddings, baptisms, and funerals. They sought a pastor, dutifully and reassuringly performing rituals, rather than a prophet pointing out where they had fallen short. Moreover, despite the fact that McGovern was juggling priestly functions, his grueling seminary studies, and responsibility for a young family, he and Eleanor were expected to lead the parish's social life. The congregants asked them to organize a youth group, oversee lay fellowship organizations, and participate in parish celebrations and festivities such as hayrides and church socials.[21]

Almost immediately, McGovern found these duties burdensome and unfulfilling. He took to performing church rituals with as little pomp as he could risk, baptizing children in their home kitchens with water from the sink and wearing tennis shoes to wedding rehearsals.[22] The only element of his ministry that he truly savored was delivering the Sunday sermon. Like his father, he meticulously typed out his words the day before and delivered them verbatim. Tittle's influence was also clear: McGovern emulated his preaching style and forthright confrontation of social issues.[23] With little tact, he began to establish a prophetic pulpit in Diamond Lake as soon as he arrived, delivering orations on concepts such as the doomsday clock and shocking his straight-laced congregation. "He was a very good minister. Very good. He kept you on the seat of your pants," remembered a congregant who was twelve years old at the time.[24] Because of his limited seminary experience, he relied on the work of Fosdick and Tittle, delivering plaintive but often cerebral sermons and dwelling in particular on Matthew 16:25: "For whosoever will save his life shall lose it: and whosoever will lose his life for my sake shall find it."[25] It became what an evangelical might call his life verse. McGovern later wrote, "That verse had intrigued me for years and still does. I called upon the congregation to understand that if we wanted to find meaning and fulfillment in our lives, we had to reach beyond immediate self-serving enrichment to consideration for the well-being of others. Peace among nations depended upon a willingness to subordinate national rivalry and commercial greed to the larger needs of the human family."[26]

The evangelist Matthew's ideal of losing one's life in the pursuit of a just cause made McGovern reconsider whether serving a small congregation was allowing him to do any greater good, and by 1947 he thought of leaving the ministry. The biographer Robert Anson came to believe that this consideration was influenced by his disgust at the Methodist Church bureaucracy. According to Anson, McGovern overheard his bishop advising a fellow minister against relocating to Minnesota because its pay scale was considerably lower than that of the northern Illinois diocese.[27] Yet while Anson argues that McGovern abandoned his career as a pastor because of this sort of financial pettiness, McGovern himself demurred: "The hierarchy I served under weren't at all like that. . . . I only left because I didn't feel I was cut out for the ceremonial functions and administrative minutiae of the parochial ministry."[28]

In 1972, Ester Mills, a Diamond Lake congregant, shared her memories of McGovern with the journalist Tom Slocum. She recalled that her young pastor thought "he could do more service by not limiting himself to the ministry."[29] McGovern was also eager to proselytize his idealistic views to a more receptive audience. He said, "I felt . . . I could really reach young minds more effectively through the classroom," where teachers could more easily discuss big ideas and students were less settled in their ways.[30] Years later, David McCartney, McGovern's successor at Diamond Lake, said that he believed McGovern had been disheartened by his unambitious congregation: "George had been led to believe the church was the hope of the world, and he found it wasn't. . . . He felt people in general did not seem to want the true teaching of the church. He felt, and told me, that the church was a country club where people wanted to receive but not to give."[31]

McGovern's decision to leave the ministry made sense to his family: Eleanor disliked the role of minister's wife, and his mother did not believe that he had a true calling to the pulpit. Yet despite its brevity, his brief career as a pastor was deeply instructive. No other major-party presidential nominee in the twentieth century had experience as a clergyman. As a pastor, McGovern struggled to find a balance between serving the ritualistic and spiritual needs of his church while delivering the social messages he felt they desperately required. Twenty-five years later, as a candidate for president, he faced a similar dilemma in his public speeches: the necessity of balancing tough messages with reassurance and validation.

McGovern believed that his time as a minister was valuable to his political career: "I learned a lot about human beings—I've never regretted it."[32] He knew that it was a mistake but recognized that it had had important, if unintended, consequences. His work had shown him that he could constructively engage with people who did not share his liberal worldview, and that lesson became a crucial element of his later political success in South Dakota.

McGovern as Historian

In 1947, McGovern transferred from Garrett Theological Seminary to Northwestern University across the street, where he took up the study of history. While his seminary studies had guided his idealism, his study of history helped him understand how it might be put into practice. During his years at Northwestern, he became fully committed to the American leftist tradition, which he saw as the best means for carrying out the social gospel. His friend Bob Pennington, who had married Eleanor's sister Ila, was enrolled in the university's sociology program, and he introduced

McGovern to Ray A. Billington, a young history professor with a reputation for spellbinding lectures. At that time McGovern was still juggling his pastorate with seminary coursework and family responsibilities, but he found occasion to visit Billington's classes and join the lively discussions the professor encouraged afterward. Jovial and gregarious, Billington helped calm McGovern's worries about forsaking the ministry, convincing him that as a professor rather than a preacher he could reach "a far wider audience with a liberal point of view."[33]

McGovern's discussions with Billington were the first in a series of fruitful working relationships with the faculty members of Northwestern's history department, which was brimming with young, charismatic, and leftist talent. Billington himself would become a legend among historians of the American West.[34] Much of his scholarship rehabilitated the famous frontier thesis of Frederick Jackson Turner, which subsequent historians had been bludgeoning since its publication in 1893.[35] Among the first generation of cultural historians, he used his study of nineteenth-century nativism to construct a staunch defense of pluralism in American society. Politically, his views were social democratic, championing personal freedoms and economic security above immediate self-interest.

McGovern's closest friend on the faculty may have been Leften Stavrianos, a historian of south-central Europe who has often been credited with launching the discipline of world history. Stavrianos studied the cultural fault lines between Christendom and the Islamic world, and he was one of the first historians to challenge students to think outside of conventional Eurocentric frameworks. He often worked in tandem with his wife, the anthropologist Bertha Stavrianos.[36] McGovern and Stavrianos frequently shared meals and discussed politics and history together. McGovern recalled that his friend "was a social activist; he believed strongly in negotiation rather than war in the settlement of problems. He wasn't a pacifist and neither was I, [but he thought] that the Cold War was exaggerated on both sides, that the fear aspect was out of all proportion to the reality."[37] His lectures and reading assignments molded McGovern's perceptions of the Soviet Union and the nature of communist expansion during the early years of the Cold War. McGovern was quick to defend Stavrianos as no "apologist for the Soviet Union" but agreed that "his lectures gave one a more balanced view of the Cold War that was beginning to develop."[38]

As he read assigned books such as E. H. Carr's *The Soviet Impact on the Western World* (1946) and Owen Lattimore's *The Situation in Asia* (1949),

McGovern began to understand that the series of foreign policy crises arising during the Truman administration were the violent manifestation of long-dormant colonial struggles. Many of the authors of these books were members of the China Hands, a group of hardened experts in Asian geopolitics whose careers often came to ruin during the McCarthy era.[39] While they generally did not sympathize with international communism, they urged their readers to recognize the Chinese population's anger over the incompetence and unfairness of Chang Kai-Shek's government. McGovern agreed with their conclusions that revolutionaries and freedom fighters in Asia were using the rhetoric of communism for nationalist ends, much as American revolutionaries had directed Enlightenment thought toward their own purposes.[40] He perceived that Asia was determined to create its own freedom, and he saw that too often his own country stood in the way under the guise of checking Soviet advancement. As he lamented in his autobiography, "Twenty-five years of misguided and failing American policy in Indochina could have been avoided if men like Lattimore had been heeded instead of hounded to the sidelines."[41] These books had convinced him that "Asia was out of control, it was throwing off imperial attachments by western powers, and . . . military masters could not control that military fervor sweeping the Asian continent; India broke away, Indonesia broke away, all across Asia, countries had been breaking away. . . . So [Lattimore's] book, which Stavrianos urged me to read, influenced my early views on Vietnam."[42] Most of the China Hands authors interpreted Soviet aggression in Eastern Europe as a defensive action after two devastating invasions from Western Europe in the course of thirty years; they did not see them as the beginnings of unchecked expansion. Altogether, the writers presented a very different stance from the school later known as orthodox Cold War historiography, which put forth a more conventional view of Soviet culpability.[43] McGovern's general agreement with their arguments gave him a new lens through which view the Cold War, one that often set him apart from hawkish hardliners in Congress.

Despite his close friendship with Stavrianos, McGovern chose Northwestern's newest historian, Arthur Link, as his dissertation adviser. Link, a biographer of Woodrow Wilson, was barely two years older than McGovern, which made their relationship more fraternal than hierarchical. Already Link was studying Wilson, and in this early stage of his career his assessments were often critical, particularly with respect to Wilson's foreign policy. His book *Wilson: The Road to the White House*, written shortly before he met McGovern, portrays a cold, impersonal, calculating politician whose actions before the election presaged his aggressions in Latin America and his violation of civil liberties at home.[44]

In time, friends and students would note that Link was beginning to resemble Wilson, becoming incrementally more like his subject (and subsequently less critical of him) with the passing of years. Both men were erudite southerners who taught at northern universities, and both were committed to the study of American political history. Link shared Wilson's pious nature and even his denominational affiliation; he was a lay leader of the Presbyterian Church throughout much of his career and for a time served as a vice-president of the National Council of Churches.[45] He even wore spectacles made in the old-fashioned style of Wilson's. Link's Wilsonian affectations in his bearing and appearance carried over to his politics. His worldview shared the progressive president's unremitting religious idealism and hopeful internationalism.

The Progressive Party

McGovern was a graduate student during the 1948 presidential election, the first of the Cold War. Support for the former vice-president and Progressive Party candidate Henry A. Wallace ran strong at both Garrett and Northwestern.[46] Indeed, sixty faculty members at Northwestern had sent Wallace a petition urging him to run against Truman, an action that Wallace himself credited with influencing his decision to enter the race. Their enthusiasm was infectious; twenty-three of the twenty-six graduate students in Northwestern's history department were backing Wallace.[47]

McGovern's time at Garrett and his conversations with Northwestern's eminent historians had convinced him of the need for large structural changes to America's economy and society. Although he had admired Dewey's toughness in 1944, McGovern was now alarmed by both Dewey and Truman's saber rattling against the Soviets. Like Stavrianos and many other professors, he believed that Wallace would question Cold War orthodoxy and revisit the wartime cooperation between America and the Soviets. The candidate awakened his sense that the social gospel could effectively be realized through politics and that politics itself could be a worthwhile cause. McGovern's enthusiasm for Wallace was not only an outcome of his new understanding of foreign policy but also a practical extension of his religious views. "I thought Wallace was the embodiment of the social gospel," he later recalled.[48]

Wallace himself had a strong pedigree in that tradition; his grandfather had been an early and prominent social gospel minister in the rural Midwest.[49] Although Wallace had taken notorious and very public forays into theosophy and mysticism, he and McGovern shared an understanding of public responsibility that was grounded in the social teachings of the Old Testament prophets, who, as Wallace wrote in the *Menorah Journal*, had been committed to "progressive religious, political and economic matters" in ways that made them relevant in the twentieth century.[50] So, heedless of the candidate's unpopularity in South Dakota, McGovern embarked on an impetuous attempt to convince his hometown neighbors to support him. "I take off my hat," he wrote in a letter to the *Mitchell Daily Republic,* "to this much-smeared man who has had the fortitude to take his stand against the powerful forces of fear, militarism, nationalism, and greed."[51]

Both George and Eleanor used their Northwestern ties to the Wallace campaign to secure positions as delegates from Illinois, and they went to Philadelphia to attend the Progressive Party's nominating convention. There, McGovern was disturbed by a communist-friendly minority among the Wallace delegates and the failure of the Vermont Resolution, a platform plank that would have clearly stated that the convention did not endorse the foreign policy of any nation, particularly that of the Soviet Union. Although some elements of the convention pleased him, particularly the folk singer Pete Seeger's serenades for social justice, all of his later official statements affirm that he left the city grievously disillusioned with the campaign's foolishly accommodating approach to the Soviet Union.[52] For the rest of his life McGovern avoided speaking about his early enthusiasm for Wallace. It was the one facet of his political career about which he was less than candid. He often claimed that, in the end, he simply could not pull the lever for Wallace in 1948.[53] In fact, however, George and Eleanor had both registered to vote in Illinois in order to take part in the Progressive convention. When Illinois successfully kept Wallace off the ballot, it was too late for them to switch back to South Dakota. Thus, while McGovern could truthfully claim he did not vote for Wallace, the reason depended on a technicality.[54]

Regardless of the outcome, the Wallace situation illustrated the tension between McGovern's conscience and his ambition. As a public man, he went out of his way to play down his youthful affection for the campaign. Ted Van Dyk records an incident in which McGovern visited Philadelphia in 1972 and was greeted on the street by aging Wallace delegates who regaled him with stories from 1948. He shook their hands dutifully, smiled vacuously, said nothing, and climbed into his car. Once inside, he confided to Van Dyk, "Truth is, I remembered them quite well. I was a Henry Wallace delegate in 1948, but no one knows it today. It's an issue I just don't need."[55]

Many years later, when the connection to Wallace could no longer hurt him, McGovern spoke more openly. In an interview for a PBS documentary on Wallace, McGovern was full of praise for him. He admitted that there were a few communist sympathizers at the 1948 convention, but they were outliers: "There are always some fringe groups like that, that turn up at any convention. They used to turn up for Roosevelt too when he was running. But the people I met at the convention were just ordinary farmers, workers, small business people, doctors and lawyers." He insisted, "I didn't see where it was any kind of Stalinist operation. That's ridiculous. These were church people, and right out of the soil of America."[56]

Openly communist Wallace supporters might have been a minority at the convention, but they were a minority that could have seriously harmed McGovern's political career. And although he would not admit it, a less radical version of Wallace's platform—less hopeful about Soviet good will but just as prophetic and agrarian—stayed with McGovern through much of his public life. He subscribed, at least in part, to Wallace's view that the Cold War was the Truman administration's choice, not a geopolitical inevitability. Long after he had retired from politics, he said, "I was never gung-ho for the Cold War from that day to this. I always thought it was vastly overdone. Each side succeeded in scaring the hell out of the other one, but neither one really had any intention of starting World War III."[57] In 1972, a fellow Northwestern graduate student recalled, "We all started off like George: liberal, idealistic, really confident in the possibilities of life. The funny thing is, though, that of all of us, George is really the only one who remained that way."[58]

McGovern's intense commitment to this worldview endured, at least in part, because his idealism had firm spiritual roots that were not easily unmoored. Nevertheless, his affinity for Wallace, whose politics were premised on hope for humanity and a populist trust in neighborliness, clashed with those of the theological giant Reinhold Niebuhr. In Niebuhr's eyes, the evil inherent in Nazi Germany and Soviet Russia meant that trust and good-faith negotiations would be folly. These regimes defied reason, mocked the idea of moral progress, and required opposition through military force. Due to humanity's inherent sinfulness, individual morality, according to Niebuhr, could not easily apply to society or systems.[59] He was an Erasmus for the Cold War era, a celebrity scholar who stubbornly reminded humanity of its capacity for folly and dismissed myopic humanism that failed to account for the fallen nature of man. Throughout his life, he somberly dismantled the utopian thinking that dominated the progressive Christianity of his day.[60]

Perhaps more than any other major liberal figure of his time, McGovern rejected Niebuhr's assertion that personal ethics such as honesty and peacefulness could be ruinous when applied to the cutthroat world of international relations. "I never understood that," McGovern said, still baffled, even decades later. "If principles are relevant anywhere, why not in foreign affairs?" He continued, "Reinhold Niebuhr was never one of my heroes" and dismissed him as "an apologist for the Cold War."[61] In fact, he rejected Niebuhr twice over—not only his neo-orthodox emphasis on original sin but also his foreign policy recommendations for dealing with the Soviet Union. Niebuhr was an early luminary in Americans for Democratic Action (as were McGovern's future friends Hubert H. Humphrey and Arthur Schlesinger Jr.), and in that role he worked hard to expel Wallace supporters and other far-left sympathizers from positions of influence in the Democratic Party. Adherents hoped that this action would defend against the Red Scare and reorient the party toward a vital and dynamic center.[62] Yet even though Niebuhr eventually shaped the foreign policy ideas of Humphrey, Scoop Jackson, and Jimmy Carter, he never convinced McGovern.[63]

In the late 1940s, as he was engaging with these political and moral issues, McGovern was also working to complete his dissertation. In those days, advisers often assigned dissertation topics to their students, and Link had given McGovern the bloody 1914 miners' strike in Ludlow, Colorado. Reading through the dissertation today, one might note many signs of the progressive school of American historiography. Progressive histories tend to be driven by conflict, especially class conflict between the people and the vested interests; and McGovern's dissertation is a legacy of his work with Billington. He was overtly biased toward the miners over the owners, whom he described as stock villains—rejecting reasonable demands, refusing compromise, and neglecting the safety and well-being of their workers and their families so as to maintain a tight grip over the mining towns. The workers, meanwhile, were "intelligent, industrious men whose dignity had not been crushed by [this] kind of industrial feudalism." In the dissertation, American corporations are social structures steeped in sin. McGovern noted, with private satisfaction, that the only religious voices supporting the miners came from Harry F. Ward and the Methodist Federation for Social Services. Most religious periodicals condemned the miners' union or remained aloof from the conflict.[64]

With his coursework and his research complete, McGovern began looking for a job. He applied for a professorship at the University of Iowa, where he was one of three finalists but lost out to an Ivy League graduate.[65] Eventually, he found work in familiar territory: he was hired to teach history and communications at Dakota Wesleyan University, and Bob Pennington also joined the staff to teach sociology. Their homecoming was not, however, entirely comfortable. In the Red Scare years, Dakota Wesleyan had became a hostile environment for a leftist of McGovern's caliber.

The university's conservative board of trustees frequently battled with Samuel Hilburn, an educational reformer from the University of Chicago who had served as president since 1946. His liberal and ecumenical spirit was a poor fit for the college, and he soon ran into difficulty. During one class, for instance, he argued that the United States and Japan shared culpability for World War II, an idea that the locals found alarming.[66] Many Americans, particularly those in the Midwest, feared the infiltration of communism into higher education, a sentiment stoked by South Dakota's two redoubtably anticommunist senators, Karl Mundt and Francis Case. Members of the local American Legion took to sitting in on Dakota Wesleyan classes, watching for subversive behavior. In a letter that found its way into the FBI's files, one student wrote that McGovern's current events courses "brainwashed [his] classes in the perfection of socialism."[67] Hilburn resisted such anticommunist vigilantism, but his efforts came at a price: feeling that their president poorly represented the college, the board elected to dismiss him. Firing off an angry missive to Arthur Link, McGovern complained, "Without any question at all, he was removed by bigoted South Dakota Republicans who could not tolerate the liberal atmosphere of the college under President Hilburn's administration. They succeeded in pulling the Methodist conference into their scheme and on carefully arranged charges were able to persuade the majority of the timid members of the board to call for the president's resignation."[68]

By now the McGovern family had expanded to three daughters: Ann, Susan, and Terry. For the moment, George seemed he have achieved a tenuous professional stability. Despite his McCarthy-era difficulties, he was respected among the students and probably could have taught at Dakota Wesleyan for as long as he wished to. He was so well liked that the students dedicated a yearbook to him as their favorite professor. But his ambition continued to burn; once again, he sought a greater audience. This time his vehicle would be the Democratic Party, which, thanks to another son of the Midwest, Adlai Stevenson, was becoming a more cerebral and idealistic organization. For McGovern, the social gospel had become a calling, and the causes that defined his time in Congress, as a Kennedy-era administrator, and as a presidential candidate were driven by his conviction that we are our brother's keeper.

3

Brother George—A Politician as Churchman

Many people forget that Christianity was an indelible element of political activity in the 1960s, and conservative voices would ever afterwards portray that period as irreligious. Although religious advocates such as Richard John Neuhaus have alleged otherwise, the decade did not usher in an era of state-sanctioned secularization.[1] In fact, those years featured sustained, even creative, cooperation between pastors and politicians, and that relationship manifests today in the form of think tanks, lobbying groups, and even the C Street house that serves as a religious fraternity for members of Congress.[2] During the 1960s, the nexus of this cooperation was the National Council of Churches, a mainline Protestant organization that shared the worldview of many leading lawmakers. Its orientation was tilted leftward; many of the council's church leaders were nearly as progressive as those whom McGovern had encountered at Garrett Theological Seminary. McGovern found a niche as a lay member of this ecumenical network, and he was not alone. In the 1960s and 1970s, many liberal church leaders and liberal members of Congress became political allies as they worked to create a progressive society that reflected their social justice ideals. Their personal faith or inward spiritual journey mattered less than their churchmanship did—that is, their sense of belonging to an established ecclesiastical tradition and maintaining ties of good will and open lines of communication among themselves.

Madly for Adlai: Becoming a Public Figure

Between 1952 to 1962, McGovern rebuilt and assumed leadership of South Dakota's anemic Democratic Party. According to Richard Dougherty, his press secretary during the 1972 presidential campaign, McGovern had an incorrigible self-confidence beneath his soft-spoken exterior, a "sense of pride more Greek than Methodist."[3] Throughout the decade, he impatiently switched jobs when he felt wasn't rising to the top fast enough or when his position failed to offer him a large enough platform to share his ideas. Growing disenchanted, first with the politics of religion and then with the politics of education, he abandoned both of those career paths and chose to enter politics directly.

When McGovern joined the Democratic Party, he was keeping a particular role model in mind. Although he had many heroes—among them Abraham Lincoln, Henry Wallace, Walter Rauschenbusch, and South Dakota's longtime progressive senator Peter Norbeck—there was no public figure he admired more than Adlai Stevenson, the governor of Illinois. This became apparent in the summer of 1952, when he and a heavily pregnant Eleanor painted the family's living room in their house in Mitchell. The couple listened to Stevenson's rousing address at the Democratic National Convention in Chicago. The oration launched Stevenson's dark horse candidacy for the presidency, but it was also a call to public service. Every note of the speech resonated with McGovern. It challenged his generation to serve a greater good, and it was filled with biblical language, ending with Micah's famous exhortation to "do justice, love mercy, and walk humbly with God."[4] Best of all, it highlighted Stevenson's stylish delivery and sprite, urbane wit. For the first time in recent memory, a man with both intellectual brilliance and powerful rhetorical control was running for president, and these qualities were not lost on a listener who had found his own voice on the debate team.

George McGovern was not the only listener who was inspired by the address. Some historians believe that Stevenson's candidacy triggered a change in the Democratic Party. Now it became known as the more intellectual of the two parties, perhaps at the expense of working-class voters, who might have preferred a party that continued to focus on pocketbook issues.[5] But McGovern was enraptured. In Stevenson he saw a man who displayed much of what he had found appealing in Wallace but who carried little of Wallace's baggage. The young professor eagerly began stumping on Stevenson's behalf—delivering speeches, writing editorials to Mitchell's daily newspaper, and demonstrating so much enthusiasm that his daughter Terry told her schoolmates that her father's three favorite people were God, Jesus, and Adlai Stevenson.[6] Indeed, he was so fixated on Stevenson that he named his son Steven, born shortly after the convention, in honor of the candidate. When Stevenson died in 1965, McGovern, who was now a senator, badgered other Democratic senators for stories of how the candidate had influenced their public careers. He was shocked to learn that, overwhelmingly, and to his mortification, they believed that Stevenson had not influenced them in the slightest. Almost all were New Dealers; and though they may have admired him, they saw him as an ineffectual buffer against the Eisenhower landslide. In their view, he was the man who had broken the Democrats' presidential winning streak for the first time since 1932.[7]

Throughout the summer of 1952, as McGovern devoted his most of his free time to helping Stevenson's cause, he attracted the attention of Ward Clark, the long-suffering chairman of South Dakota's Democratic Party. Delighted to discover this young advocate with a passion for public speaking, he asked McGovern to leave his job at Dakota Wesleyan to become the state party's secretary. The job was not glamorous. McGovern would need to raise his own salary by soliciting donations and selling campaign memorabilia, and he would need to commit to driving repeatedly across a huge, sparsely populated state inhabited mostly by lifelong Republicans. Although his colleagues at the college urged him to not leave a secure job to support a state party perpetually in the minority, McGovern decided to accept Clark's offer and became an evangelist for the Democrats.

So began a whirlwind four years in which McGovern quit his job as a professor, built South Dakota's nearly defunct Democratic Party from the grassroots up, and became the state's first Democratic congressman in a generation. In 1952, South Dakota was almost monolithically Republican. Hutchison County, for instance, had three registered Democrats among its 11,000 residents. A former Democratic leader told McGovern's biographer Robert Anson that, in those days, if you joined the party, "people didn't regard you as a social menace or anything; they just found it hard to take you seriously."[8] But McGovern was undeterred. He crossed the state in a beat-up car, visiting local chairs, raising money, registering voters, and gauging interest at business lunches, county fairs, general stores, and, most importantly, churches.

In 1956, McGovern was elected to the US House of Representatives for South Dakota's first congressional district, which covered the state east of the Missouri River. While his hard work as a state organizer certainly factored into his success, the unpopularity of Eisenhower's farm policy may have tipped the election in his favor. Eisenhower's secretary of agriculture,

Ezra Taft Benson, was a Mormon apostle whose free-market philosophy was reviled in the Dakotas, which were heavily dependent on subsidies. Benson had even been pelted with eggs on a visit to Sioux Falls.[9] During his campaign, McGovern had staked out a different position: rather rise and fall in an unforgiving market, his state's farmers should be paid a fair price to produce as much food as they could for the benefit of all.

McGovern's conspicuous churchmanship helped him successfully artic-ulate that point in a state not accustomed to voting for Democrats. Aware of his disadvantage, he used what the historian Jon Lauck calls the "social capital" of the prairie's churches—their tradition of republicanism and civic-mindedness that had been vital to the state's political culture since its days as a territory.[10] Being a good citizen meant participating in an active—and invariably Protestant—church life. As such, churches were technically nonpartisan sanctuaries on Republican turf. McGovern could present his concerns in a church fellowship hall, articulating them not as Democratic ideas but as humanitarian ones in the Judeo-Christian tradition.[11] In other venues, Candidate McGovern might be ignored, but he could often reach a sympathetic ear as Brother McGovern. Throughout his time in Congress, he regularly visited small church organizations with civic missions, such as the Baptist Church Young Adults Group, the Presbyterian Men's Club Dinner, and the Methodist Youth Fellowships. He never failed to send a telegram of congratulations whenever a new church opened in South Dakota or a pas-tor had been promoted. These visits and communiqués demonstrated that he stood firmly within the state's Protestant cultural and social milieu and allowed him access to a wider range of voters, including the independents and Republicans whose votes he would continue to need.

A good example of this approach occurred in 1964, when McGovern, then a senator, delivered a sermon to an Episcopal congregation titled "Christian Citizenship Responsibilities." In this address, given a week before the presidential election (and subsequently the only time in McGovern's adult life when most South Dakotans voted for the Democratic presidential candidate), he pledged that his audience would "hear no hint of partisan-ship from me." Nonetheless, his speech was brimming with political ideas rooted in the social gospel. "No one can entirely separate his concern about the welfare of his church and health of his family from politics, for politics touches our lives at every point," he argued before the congregation, call-ing for a dialogue between the affairs of the soul and the affairs of state. The address was a plea for "appreciations of the enduring values of life," including the human dignity available only to well-fed, well-educated citizens living in peace.[12]

McGovern needed all the church support he could get; for as a congressman, he had been pilloried for his belief that communist China should be permitted to join the United Nations and be recognized diplomatically. Again and again, he had argued that American military aid was misplaced and that humanitarian aid was the better way to promote sound international relations. In his first roll call vote as a congressman, he was among a handful of members who had voted against a resolution that would grant President Eisenhower the ability to intervene in the Middle East.[13] During his 1956 campaign for the House, charges that McGovern was soft on communism were so persistent that Frank Lochridge, the Methodist minister in Mitchell, had to publicly vouch for the candidate's Americanism.[14]

One of McGovern's most common counter-arguments centered around the notion of using the Dakotas' agricultural abundance as a weapon in the Cold War. On the House floor, he urged the government to purchase surplus grain for distribution to the hungry people of the developing world, arguing that, "properly utilized, our agricultural abundance can be a blessing to us and to the world." In his view, "surplus food can be a great instrument to relate our spiritual heritage and moral precepts to a suffering mankind. Surely we do not want to hide the candle of compassion under our bushels of surplus food? Would we not better fulfill our role as a great democratic Nation by following the timeless advice: Thou shalt open thine hand wide unto thy brother, to thy poor, and to thy needy?"[15]

McGovern's strategy, expressed in King James parlance, would have had two beneficial outcomes in a state where anticommunist sentiment ran high. Not only would it open even more markets to South Dakotan farmers, but it would use the state's agricultural fecundity to demonstrate America's superiority at the zenith of the Cold War.[16] The churches, McGovern argued, would play an important part in this humanitarian action, given their history of relief work and their ability to organize charitable labor. He praised the churches' efforts in those areas as "one of the most inspiring . . . in the world today."[17] Thus, McGovern succeeded in South Dakota by turning an apparent disadvantage into an advantage. In an editorial in support of his strategy, he wrote, "I don't think any of us could conceive of the politicians in the Kremlin wringing their hands over a food surplus. You could bet if they had it they would be using every bit of it to advance Communists' aims and objectives in the uncommitted areas of the world."[18]

Aided by these acts of prairie republicanism and strategic churchman-ship, McGovern was successful in the House and was handily reelected in 1958. Yet he was tired of serving on ineffectual committees and yearned for higher office. His best chance to advance was through the Senate, which McGovern believed would be a citadel for debate. Moreover, he knew that coming from a sparsely populated state would be no disadvantage in com-mittee work (as it could be in the House) because each state was represented equally. Unfortunately, in 1960, his ambition to enter the Senate also meant taking on the popular Republican incumbent, Karl Mundt. McGovern's decision to run was a poorly calculated move rooted in his scorn for Mundt, whom he saw as a mean-spirited McCarthyite reactionary. Moreover, with John F. Kennedy's name at the top of the Democratic ticket, the race was even more difficult. Even McGovern's conspicuous Methodism could not negate the prairie voters' lingering distrust of Catholicism, which many saw as suspicious, foreign, and far too deferential to Rome. Some of McGovern's less scrupulous opponents slyly hinted that he himself was a Roman Catholic, pointing out his Scots-Irish surname and his brood that now included five children.[19] In a letter to Arthur Link, McGovern com-plained, "It would be hard for me to describe the intensity of the religious hysteria that struck this state in the closing days of the campaign. Mundt skillfully combined this with traditional fears and anxieties of conservative South Dakota Republicans. I regard the man as an evil genius in the art of fear-mongering."[20]

McGovern lost the election and was now out of office, but the man who might have cost him his chance at the Senate offered him a consolation prize. President-elect Kennedy invited him to lead the new Office of Food for Peace, an agency that would distribute American food to the developing world, using agricultural surpluses as leverage in the global contest against the Soviets.[21] Kennedy's advisors believed that extra food would free fledg-ling nations to focus their resources on technological advancement. The post was an ideal fit for McGovern. Although he was easily bored by its administrative detail, Food for Peace allowed him to pursue the social gos-pel's priority of meeting human need while boosting his standing in South Dakota, which would be necessary if he were to try again for the Senate. To that end, he successfully requested the job title of "special assistant to the president" so as to raise his public visibility.

In the two years that he worked for Food for Peace, McGovern con-centrated on shipping farm surpluses to the world's hungriest regions and advocating for international school-lunch programs.[22] The agency quickly became what his biographer Thomas Knock calls "the most intensive foreign aid program of its kind of the twentieth century."[23] It created a global food bank, and proceeds from food sales were channeled into sorely needed developmental aid. At one point, 20 percent of schoolchildren in India received school lunches through Food for Peace. McGovern's leadership burnished both his humanitarian and anticommunist credentials. He boasted, "American food has done more to prevent . . . communism than all the military hardware we have shipped around the world," and he framed South Dakota's farmers as the first line of defense against that ideology.[24] One South Dakota churchwoman, Lillian Stewart, wrote an effusive letter to McGovern comparing him to Joseph, the Old Testament patriarch who generously gave a nation's overabundance of grain to neighbors in need. "We believe you are a person who looks to God for wisdom," she concluded and said that she hoped President Kennedy would make use of his counsel.[25] In his responses to Stewart and others like her, McGovern proudly wrote, "The program is based on a Christian humanitarian concept."[26] In the meantime, he continued to use his high profile as groundwork for another try at the Senate.

Mainline Churches: The Original American Social Network

McGovern's Food for Peace efforts ushered him beyond the parochial, republican church life of South Dakota and into a national ecumenical network of churches. The program relied heavily on the volunteerism and positive publicity of both mainline Protestant and Catholic churches. Religious agencies such as the Church World Service, Catholic Relief Services, and Lutheran World Relief did a great deal of the legwork in organizing volunteers to distribute food in developing countries. McGovern's staff prepared dossiers about the program for religious magazines in hopes that they would use them as the basis for favorable articles, and McGovern himself told an approving Methodist cleric that he was "enthusiastic about the possibility of a story on Food for Peace" in a Methodist magazine.[27] Intrigued by the program's humanitarian successes as well as the possibility of further church partnership in public affairs, the Methodist magazines *Concern* and *Together* eagerly praised Food for Peace and McGovern's leadership.[28] The *Register* and *Our Sunday Visitor*, both Catholic magazines, followed suit, stressing the role of the Catholic Relief Services in these efforts. Such responses convinced McGovern that religious organizations were valuable partners in his office's humanitarian mission. Later in the 1960s, he recalled watching church-based volunteer organizations distribute food and medical aid "not on a mechanical basis, but on a warm human basis where you actually feel the warmth of a human being involved in the sharing of food."[29] In his years on the job, he followed progressive religious print culture closely, subscribing to and regularly reading the *Christian Century, Christianity and Crisis,* and the Catholic journal of social justice, *Commonweal.*

Theodore Palmquist, the pastor of Foundry Methodist Church, the denomination's most prominent church in the Washington, DC, area, offered his congratulations on McGovern's appointment to the Office of Food for Peace, writing that "the hungry man in the world today may determine the future of civilization tomorrow" and inviting McGovern to attend his church.[30] From then on, McGovern regularly attended Foundry when he was in the city, and this choice strengthened his ties to the national Methodist leadership when he successfully ran for the Senate in 1962. That same year, Cameron Hall, the executive director of the National Council of Churches, invited him to deliver a keynote speech at a seminar titled "The Christian Farmer and His Government."[31] These small invitations were McGovern's first openings into what became a growing relationship with the larger world of mainline American Protestantism.

Central to this network was the National Council of Churches (NCC), which positioned itself as America's ecumenical conscience throughout the 1950s and 1960s. In the aftermath of World War II, mainline churches in the United States had enjoyed a revitalization. Young American adults who had weathered the war began to settle down, raise families, and attend worship services regularly to set a good example for their children. A new spirit of ecumenism reigned: the forces that were pushing for the global forum of the United Nations were prevailing in the religious sector as well. The NCC was formed in 1950, reforged from the Federal Council of Churches, founded in 1908 as a coalition of America's most established and prestigious denominations. In 1958, no less a figure than President Eisenhower headlined the dedication ceremonies for the NCC's Interfaith Center, located next to the ornate Rockefeller-funded Riverside Church in New York City. As the president's participation suggests, a large number of prominent laymen were also ecumenical church figures. This was true even within Eisenhower's own cabinet. Arthur Fleming, his secretary of health, education, and welfare, was president of the NCC; and John Foster Dulles, his secretary of state, chaired an NCC committee on peace.[32] The mainline churches were centers of established power, for most prominent men and women in public life belonged to one of its denominations. So did much of the American public: 40 million people, nearly half of all voters, were members of an NCC-affiliated church.[33]

The churches' spirit of ecumenism had expanded globally. The NCC's international equivalent, the World Council of Churches (WCC), met regularly every seven years, uniting diverse nations and denominations to create a collective voice for justice and conscience. As the Presbyterian churchman Robert McAfee Brown explained, the WCC conceptualized the global church as "an international body cutting across race, class, and privilege, and avoiding the dreary parochialism of so many long-established churches."[34] As centuries of imperialism and sectarian divide seemed to draw to a close, the WCC was working to establish a truly international and vibrant church.

Many of the mainline churchmen were from theological backgrounds similar to McGovern's, which stressed a religious commitment to solving the age's great challenges. Not only were they also committed to liberal causes, but they had already established themselves in the nation's capital, often borrowing space in the Methodists' downtown offices. The United Methodist Building, located close to the Supreme Court Building, had been the home base of a corps of lobbyists since the 1950s. By 1960, these lobbyists were advocating on behalf of migrant labor, black civil rights, and the urban poor, even though these issues were often outside the experience, and in some cases the concern, of many of their congregants.[35] "Previously the parish had been their world," said the NCC negotiator John P. Adams. "When the challenge came, the world became their parish."[36]

As the conscience of the churchgoing public, the NCC may have had its greatest success during the civil rights movement.[37] The organization's Board of Religion and Race encouraged local congregations to take part in the freedom struggle, declaring that "the Church [is] called upon to put aside every lesser engagement [and must] confess her sins of omission and delay" in order to right racial injustice.[38] NCC leaders participated in peaceful demonstrations in the South, among them Robert McAfee Brown, a professor at Union Seminary. He described the freedom rides as "an experience that erases naivety" and believed that such actions were making made the institutional church a vibrant part of transforming the world.[39] In an attempt to integrate a historically white church, two

Methodist bishops—James Mathews, a white man; and Charles Golden, a black man—walked together into an Easter morning service in Jackson, Mississippi, only to be blocked by ushers.[40]

Missives from the Board of Religion and Race implored parishioners to write to their congressional representatives to support civil rights; and in 1964, fully 42 percent of such letters came from men and women who were writing on behalf of or in cooperation with a place of worship.[41] That same year, after cloture was invoked in the Senate to end a mostly southern filibuster, a meaningful civil rights bill finally made its way through the congressional stalemate.[42] It did so with the usual votes from Congress's northeastern and Pacific coast members, but it also received support from heretofore reluctant small-government conservatives in the West and the Midwest, where membership in the mainline denominations was particularly strong. Milton Young, Roman Hruska, Wallace Bennett, and McGovern's nemesis Karl Mundt—all of them conservative senators—voted for the bill, partly because of their constituents' strong support. As Richard Russell, the Senate giant who led the opposition to the bill, later complained, the logjam broke only after "those damn preachers got the idea that it was a moral issue."[43]

In fact, leaders in the NCC had gotten the idea that a great many issues were moral. From the spires of their Riverside Drive headquarters, they began regularly wading into controversy, issuing left-of-center resolutions and policy outlines for public consideration. In the 1950s and early 1960s, they brought the weight of the church to bear on civil liberties and civil rights issues before turning their focus to the escalating war in Indochina.[44] In their efforts to persuade, these leaders relied on the mainline Protestants in the halls of Congress. These allies included a number of liberal Democrats, many from the Midwest. Birch Bayh and John Brademas of Indiana, Walter Mondale and Hubert H. Humphrey of Minnesota, and Robert W. Edgar of Pennsylvania all shared the intellectual and spiritual culture of the mainline Protestant leadership.[45]

The Methodist pamphlet *Register Christian Opinion* defended this approach, declaring that "peace, freedom and justice are most likely to triumph when spiritually motivated persons use their political freedom effectively to translate their ideals into constructive legislation and national politics."[46] The close relationship in the 1950s and 1960s between mainline leaders and policymakers demonstrates how church members became, at least in their own eyes, devout helpmates in the legislative process. James

Mathews, the Methodist bishop who had tried to integrate the Mississippi church, recalled in his autobiography that it "was my practice to quietly cultivate such avenues and access as might be helpful for the Church to both houses of Congress and to the White House itself," including friendships with McGovern and Brademas. McGovern often attended Mathews's church in Washington, DC, and on the Sunday after Kennedy's assassination the bishop invited him to read the gospel lesson. Yet even though Mathews sought friendships with members of congress as part of his ministry, he did so with caution, given the constitutional separation of church and state: "I soon discovered that no political leader wants to appear beholden to a religious leader."[47]

The NCC church leaders drew McGovern into activist strands of mainline Christianity that were national or global in their focus. Their apparent victory in the civil rights struggle gave them the confidence to expand and embolden their relationship with lawmakers; and given McGovern's ties to Methodism, his seminary studies, and the close association between churches and Food for Peace, they believed he was their kind of man. In 1964, Methodist leaders invited McGovern and his decidedly less Methodist colleague, Jacob Javits, to attend a forum on disarmament and world peace sponsored by the denomination's Board of Social Concerns.[48] The board's pastors and activists were delighted to have a prominent dove such as McGovern working with them. By 1970, the senator was in frequent correspondence with major figures in the antiwar movement, such as William Sloane Coffin Jr., the chaplain of Yale University, and J. Brooke Mosley, the president of Union Seminary. Many of the movement's leaders came out strongly for McGovern during his 1972 campaign and exhorted their fellow clergy to do the same. In this way, they created a reserve of spiritual capital.

Given these connections, McGovern had easy access to mainline Protestant print culture, where he often expounded on his belief in a more compassionate political process. In *Theology Today*, he argued that Christians know that "it is just not possible for human life to flourish on this increasingly crowded planet unless we come to understand that brotherhood is the prime condition of our survival."[49] His article listed a series of maladies that required federal action rather than abstract goodwill: nutritional deficiencies, rickets, goiters, and tooth decay. In *Congress and Conscience*, Congressman John B. Anderson's edited volume on how religious faith guides lawmakers, McGovern expanded on these ideas. Knowing that he was writing for an audience dominated by Anderson's fellow evangelicals,

McGovern was unapologetically liberal. He made clear his belief that the state had an obligation to step in on behalf of those who could not speak for themselves. He cited the biblical passages that address poverty directly, condemning inaction in the face of human need. A passage from Matthew 25:41–45 read: "Depart from me, ye cursed, into everlasting fire, prepared for the devil and his angels, For I was hungry, and ye gave me no meat, thirsty, and ye gave me no drink." Another, from Isaiah 58:6–8, read:

> Is not this the fast that I have chosen? To loose the bonds of wickedness, to undo the heavy burdens, and to let the oppressed go free, and that ye break every yoke? Is it not to deal thy bread to the hungry, and that thou bring the poor that are cast out to thy house? When thou seest the naked, that thou cover him; and that thou hide not thyself from thine own flesh? Then shall thy light break forth as the morning, and thine health shall spring forth speedily: and thy righteousness shall go before thee; the glory of the Lord shall be thy reward.[50]

These passages, the senator argued, did not pertain principally to private almsgiving but to civic generosity. In his view, mere charity had "not made a significant dent in the problem of widespread hunger and malnutrition."[51] Instead, he conceptualized the state as a guarantor of the commonweal because it was the only institution with the resources to effectively address the scale of the crisis. Recognizing that his audience was religious, he knew these passages would help him explain and promote his philosophy of using good governance as a lever of social justice.

Uppsala and the World

Mainline organizations often invited political figures to serve as board members or honorary chairs, a mutually beneficial arrangement for both churchmanship and statesmanship. Thus, in 1968, the Methodist Council of Bishops invited McGovern and John Brademas to attend the meeting of the World Council of Churches in Uppsala, Sweden. The month-long event was one of the decade's most significant gatherings of Christians; and even though McGovern was able to attend only a small portion of the proceedings, he was still able to establish friendships with a number of prominent mainline Protestant leaders, including James Armstrong, an Indiana pastor who would become one of his closest friends.

Many of the Uppsala attendees advocated reform from below, ideas that later coalesced into what is now known as liberation theology. According to an article in *Theology Today,* the most distinctive trait of the assembly was how it prioritized "concern with contemporary social and economic issues" as privileged westerners and participants from the developing world came into contact with one another.[52] In 1968, many global issues were vying for attention—among them, riots in Paris, the short-lived Prague springtime in Czechoslovakia, apartheid in South Africa, the reviled war in Vietnam, and numerous uprisings in colonies throughout the world, in Asia, Africa, South America, and the Middle East. Given the array of global voices represented in Uppsala, many attendees believed that prophetic action could no longer be the gentle corrective of Rauschenbusch but must become a revolutionary force at work in the world. One speaker cried, "No . . . ecclesiastical, industrial, governmental, or international [structures] lie outside the scope of the churches' task as they seek to carry out their prophetic role in understanding the will of God for all men. The churches should constantly evaluate such structures and foster a willingness to accept change and even to promote it."[53] Another declared, "The capacity of the Church to exercise its prophetic ministry in the revolutionary world in which we live depends upon the Church renewing its prophetic being, that is, its being in Christ for every man and for all mankind."[54]

The council took place in the wake of both the Martin Luther King Jr. and Robert Kennedy assassinations, and the way in which many attendees were challenging the world order discomfited some members of the American delegation. Voices from around the globe unleashed prophetic outrage against American foreign policy excursions and the nation's culture of violence. Echoing King's 1967 address at Riverside Church, in which the pastor had called the United States the greatest purveyor of violence in the world, O. Frederick Nolde of the Lutheran Church in America struck a confrontational tone: "The U.S. citizens must bow in shame when they recall the assassinations of President John F. Kennedy, Dr. Martin Luther King, Sen. Robert F. Kennedy. The War in Vietnam, portrayed on TV in all its bloody cruelty, makes its derisive debilitating impact."[55]

While this language was not wholly different from McGovern's outcry against the Vietnam War, such statements put him into a difficult position. His service as an elected officeholder from a conservative state would be jeopardized if he did not respond to such blanket condemnations of the United States on foreign soil. Mindful that he was up for reelection, he hastily called a press conference and share his concerns in front of 250 journalists from around the world. As he explained years later, he wanted to remind the foreign press that "their history too was filled with blood and unnecessary wars—we've all sinned against humanity—and [used] military methods to try to resolve problems—and it's much more complicated than that—every country I could see at that press conference was up to their elbows in blood in their history, and a word of caution might be in order."[56] The senator admonished some of his fellow WCC delegates: "I am bothered by [their] self-righteousness and intolerance. I do not want to be ungenerous, but it is a fact that no nation comes into this assembly with clean hands." He asked the delegates to remember that the United States, too, had a prophetic tradition and that "the interaction of the Judeo-Christian conscience and the political process" had driven reform in civil rights.[57] Despite these caveats, McGovern did not shy away from his involvement in the conference, and he saw churchmanship as a serious conduit for discussion in public affairs. In a constituent mailing he sent from Uppsala, he explained, "Every major political question is at bottom a moral issue which challenges politicians to draw on the insights of the church."[58] Once again, he drew a link between himself and the conservative churchgoing South Dakota public, making his humanitarian liberalism an asset rather than a disadvantage.

Despite the turmoil surrounding his visit to Uppsala, McGovern agreed to chair the WCC's Council on Racism in 1969.[59] This gathering at Notting Hill in London was the first in a series of WCC councils to study the issues of racial oppression in the developing world that African and Asian voices had raised so urgently in Sweden. The forum included a constellation of international activists, including Michael Ramsey, the archbishop of Canterbury, and Oliver Tambo, the president of the African National Congress. Yet the council's focus on the problem of "white racism" did little to counter conservative accusations that liberal church councils were finding fault with Middle American institutions.[60]

During this visit to Europe, McGovern had other responsibilities, and so was absent for the most controversial moments of the forum. He split his time between Notting Hill and Paris, where peace talks with the North Vietnamese were under way. During one of his absences, Tambo harshly condemned the tepid and incrementalist responses from the West, which in his view encouraged patience and forbearance while castigating South African revolutionaries as violent political actors. He exhorted, "The situation can no longer be contained by pleading caution or advocating patience. Direction and practical involvement on the right side is the only realistic way of fighting racism and colonialism. To stand aloof is to court disaster."[61]

Tambo's strong words were echoed by the actions of black militants, who at points during the conference seized the podium and proffered a list of demands. These unplanned incidents gave the proceedings an unwelcome atmosphere of sensationalism. One British tabloid described the council as "part teach-in, part penitence, part act of redemption and part morality play with unscripted episodes from black power."[62] The council agreed to a series of resolutions that did not go as far as Tambo had hoped, but they did include reparations, sanctions against nations and businesses engaged in racial injustice, and a provision supporting violent revolution as a last resort.[63]

McGovern was a churchman, but he was also a politician. The global church was taking up causes that he supported but was also using problematically radical language, creating bad publicity, and favoring untenable solutions. In both Uppsala and London, he had attended meetings as a Methodist emissary in good faith, but he was careful to keep his distance when the church gatherings became too controversial or were no longer politically advantageous. He was much more intentional about fostering warm relationships with ecumenical leaders, especially as their opposition to the Vietnam War grew. Sometimes their correspondence was endearingly personal and humorous. This can be seen in a letter congratulating Mosley on his installation as Union Seminary's president. McGovern warmly recalled their time together at Uppsala and in a postscript used revivalist language to joke about the Senate's recent vote against one of President Nixon's Supreme Court nominees with segregationist baggage. "We just defeated Brother Carswell, 51–45. Hallelujah! Hallelujah!"[64] McGovern knew that Mosley and other like-minded churchmen would share his own opinion about Carswell's antiquated and regressive views on race.

By the end of the 1960s, McGovern's beliefs in Christian humanism and the salutary role that politics could play in alleviating suffering were as strong as ever. Now they were rerouted through the machinery of the mainline churches and were important elements of his relationships with their leaders. Those relationships were not seamless, and at each turn McGovern prioritized being a successful senator over being a dependable churchman. Still, more often than not, he and his mainline allies shared a set of ideals, and nowhere was this more apparent than in the common issue that drew their righteous ire: the war in Vietnam.

4

Pastors, Public Men, and Peacemakers

Throughout the 1960s, George McGovern was part of a rich network of prominent mainline pastors and influential liberal politicians. This web of allies was staunchly opposed to the Vietnam War, and McGovern's close friend, the Methodist bishop James Armstrong, played an especially pivotal role. As he explained in a 1972 speech, he believed that working "within the vineyards of the establishment" was not just a ministerial right but an obligation.[1] Like McGovern and many other liberal Protestants, Armstrong had visited Vietnam, and the experience transformed his understanding of the conflict from an abstraction of Cold War policy into a crisis of the American spirit that demanded conscientious opposition. He and other religious voices of dissent worked with antiwar politicians to hone a prophetic critique of American involvement in the war. Yet their activism came with a cost. Some members of the public believed that liberal politicians of McGovern's ilk were naïve or cavalier about the geopolitical realities of the Cold War, and mainline Protestant leaders earned a reputation as meddlers in the political process, thus damaging their historical role as arbiters of American conscience.

Armstrong and the Prophetic Ministry

The activist clerics of the 1960s and 1970s have become romantic figures, immortalized in Paul Simon's song "Me and Julio Down by the School-yard" and satirized as the hip Rev. Scot Sloan in Gary Trudeau's comic strip *Doonesbury*. Their real-life counterparts are easy to recall: the Catholic

Berrigan brothers and the liberal Protestant William Sloane Coffin Jr., all of them men of the cloth who were also eloquent members of the anti-war movement. Iconoclasts in clerical collars, they saw their acts of civil disobedience as discipleship against an oppressive and violent structure.[2] Daniel Berrigan famously broke into a draft office and stained its records with sheep's blood, a theatrical act of disruption that echoed both the Bible and Yippie protest. Coffin, for his part, was arrested for helping young men evade the draft. In both cases, these acts were archetypes of radical opposition to the Vietnam War from within the ministry.

Alongside such colorful, law-breaking contemporaries, Bishop Armstrong may sometimes be forgotten. Yet he was a prolific author and a prophetic minister who tried to work within established systems of power rather than make use of civil disobedience and street theater to achieve his ends. His public life was filled with apparent conflicts of interest as his moral compass led him into seemingly divergent and contradictory roles. He surfaced as a citizen-pastor, a lobbyist-counselor, and, most importantly, a prophet-adviser, a gregarious man who socialized easily within the establishment while often acting as one of its fiercest critics. Armstrong was fervently engaged in civic life. He bargained with mayors, served on blue-ribbon committees, and accepted invitations to speak all over the country. He was also one of McGovern's closest friends and most emphatic supporters. With similar backgrounds in the social gospel and the midcentury ecumenical movement, they navigated the crises of the 1960s and 1970s together and became lifelong confidants. Their relationship was symbiotic: McGovern had a statesman's ability to shape public policy, while Armstrong was an important player in the Methodist Church. Their friendship was a meeting place of political power and moral authority, but that did not make it any less sincere.

Two years McGovern's junior, Arthur James Armstrong was born in 1924 into a Hoosier family with a history of pastoral ministry in the Methodist Episcopal Church. Intending to follow his father into the ministry, Armstrong completed his education at Emory University's Candler School of Theology. Emory's approach tended to be liberal and included a blend of prophetic preaching and personalist thought that was similar to what McGovern had encountered at Dakota Wesleyan and Garrett. A telltale passage in Armstrong's later work suggests that he had a personalist understanding of the divine as unlimited in its capacity for love and accordingly finite in its ability to prevent evil. "If God and love are one," he wrote in

1969, "then the blame for irrational and heartbreaking tragedy cannot be placed at the feet of God. *Better to have a limited God than a demonic one.* In trying to make God all powerful we have (without meaning to) accused him of being perverse. In underlining his sovereignty we have erased his love."[3] Like McGovern, Armstrong saw personalism as a theological impetus for social change because it placed the burden of action on an informed and transformed humankind, not on an intercessory God. McGovern and Armstrong were scarcely alone in this conception; personalism was also a crucial component of Martin Luther King's theology, which tempered hope with committed action.[4]

Armstrong, like McGovern, believed that politically liberal causes that brought about positive reform could actualize the kingdom of heaven. He also learned to borrow language from the Old Testament prophets, choosing passages rooted in a sense of community and nationhood as models for encouraging the common good. He wrote, "We have neglected the Old Testament; many of us have eliminated it from our lectionaries. So, relying upon a distorted view of the New Covenant, our faith has become more individualistic, more self-serving, more comfort-oriented and acculturated, while the stern and righteous judgments and the sense of collective responsibility implicit in the Old Covenant have been conveniently brushed aside."[5]

For Armstrong, "collective responsibility" usually meant taking an active part in politics; and as a student pastor in Florida, he took his first step into partisan waters. His time there coincided with one of the most contentious races in Senate history, in which the urbane George Smathers challenged New Deal liberal Claude Pepper from within his own party.[6] Smathers race-baited shamelessly throughout the 1950 primary election, particularly in Florida's conservative panhandle. Repulsed, the young pastor wrote a strong letter to Smathers condemning the racially charged tone of his campaign. The future senator's office responded with a similarly sharp missive, curtly questioning the propriety of sending such a note on church letterhead.[7] This incident would have been purely anecdotal if it had not anticipated a dilemma that would follow Armstrong throughout his public career. Should the clergy take part in electoral politics when issues of grave moral concern are at stake? If so, how can they avoid compromising the mission of the church or presuming to speak for the church as a whole?

Armstrong's concern about the politics of race did not abate when he left the South in 1958 for Broadway Methodist Church in Indianapolis.

The denomination's largest church in the state, it boasted more than 3,000 registered members.[8] The church was popular among the Indianapolis elite, with parishioners including Mayor Charley Boswell as well as the city's Democratic and Republican party chairs. At a time when affluent people were leaving the inner city in droves, Broadway Methodist was a thriving place of worship near the city center. Yet like other well-to-do churches in similar areas across the country, the congregation was becoming majority-minority, much as the neighborhoods were. As white flight took hold, former congregants moved to, and often worshipped in, more bucolic settings outside the city limits.[9] Broadway Methodist's first black family joined in 1961, and by the time Armstrong left in 1969, it was about 85 percent black, roughly proportionate to its Fall Creek neighborhood.[10]

Armstrong personally welcomed the first black family to move into Broadway's vicinity and, thanks to his contacts with the mayor, secured police protection for their house.[11] In the spirit of the social gospel, he and others at the church aimed to alleviate the material need, the lack of education, and the boredom that were contributing to cycles of crime and poverty. The church instituted athletic programs for inner-city teens, established tutoring programs, and administered inoculations to poor children throughout the city.[12] He also rallied the largely minority citizens of Fall Creek to stand up against the expansion of freeways and state universities, which, under the guise of urban renewal, would have broken up their communities, effectively evicting the residents without fair recompense. As a liaison between the black community and the mayor's office, Armstrong was trusted implicitly by both parties, and this work framed much of his activism throughout the 1960s. To resolve a discriminatory zoning law or the lack of municipal services in a rundown part of town, he always made a beeline to the city's most prominent men, yet he was careful to avoid being too familiar or too forward. He wrote, "If we are to stand by the sides of those called upon to lead their people in such an hour, we must earn our places with clarity of thought, decisive action, and a willingness to run the same risks and be judged by the same standards as other partisan activists."[13]

As his reputation in United Methodism grew, Armstrong began developing friendly relations with Indiana politicians, including Vance Hartke and Birch Bayh, both liberal senators in a conservative state. Although Bayh was an Episcopalian, he asked Armstrong to baptize his young son, the future senator Evan Bayh. Armstrong cemented such friendships by participating in a number of civic organizations. An ecclesial cog in the machinery of civic power, he became an important member of Indianapolis's Urban League, its Community Service Council, and the Mayor's Progress Committee. In 1964, President Lyndon Johnson appointed him to the National Citizens' Committee for Community Relations.[14]

However, in Armstrong's view, a minister was more than a Rotarian in a clerical collar; he also had prophetic obligations to challenge injustices before the law. "The pastoral role dare not be minimized," he maintained later in his career, "but anything less than prophetic witness is sub-Christian. And the pulpit must reflect this fundamental truth."[15] Armstrong believed that speaking out on behalf of a disadvantaged group was a vital component of the practice of Christianity. He explained, "When the servant of God pleads for justice, when he talks about human rights, the liberation of oppressed people, the preservation of this good earth, corruption and ethical blindness in high places, greed and avarice among us all, the sins of war-thinking and war-profiteering and war-making, he is not adding his own divisive notions to the gospel; *he is preaching the gospel.*"[16]

This approach made Armstrong a natural candidate for Methodism's Board of Christian Social Concern, the denomination's loudest mouthpiece on issues of justice.[17] The church hierarchy also chose him as a delegate to the 1968 World Council of Churches meeting in Uppsala, where he encountered the African American novelist James Baldwin as well as Barbara Ward, an economist specializing on the developing world, and Martin Niemoller of Germany's Nazi-opposing Confessing Church. All made the case for the global connections among race, war, and injustice.[18] But this forum also had a significant impact on Armstrong's ministry among American lawmakers. Given their common ecumenical ties and their shared internationalism, it was fitting that he met the man who would become his closest political ally, George McGovern, in Uppsala. McGovern, as Armstrong recalled, was eager to be photographed with Michael Ramsey, the archbishop of Canterbury, and asked Armstrong, standing nearby, to take the picture.[19] Neither man knew that Armstrong would become McGovern's bishop in a matter of months and that they were beginning a friendship that would last until the senator's death.

The tense atmosphere of 1968 convinced Armstrong to use his stature to further the causes of left-leaning candidates. He began by supporting Eugene McCarthy for president, although he eventually concluded that the Minnesota senator was temperamentally the wrong man for the job despite his stern indictment of the war in Vietnam. By the time the primaries were over, he found McCarthy "insulated from harsh, cultural reality, scorning team play and staff resources, and betraying a strange, messianic diffidence to the outcome of the enterprise."[20] In 1970, Armstrong openly endorsed Hartke in his difficult but ultimately successful bid for reelection to the Senate. To help him, Armstrong circulated a lengthy missive praising Hartke as a rare forward-thinking leader, one who had been warning against escalation in Vietnam since 1966 and who had spoken in favor of a Department of Peace as a counterbalance to the Department of Defense.[21]

While Armstrong was engaging in an unusual level of partisan activity, his efforts were not conducted under an explicitly religious banner. Rather, he took part in electoral politics through wholly secular citizens' organizations: the National Coalition for a Responsible Congress (for Hartke) and Hoosiers for a Democratic Alternative (for McCarthy). By doing this, Armstrong characterized his involvement as a private civic act that was informed by religious sentiment rather than an overtly religious attempt to Christianize the public sphere. As he explained many years later, "a clergy doesn't surrender his citizenship when he or she becomes a clergy. And as a citizen, theoretically, we are trained, and theoretically we have minds, so why not use our minds and our training for public life?"[22] Yet his growing concern about Vietnam was forcing him to frame his political involvement in terms of moral urgency, although it remained outside the formal purview of the church.

With his national visibility on the rise, James Armstrong faced a sudden transition in his career: promotion. In 1969, the United Methodist Church bestowed on him the office of bishop and assigned him to a sprawling diocese spanning both North and South Dakota. At the age of forty-three, Armstrong had become one of the youngest Methodist bishops of the twentieth century. Yet if church leaders had hoped that the assignment would keep Armstrong out of trouble, they were disappointed. The move was, he recollected, "the best thing that could have happened" to him, given how few Methodist churches there were to oversee in the Dakotas.[23] He now had far more time to address social issues and take part in ecumenical church activity. Ironically, by consigning him to the hinterland, the Methodist hierarchy gave him the freedom to engage in greater, and in some ways more politically active, social witness.

Armstrong's promotion and relocation also made him McGovern's bishop. What had begun, after Uppsala, as a cursory exchange of letters and courtesy calls deepened into personal affection and a close friendship bound by a common set of values. Armstrong recollected, "I came to learn more about him, and I realized we were playing from the same page on national and international issues, and that helped to bond the friendship."[24] By the end of 1969, he had convinced McGovern to write the foreword to his collection of sermons, *The Urgent Now*. In it, McGovern praised his friend as "at once preacher, philosopher, poet, prophet, and political activist," one who "proclaims in the highest traditions of great preaching the enduring claims of love over hate . . . [and] the imperatives of brotherhood over the folly of war."[25] Within a year of beginning their correspondence, "Bishop Armstrong" and "Senator McGovern" had become "Jim" and "George."

By 1970, the two were conversing weekly about national issues. Many of these discussions were face to face, as Armstrong's work on the Methodist Board of Church and Society frequently brought him to Washington, DC. These talks, according to Armstrong, involved "little theology in the abstract sense, but dealt with ethical and social issues in a political context."[26] During the fall of that year, when McGovern was first mulling over a presidential campaign, he had Armstrong's full encouragement, even though the role the bishop might play remained ambiguous and constrained. "I recognize that there are limitations to the extent and kinds of activities you can become involved in," McGovern wrote to his friend.[27] Armstrong spent the next two years testing the boundaries of those limitations.

Vietnam as a Moral Crisis

Until 1969, race relations in urban areas had been Armstrong's signature issue as a social activist pastor. Despite his temporary affinity for McCarthy, he was not seen as an antiwar minister in the vein of pastor-activists such as Coffin and the Berrigans. His priorities shifted when he was named to the US Study Team on Religious and Political Freedom in Vietnam organized by the venerable ecumenical peace organization Fellowship of Reconciliation (FOR). The team was charged with exploring conditions in South Vietnam prisons, and its members included Representative John Conyers of Michigan, future congressman and Jesuit priest Robert Drinan, and FOR secretary Alfred Hassler. What they found was an arbitrary and ruthlessly efficient form of justice in which all manner of prisoners were summarily tossed into jail without due process under the ambiguous category of "civilians related to communist activity."[28]

Not only did team members see despotism at work inside the prisons, but they also saw the bald and pointless destruction outside them. Armstrong was shocked: the country's landscape was ruined, and its military rulers were growing increasingly oppressive. As he recorded in *The Urgent Now*, Vietnam's rural areas had been "laid to waste," and its urban centers were "glutted with millions of nameless refugees."[29] In Saigon, Armstrong's delegation visited the surgical unit of a children's hospital and found the ward filled with young Vietnamese who had suffered disfigurements, burns, and amputations as the military had worked to contain and bomb the Viet Cong. Heretofore Armstrong's opposition to the war had been abstract and academic, but the trip transformed him into a passionate and prophetic activist against the conflict.

His antiwar activity included both political and pastoral elements; he wanted to stop the war while aiding those caught in its orbit. As part of this ministry, for instance, he and Harvey Cox, the chair of Harvard Divinity School, traveled to Europe to comfort and counsel young Americans who had left their own country rather than be drafted.[30] In the Old Testament prophets Armstrong found a language for confronting civic leaders and making a moral case to congregations who preferred not to hear about the horrors of Vietnam on Sunday morning. The prophets, he tried to explain, "cried against specific deeds and practices, specific attitudes and policies, against the unrighteousness of both their own people and of others." In words that seemed to be directed at both Saigon's and Washington's policymakers, Amos, in his short book of prophecy, was "cataloging their rapacious conduct in war and their brutalization of persons. Hosea the prophet shook a finger of judgment in the faces of the judges and princes, the insensitive bureaucracy of this land."[31] Armstrong acknowledged Elijah, Nathan, Isaiah, Josiah, Hosea, and Amos as exemplary figures whose ire "zeroed in on their own land."[32] The Hebrew prophets, he wrote, were "not intimidated by those in high places," a dig at the sycophantic ministers he saw around President Nixon. On the contrary, they "cried out against the greed and blindness of the rich; against the tyranny of courts and princes; against the callous inhumanity of the powerful."[33] Armstrong's zeal against the war was manifested in one of his breakout moments as a national figure, when he delivered his oration "Is 'Peace' a Dirty Word?" to the Methodist Church's General Conference in St. Louis in 1970. The speech decried not only the presence of war but an American society predicated on Cold War militarism. "If peace is a dirty word," he exhorted, "then Christ was a dirty liar and history is a dirty joke. . . . No! This we do not believe. We are

Christians—United Methodists—and we have been raised up for such a time as this. We believe in God. And, as we are faithful and obedient, he will be with us, believing in us, empowering us, enabling us to join him in extending the boundaries of his kingdom in his world."[34]

As Armstrong criticized American war policy, voices among the laity challenged his activism—some because they disagreed with his politics, others because they felt that a bishop should put pastoral efforts and church administration before social reform. Speaking to a gathering of church members in western Pennsylvania, Armstrong shared a horrific account of his visit to Vietnam. Midway through his talk, he asked rhetorically, "Does a sermon like this have any place at an Annual Conference?" In response, a voice in the back of the room shouted a defiant "NOOOO!"[35] In another encounter, this time at the 1968 Methodist General Conference, which supported civil disobedience with qualifications, a former parishioner from Cincinnati acrimoniously left the gathering, telling Armstrong, "I just want you to know, I love my country more than I love my church."[36] The exchange highlights Armstrong's conflicted attitude toward his congregants and toward Protestant America in general. As he saw it, ordinary congregants sought comfort from their church but were unwilling to engage in the great issues of the day, unwilling to make sacrifices for people who were different from themselves.

Armstrong's journey from a skeptic of the war to a vocal critic paralleled the journey made by other leaders in the mainline churches, as well as by George McGovern himself. Throughout his early political career, McGovern tended to see military adventurism as a waste of resources and, as a freshman senator, questioned the use of American military aid in the Indochina region. His first public critiques of US involvement took place even before Kennedy's assassination, when Vietnam was hardly a matter of pressing public concern. The funneling of weapons and advisors into Vietnam had been "a clear demonstration [of] the limitations of military power," with little progress made and Ngo Dinh Diem's government as hated and unstable as ever.[37] But with the strikes on the Gulf of Tonkin in 1964, the calculus of America's involvement in Vietnam changed greatly. At President Johnson's request, a resolution was brought before Congress granting the president wide clearance to deploy military personnel and equipment. McGovern was not entirely convinced this move was wise or necessary. Yet he was ultimately persuaded by J. William Fulbright, the chair of the Senate Foreign Relations Committee, who assured him that the resolution would be limited in scope. It was theater for domestic politics, Fulbright argued, designed to shield the president from accusations of "losing Vietnam" before his 1964 campaign against the hawkish Barry Goldwater.[38]

The vote was a test of profound political foresight and moral courage, and McGovern failed it when he reluctantly voted for the resolution. As a consequence, the Gulf of Tonkin Resolution allowed Johnson to conduct military action in Vietnam without a formal declaration of war and with little congressional oversight. McGovern agonized about his decision long after, characterizing it as the biggest mistake of his career, one that taught him to never mistake "what I see as the truth for a winking assurance in a back room."[39] "What I regret," he explained to the historian Robert Mann, "is telling audiences all over the country that Johnson would not expand the war and that he would not engage in bombing, he would not attack the northern cities, he would not escalate—all those things that proved to be wrong."[40] Only two senators—Ernest Gruening of Alaska and Wayne Morse of Oregon—voted against the resolution. Both committed political suicide in doing so; neither was reelected.

Recognizing their mistake by 1965, McGovern and another western-state liberal, Frank Church of Idaho, called for a negotiated settlement to end the conflict between North and South Vietnam. McGovern's critical attitude toward military action in Indochina was informed by his graduate-school readings about the Cold War, which Arthur Link and Leften Stavrianos regularly supplemented throughout his public career. In particular, he was persuaded by Bernard Fall's critique that American strategists were repeating French mistakes, using firepower and airpower strikes against an elusive enemy that was fighting a guerrilla war and defending a homeland.[41] By trusting to superior firepower, American forces forfeited the chance to win trust on the ground. For McGovern, what was happening in Vietnam was clearly not a classic domino-theory scenario of Soviet and Chinese influence over Vietnam but was shaped by the particular histories of North and South Vietnam. He viewed the Viet Cong as nationalist in character, not as Chinese surrogates. To him, their actions made sense only in the context of decades of French domination, centuries of Chinese domination, and fear of possible American domination.[42]

McGovern arranged two private meetings with Johnson—one by himself, the other with Frank Church. In them, he reminded the president that Vietnam had been historically defined by its resistance, not its acquiescence, to Chinese imperialism. He argued that, as a Vietnamese nationalist, Ho

Chi Minh would not look to China for assistance unless American attacks made him feel that he had no alternative. In McGovern's opinion, instead of sending fighting forces, the United States should advocate for an agreement along the lines of the Geneva Convention, one that would allow North and South Vietnam to exist as a united country but under local autonomy to account for the different political proclivities in each region. In truth, however, McGovern and Johnson viewed Vietnam through very different lenses. Whereas the senator interpreted North Vietnam aggression as a manifestation of nationalism and anti-imperialism, the president saw it as a containment problem with politically salient ramifications at home. After McGovern explained his point of view in their final White House meeting, Johnson snapped, "Don't give me another goddamn history lesson. . . . I don't need a lecture on where we went wrong. I've got to deal with where we are now." He assured the senator that the war was under control. "I'm going up old Ho Chi Minh's leg an inch at a time," he boasted. McGovern rejoined, "Well, Mr. President, sometimes when we go up a leg we get slapped."[43]

McGovern's reservations about Johnson's war policy increased after he took his first trip to Vietnam in 1965. As Armstrong would do in 1969, he credited his experiences in Vietnam with transforming him from a war skeptic to a war opponent. In a hospital for civilians, he was appalled by the maimed infants he saw. Patients, many with horrific injuries caused by American bombs and shrapnel, were packed in two per cot. Some were lying outside, exposed to the elements because there was no room inside. The visit also vanquished his lingering doubts about whether or not the South Vietnamese government had the confidence and support of its people. In his autobiography, McGovern described these revelations in expressly religious terms, saying that they committed him "not merely to dissent, but to crusade."[44] Years later, he compared his hatred of the war to "an obsession" that he carried in his "stomach and heart and mind for ten years."[45] In a public break with the administrative line, he declared on a 1966 episode of *The Today Show,* "I don't see how either . . . side can score a decisive military victory." Moreover, given Vietnam's difficult terrain and the challenge of telling friend from foe, "if we were to destroy the Viet Cong, we'd have to destroy a large part of the civilian population."[46] Although he was careful to avoid criticizing Johnson outright, he had become persona non grata at the White House. He was not invited into the executive mansion until Gerald Ford took over as president, after the war had drawn to a close.

The Churches' "Vietnam Problem"

The Vietnam War also became a trial of credibility for the leadership of the mainline Protestant churches. Their actions against it limited their access to power and frayed the bonds of trust they shared with their congregations. Paralleling the senator's path, many mainline church leaders transitioned from skeptics of the war to critics and finally to outright dissenters as the Johnson and Nixon administrations refused their advice and spurned their counsel. Like McGovern, they were influenced by the milieu of liberal Protestantism, and their criticisms and skepticism were corroborated by what they saw on the ground. As early as 1965, an editorial in the *Christian Century,* which had long been a mouthpiece of the religious establishment, was urging a settlement and hoping that Johnson would not confuse "negotiation with retreat." Noting, as McGovern did, that the situation in Vietnam was more of a nationalist struggle than a Cold War front, the editorial argued, "There is little for foreigners to 'win' in such a conflict, for, short of destroying perhaps a majority of the Vietnamese people, it is unlikely that we will ever succeed in molding a Vietnam tailored to American desires!"[47]

Long before the public turned against the war, the ecumenical movement was at the front lines of proactive peacemaking. In 1965, the year of McGovern's first visit, FOR sent a delegation to Vietnam and came back with similar reservations about General Nguyen Van Thieu's regime. By mid-1965, the NCC was spearheading an event in which sixty major religious leaders, not just Protestants but also Catholics and Jews, would seek out lawmakers to "express their concern about the war" and push negotiation as the wisest course.[48] An article in *Time* noted the early tremors of this movement: "Civil rights is old hat. Now, the area in which clergymen are seeking to prove the contemporary relevance of Christianity is foreign policy."[49]

Johnson was not happy about the NCC's position, but he was indebted to its leaders for their valuable assistance in passing civil rights legislation. In 1964, editorials in the *Christian Century* had endorsed him for president over Barry Goldwater. In an act that caused the magazine to briefly lose its tax-exempt status, its editors had declared that Goldwater's election would ruin American credibility across the globe and set back the cause of civil rights by decades.[50] Thus, in 1967, key ecumenists easily secured face-to-face meetings with the administration's highest officials. Secretary of Defense Robert McNamara, for instance, met with William Sloane Coffin Jr., Rabbi Abraham Heschel, and Robert McAfee Brown. According to

Brown, McNamara, a "sometimes Presbyterian," began the interview "by acknowledging that it was perfectly appropriate for us to be there."[51] The three religious leaders left believing that Johnson would support a negotiated settlement with sufficient public support. They did not know that McNamara's goodwill had largely been for show; the outcome of the conflict would be determined on the ground, not around the negotiating table.

As the war escalated, the church leaders' relationship to the president grew frostier. With the churchgoing public also becoming more hostile, both McGovern and mainline leaders took a prophetic turn. In the aftermath of Tonkin, they had pushed for a negotiated settlement rather than a military solution. But as casualties mounted and more troops were committed to Indochina, they called for outright withdrawal and began publicly criticizing the president's war policy.[52] Looking for a way to safely express his moral opposition to the war, McGovern decided to made his first call for troop withdrawal at the annual conference of Dakota Methodists in Aberdeen, South Dakota, on October 7, 1967. As he told his co-religionists, "to remain silent in the face of policies we believe to be wrong is not patriotism; it is moral cowardice—a form of treason to one's conscience and to the nation."[53]

Such language came easily to religious people of both parties; McGovern remembered Ernest Tittle's prophetic torrents against Red Scare tactics during the 1950s, and many mainline ministers had recognized the value of speaking truth to power during the civil rights movement.[54] But when Protestant ministers were speaking out against McCarthyism or Jim Crow, they had received significant help from the president's administration and a good deal of congregational support. Now they had few such advantages; on the contrary, they faced overt opposition from the White House, and Johnson was a formidable enemy. As a way to focus on Vietnam and protect the NCC from criticism, many antiwar ministers organized under the aegis of Clergy and Laity Concerned about Vietnam (CALCAV). Significantly, CALCAV was one of the first organizations to articulate its dissent prophetically, and by 1967 it was openly endorsing acts of civil disobedience as its members shifted from counseling peace to demanding peace. In the 1968 publication *In the Name of America,* CALCAV condemned US activity in Indochina, calling it a "consistent violation of almost every international agreement relating to the rules of warfare" and going on to describe the treatment of prisoners, the brutal killing of civilians, and the effects of American napalm on the human body.[55]

Arguments that had once taken place behind closed Oval Office doors were spilling into the street, and laypeople watched nervously as church leaders mobilized behind antiwar activities. In 1967, partly in response to official Methodism's growing advocacy of peace in Vietnam, a group of Methodist laypeople formed the organization Good News. Their goal was to "reclaim" Methodism for local (and usually more conservative) congregations and to challenge the influence of over-politicized church leaders with liberal seminary backgrounds.[56] By framing the notion of ordinary, commonsense Americans taking stand against a tiny corps of leftist elites working against their interests, Good News anticipated Nixon's approach to politics. The laity and the more conservative clergy were resisting what they saw as a bureaucratic church culture that forfeited pastoral responsibilities to chase after leftist causes célèbres. As the church historian Martin Marty suggested, "everybody knows that when the mainline churches take a position, it is only six people in a room on Riverside Drive."[57] In a 1970 Methodist magazine article, such cynicism was poignantly encapsulated in the words of a Minneapolis man. Alluding to the NCC's support of Cesar Chavez's activism among migrant workers, he complained, "I used to go to church and the preacher would talk about God, Jesus and the Bible. Now he tells me why I shouldn't buy grapes."[58] For a generation of churchgoers, their pastors and denominational leaders seemed far more engaged in social crusades than in the spiritual well-being of their flocks.

Contemporary statistics confirmed this growing chasm. One poll from the late 1960s found that 85 percent of Lutheran ministers respected a protestor's right to actively disagree with government policy; in contrast, 58 percent of lay congregants did not respect that right.[59] A similar poll in 1974 revealed the divide between more conservative congregations and pastors who had been educated in liberal-leaning seminaries. Among Presbyterians, 47 percent of ministers said that military spending was too high, but only 13 percent of their church members agreed.[60] These disparities disturbed John Wesley Lord, the aptly named Methodist bishop who presided over the Washington, DC, area for several years in the 1960s. Reflecting on the painful choice between speaking out against the war and risking the loss of congregants, he wondered if the church could retain its influence under these conditions. "Will faithfulness to the gospel survive future Viet Nams? In this last chance that history affords, will religion be able to shape public opinion and create a climate in which theology can give direction to the course of human events?" he asked in the Methodist family magazine *Together*.[61] The clergy, he feared, were losing their capacity to influence the moral compass of the rank and file when controversial issues were at stake.

Faithfulness to the gospels compelled CALCAV, the NCC, and the mainline church leaders to press on, not least because the laity disagreed with them so vehemently about Vietnam. Many felt it was their prophetic obligation to call congregants to social righteousness, to compel them to address the effects of American bombings and the treachery of the South Vietnamese government. To facilitate these conversations, CALCAV published a ten-page brochure for the 1968 presidential primary season. Titled "Who's Right, Who's Wrong on Vietnam" the booklet was loaded with germane quotations from the major candidates, and its intent was to steer voters toward either Eugene McCarthy or Robert Kennedy, the two candidates who were denouncing the war in the strongest terms. "We sent it to every barber shop and beauty shop in America," remembered CALCAV's director Richard Fernandez. But much of the reaction was viscerally negative: "We got more hate mail. . . . We got shit in the mail, literally dung."[62]

Still, unlike some elements of the antiwar Left, these church-based organizations remained wary of revolution. McGovern, too, insisted on working within the extant political system. In 1967, he met with the activist Allard Lowenstein, who urged him to challenge Johnson in the 1968 primaries as an antiwar candidate. McGovern demurred, dreading the choice between reelection to the Senate and a presidential campaign. Instead, he recommended McCarthy, an eloquent senator with a strong Catholic background who also hated the war with a deep spiritual revulsion.[63]

A summer of turmoil and assassinations—including the murder of his friend Robert Kennedy—soon led McGovern to reconsider his initial refusal to run. As he recounted in his autobiography, his decision to seek the nomination as a long-shot candidate was spurred by an alarming conversation with McCarthy in which he learned that the senator was making no attempt to secure Kennedy's delegates and thus was effectively ceding the nomination to Vice-President Humphrey.[64] McGovern hoped that he might unite the delegates committed to McCarthy and Kennedy, whose factions deeply distrusted one another. Yet even though he received 146.5 votes at the Democratic National Convention in Chicago, they were not nearly enough to challenge the accumulated might of the state chairs and political machines, and Humphrey was awarded the nomination. Similarly, McGovern's efforts to put forward a peace plank at the convention were defeated. The platform of a candidate beholden to Johnson's war policy flatly rejected any bombing halts, and antiwar Democrats left Chicago battered and the party's reputation damaged.

Although Nixon and Humphrey both promised some form of disengagement from Vietnam, Nixon's victory in 1968 did little to convince the mainline clergy that an end was in sight. It soon became clear that Nixon's promises to end the war in Vietnam had been a cynical campaign tactic. As a token gesture, his administration granted NCC leaders a meeting— not with the president but with the point man of his foreign policy, Henry Kissinger, then the director of the National Security Agency. The meeting was unproductive, as was a subsequent meeting with Secretary of State William P. Rogers. Howard Schomer, a church layman who attended the second meeting, recalled that Rogers was both dismissive and standoffish. He clearly had not read the memos that NCC had sent beforehand, which at least Robert McNamara had had the courtesy to do in his 1967 meeting with NCC representatives. Instead, he harped on their duty as "potential public opinion makers" to support the president, all the while denouncing McGovern for "collusion with the enemy."[65]

By 1969, William Sloane Coffin Jr. had become one of McGovern's key allies. Pastors, Coffin believed, had a prophetic obligation to challenge the war effort. From their unique position in society, they "could speak out against the herd mentality that tends to dominate any nation in wartime." As a motorcycle-riding war protestor, he was comfortable within the counterculture, yet he was equally at home in the highest rungs of the Protestant establishment. (The first sentence of his autobiography reads, "Mademoiselle Lovey was our Swiss governess.")[66] Coffin worked easily with likeminded lawmakers, and he collaborated with McGovern often. Throughout 1969, they met several times to coordinate the senator's activities with CALCAV's. Partly under Coffin's advisement, McGovern spoke on October 15 before 100,000 antiwar demonstrators at an event known as the Moratorium to the End the War in Vietnam, held on Boston Common. He spoke again on November 15, this time in Washington, DC, at a demonstration involving nearly 300,000 people, sponsored by the National Mobilization Committee to End the War in Vietnam. In each case, he lambasted the war and thanked the protestors for having "faced up to their responsibilities. This is the highest form of patriotism." He insisted that the war's evil lay partly in the prioritizing of weapons above humanitarian efforts. The focus on saving Asia from communism had left "15 million

Americans defenseless against malnutrition" and was symptomatic of an "economy of death" snuffing out an "economy of life."[67]

These demonstrations, known as the Moratorium and the Mobilization, were among the greatest gatherings of antiwar voices in the history of the movement, although they were different from one another in many respects.[68] The Moratorium was more moderate, with a strong link to McCarthy's campaign and other forces that wanted to work within the two-party system. It was also significantly larger and more evidently successful: the gathering on Boston Common was the biggest of two hundred major demonstrations taking place simultaneously on October 15.[69] In contrast, the Mobilization, whose long history had begun with the work of the pacifist minister A. J. Muste, had attracted a radical contingent, including the Weathermen, who were attempting to upend the system.[70] During the November 15 demonstration, a branch led by the Yippies had a violent altercation with the police, and a hundred people were arrested.

McGovern's prominent speaking role at these protests put him into a new dilemma: he was taking part in events that were too radical for most South Dakotans' comfort, and he was too associated with the two-party system to please the revolutionary voices at the gatherings. McGovern may have been the most leftwing candidate ever nominated by a major US party, but he was no subversive. His address to the Mobilization rang hollow in a crowd filled with young people whose faith in traditional politics was fundamentally broken. They shouted over his speech, and he failed to make a significant impression on his listeners.[71] At the more moderate Moratorium, Peter Camejo of the Socialist Workers' Party received cheers when he declared, no doubt with McGovern in mind, "Watch out for the politicians who turn up now. They'll never march with you in the streets."[72]

McGovern's aides had warned him not to attend these demonstrations. His constituents, they argued, would see his activism as un-American and neglectful of his duties to his home state. Although McGovern had comfortably won reelection in 1968, he knew that South Dakotans had long memories and were suspicious of out-of-state influences. His fears were justified when a state newspaper chastised him for consorting with "flag burners and other assorted long-haired peace creeps."[73] Coffin tried to console him. "Outraged respectability is hardly a creative response to the vocabulary and acts of desperate students," he told the frustrated senator in 1969.[74] Middle American disapproval, the pastor argued, should not intimidate McGovern into stepping away from a position of leadership in the antiwar movement.

After the Moratorium protests, President Nixon began to publicly con-
flate opposition to his Vietnam policy with disloyalty to the country. On
November 3, 1969, he addressed the "silent majority" of Americans who did
not take to the streets: "The more support I can have from the American
people, the sooner that pledge [to withdraw with honor from Vietnam]
can be redeemed; for the more divided we are at home, the less likely the
enemy is to negotiate in Paris. Let us . . . understand: North Vietnam cannot defeat or humiliate the United States. Only Americans can do that."[75]
In other words, Nixon argued that lack of progress in the war was caused by
domestic opponents who had sapped America's strength at the negotiating
table. Behind the scenes, he encouraged White House proxies to attack the
institutions that were most critical of his presidency, including the mainline churches. Vice-President Spiro Agnew, the administration's designated
hatchet man, satirized these ministers as that "pleasant clergym[a]n who
lifts his weekly sermons out of old newsletters from a National Council
of Churches that has cast morality and theology aside as not relevant and
set[s] as its goal on earth the recognition of Red China and the preservation
of the Florida alligators."[76]

Clearly, this White House administration was different from Johnson's.
Rather than merely ignoring the NCC when it no longer served his purposes, Nixon actively undermined the organization and encouraged the
public to turn against its leaders. He harbored an intense hatred of the
social elite, a reaction dating back to his days at Whittier College, where
student affairs were run by a well-to-do clique called the Franklins. Nixon
had undercut their campus dominance by forming a rival faction he called
"the Orthogonians," populated with the salt of the collegiate earth.[77] As
president, he viewed the ecumenical leaders in the same light, treating them
as a self-important group that he had to outmaneuver. He began meeting
regularly with prominent evangelicals who were generally more support-
ive of the war, often inviting them to host a Sunday service at the White
House. Mainliners recognized that they had lost their customary privilege
of calling on the president. Eugene Carson Blake, the general secretary of
the WCC, made several attempts to meet with Nixon but was rebuffed with
polite form letters. Eventually he complained in the *Christian Century* that,
"from the beginning, the actions of the Nixon White House have worked
to downgrade the basic mainline Protestant leadership. And that is because
this leadership was critical of the government's Vietnam policy."[78]

Yet these leaders persevered in their work. In 1970, several Fellowship of

Reconciliation members, including Armstrong, Father Robert Drinan, and Alfred Hassler, joined McGovern and Representative John Conyers at a religious press conference. They asserted that General Thieu's regime in South Vietnam had "surpassed Diem's worst," with regular murders, tortures, and violations of due process.[79] Fellowship members argued that Thieu's anticommunism alone did not warrant US support, given his egregious human rights violations. If this was the regime Americans were dying to uphold, they argued, it would be better to get out and rescind our support.

That same year, the antiwar movement was suddenly rejuvenated by Nixon's announcement that he would expand the war into Cambodia. During an antiwar demonstration at Kent State University, the Ohio National Guard fired on the assembled protestors, killing four students. When John Lindsay, the mayor of New York City, flew the American flag at half mast in honor of the Kent State victims, enraged construction workers stormed City Hall, assaulting antiwar protestors in what became known as the Hard Hat Riot. Amid the unfolding chaos, McGovern recognized that the Senate's duty to "advise and consent" now meant revoking the impulsive decision that had allowed Johnson to send troops to Vietnam. Congress needed to end the conflict because Nixon had abdicated that responsibility. McGovern teamed up with Senator Mark Hatfield, a vocal antiwar Republican and the most famous evangelical in public office.[80] As the governor of Oregon, Hatfield had refused to support the Gulf of Tonkin Resolution, making him the lone gubernatorial holdout. Now he and McGovern, along with their staffs, crafted an amendment to an otherwise standard military appropriation bill. The amendment cut off funds for military action in Southeast Asia by the end of 1970 and mandated a withdrawal before July 1971.

Although some polls showed that the public supported the measure, the amendment did not pass in the Senate, failing thirty-nine to fifty-five, with only eight Republicans and thirty-one Democrats voting in its favor. Wes Michaelson, a young Hatfield aide, watched with disgust as Nixon bought off congressional voters in order to embarrass McGovern and truncate the effort. For instance, he overheard Vermont senator George Aiken, a known critic of the war, discreetly talking on the phone with a Nixon operative and agreeing to vote against the amendment if price supports for milk were raised.[81]

In such an atmosphere, mustering thirty-nine votes in favor of decisive de-escalation was a considerable feat, and it demonstrated the war's growing unpopularity in Congress. But its failure deeply troubled McGovern, particularly because he knew that senators with grave reservations about the war had voted against his amendment to protect their reelection bids or avoid running afoul of Nixon. One Democratic colleague even told him, "Well, you're right, but I just can't interfere with the president's prerogatives." His aides took note of his fury; "he thought he saw it so clearly that he couldn't understand for the life of him why everybody else couldn't."[82] After six years of warning against the entanglement in Vietnam, he had lost his patience, and on September 1 he launched into one of the most emotionally charged speeches of his career. On the Senate floor, he attacked the lawmakers who would not end the conflict or rein in the president. He was no longer condemning the war but condemning those who had voted for its perpetuation:

> Every senator in this chamber is partly responsible for sending 50,000 young Americans to an early grave. This chamber reeks of blood. Every senator here is partly responsible for that human wreckage at Walter Reed and Bethesda Naval [veterans' hospitals] and all across our land—young men without legs, or arms, or genitals, or faces, or hopes.
>
> There are not very many of these blasted and broken boys who think this war is a glorious adventure. Do not talk to them about bugging out, or national honor, or courage.
>
> It does not take any courage at all for a congressman, or a senator, or a president to wrap himself in the flag and say we are staying in Vietnam because it is not our blood that is being shed. But we are responsible for those young men and their lives and their hopes.
>
> And if we do not end this damnable war, those young men will someday curse us for our pitiful willingness to let the Executive carry the burden that the Constitution places on us.
>
> So before we vote let us ponder the admonition of Edmund Burke, the great parliamentarian of an earlier day: "a conscientious man would be cautious in how he dealt in blood."[83]

This oration is perhaps the most famous of McGovern's career, and it is easy to overlook its religious undercurrents. But it was a prophetic moment as the senator let loose a torrent of righteous anger at an unjust war and the men who were allowing it to continue. For a few minutes, McGovern was a modern-day Amos, pointing fingers at the powerful as he advocated for the forgotten. The senators were stunned at this address from their ordinarily mild-mannered colleague. When one protested that he had been offended by the speech, McGovern brusquely retorted, "That's what I meant to do."[84]

Most liberal Protestant leaders shared McGovern's frustration. Unable to sway their congregations or the administration, they had little payoff for their tentative progressive Christianity except for an intrinsic belief that they were doing what was right. In his book *Mission: Middle America*, Armstrong lashed out against what he saw as a callous and disinterested laity, decrying the conflation of patriotism with Christianity, of dissent with blasphemy. "More and more people are worshipping at the shrine of God and country," he lamented. "The cross and flag stand side by side on their altars, but the flag always seems to stand a bit taller and its claims and disciplines more binding."[85] He hoped that churchgoers might realize that "salvation cannot be grasped and smothered by the individual alone. It must be offered and applied to the larger, fragmented world to which he is a part."[86]

Nonetheless, CALCAV and other ecumenical voices had played a crucial role in the wider antiwar movement, even as their activities had repulsed Nixon's so-called "silent majority." During the hectic months of 1972, McGovern found time to thank CALCAV members for their "gallant, wise, and successful" work in peacemaking, and for encouraging him to speak at the Mobilization: "At a time of national crisis, you assumed the lonely burden of testing the promise of [Ralph Waldo] Emerson: 'If a single man plant himself on his convictions and then abide, the huge world will come round to him.'"[87] Despite setbacks, neither McGovern nor his mainline allies had abandoned the prophetic stance of speaking truth. And now they had shifted their thoughts to another way to withdraw from Vietnam—a faint and improbable option but a possibility nonetheless. George McGovern had his eyes on the presidency.

5

Calling America to Come Home

Sometimes the path to historic significance lies through defeat. Barry Goldwater's failed 1964 bid, for instance, triggered the rise of conservatives who would eventually wrest the Republican Party from eastern moderates at peace with the New Deal.[1] Howard Dean's 2004 attempt was the first truly online campaign and offered lessons in how to use the Internet to raise funds and mobilize volunteers.[2] Ron Paul's long-shot bids in 2008 and 2012 reinvigorated the libertarian movement among younger, more tech-savvy voters. Likewise, George McGovern's 1972 candidacy gave voice to social and political issues that would later become mainstream concerns. Not only did it call forth a new version of political participation that was closely linked to identity politics, but it also embodied progressive Christianity in a way that was exceptional in postwar electoral politics. Today the campaign is remembered most for its leftist and anti-establishment themes, yet its spirituality and social Christianity were the elements that made it unique.

The 1972 election coincided with an important transition in progressive Christianity. Chronologically, the campaign was positioned between the ecumenical, mainline leftism of the 1960s and the "resident alien" motif that many progressive Christians, especially those on the evangelical Left, adopted in response to the blue-collar populism of the 1970s.[3] While McGovern's bid inspired many Christians from both mainline and evangelical branches to participate more vigorously in public affairs, it also demonstrated the limits of prophetic action as a tool to win elections. Never again did progressive Christian voters mobilize so eagerly.

During an interview, Gordon Weil, McGovern's adviser and personal assistant throughout the 1972 campaign, reminded me that "the candidate is not the campaign; he's only a part of the campaign."[4] In other words, the person who is running for office can get lost in a labyrinth of aides and party functionaries. Yet within a complex campaign, McGovern strove to stay true to his worldview, and his bid for the presidency was underscored by the ethics of liberal Christianity that he had embraced throughout his public life.

According to the theologian Gary Dorrien, the social gospel centers around the idea that Christianity should transform both hearts and social structures; it should bring the kingdom of heaven closer to fulfillment.[5] McGovern construed his bid for the presidency partly as a campaign to restore his country's social institutions by way of compassion and peace. As he crossed the nation in search of delegates and votes, he used his missionary fervor to spread these ideals throughout the American electorate. He called on the lessons he'd learned as a preacher's son, as a student debater, as the pastor of a complacent congregation, as a historian, as a party organizer, as an ecumenical churchman, and as a senator. In other words, many of the idiosyncrasies of his campaign were rooted in his ethos of interpersonal responsibility: that we are our brother's keeper.

The senator and his supporters were convinced that they were speaking hard truths and calling America back to an earlier state of virtue. But the wider electorate saw McGovern as a shrill moralizer with a radical-chic following and an unstable running mate. He ended up winning only one state and only 37.5 percent of the popular vote, by some metrics the worst showing by a major-party candidate in the history of American presidential elections. Although his prophetic tone may have been acceptable in a conscientious senator, it was problematic in a presidential candidate who was expected to reassure rather than remonstrate. McGovern saw the nation's interventionist foreign policy as a historic aberration. He challenged listeners to perceive the Cold War through the lens of compassion rather than as a struggle to keep hordes of wicked communists at bay. As Herbert Schell, a professor at South Dakota University, argued in 1972, McGovern "is the only nominee of either major party since World War II who has not accepted the assumptions of the Cold War."[6] At a time when policymakers were stigmatizing the poor, railing against quotas, and interpreting feminism as an attack on the family, McGovern called for government to take a greater role in alleviating the misery of its least privileged citizens. Worse, he urged such changes at a moment of intense insecurity, when the chief signposts of American superiority—technological prowess, economic stability, and social cohesion—were showing signs of strain.[7]

For the Commonwealth

On the night of Nixon's surprisingly narrow 1968 victory, McGovern decided that he would run for president in the next election. In the aftermath of that year's disastrous Democratic Convention, in which Humphrey had cruised to the nomination without having competed in the primaries, the Democratic Party had charged McGovern and Representative Donald Fraser of Minnesota to devise a more sensible and transparent primary system. Ironically, party leaders gave this job to McGovern as a sop to the antiwar Democrats, believing that such candidates would never themselves be nominated, even with a different set of rules in place. Yet the McGovern-Fraser Commission not only developed a system that would give a dark horse candidate a sporting chance to become the party nominee, but it also mandated that state delegations must include more representative proportions of women, racial minorities, and citizens under the age of thirty to amend the overwhelmingly white, male, and middle-aged biases of previous conventions.[8]

These changes combined enlightened self-interest with a desire to reach out to historically underrepresented segments of American society. During his 1972 campaign, McGovern's team worked hard to thwart some of the radical planks proposed by the gay, feminist, and racial minority groups that were drawn to his campaign. Nonetheless, he was the first viable candidate to offer them a seat at the table.[9] The McGovern-Fraser changes were a benchmark in party reform and an important step in curtailing white male control of the electoral process. As he boasted in his autobiography, "the guidelines of the McGovern Commission wedded the party to the principle of participatory democracy."[10] McGovern's campaign was also helped, at least in theory, by the passage of the Twenty-sixth Amendment in 1971, which lowered the voting age to eighteen. Thus, most antiwar undergraduates became eligible to vote in the upcoming election.

McGovern's transition into a presidential aspirant was accompanied by changes in his personal appearance. He grew out his cropped hair, as if to demonstrate solidarity with the young antiwar crowd, and added a formidable set of sideburns, "as lush as he could grow them without impairing his hearing," wrote the columnist Mike Royko.[11] He fixed his unsightly teeth, began wearing more stylish suits, and considered acquiring a toupee, though he ultimately chose an unconvincing combover to cover his thinning pate.

On January 18, 1971, McGovern formally announced his bid for the presidency during a low-key appearance on a local Sioux Falls television program. As he would do throughout the campaign, he articulated his vision in language that imagined the restoration of American virtue. Hearkening back to a mythic, egalitarian past, he pledged to "seek to call America home to those principles that gave us birth. I have found no better blueprint for healing our troubled land than is contained in the Declaration of Independence, the Constitution, and the Bill of Rights. And I find a nation drifting so far from those ideals as to almost lose its way." The speech was layered with biblical allegory, as if McGovern were suggesting that the American people, like the wayward tribes of ancient Israel, had strayed and must return to an earlier state of grace. Drawing on exilic themes, he promised to help Americans "seek a way out of the wilderness." "For my part," he solemnly intoned, "I make one pledge above all others—to seek and speak the truth with all the resources of mind and spirit I command." He declared, "We need to harness the full moral force of our nation to put an end to the most outrageous moral failure of our history—the lingering curse of racism. We must end, too, the blight of hunger, bad housing, and poor health services."[12]

Despite McGovern's reputation as a radical, much of the language and imagery in this announcement was strikingly backward-looking, pitting a troubled present state against an idealized past. Members of the press perceived how unusual it was for a candidate to make a national altar call to forsake militarism and backlash politics. Burton Carlson of the *Christian Century* observed that McGovern was waging "a campaign with a simple moral fervor no public figure has attempted since William Jennings Bryan."[13] The *Christian Science Monitor* reached a similar conclusion, reporting that "the McGovern stumping style remains somewhat ministerial. He often sounds like an old-time preacher delivering a sermon."[14] *Time* equated the candidate's "messianic drive to unseat Nixon" with his "personality-oriented, almost evangelical appeal for faith in a candidate [of integrity]."[15] Don Oberdorfer of the *Washington Post* noted that, "unlike most other political figures, he speaks of morality and justness, and has taken to closing his stump speeches with [a] passage from Deuteronomy."[16] Collectively, these journalists recognized that McGovern was gambling on the hope that Americans would see their choice as one that involved faith to principles. He had made his moral credibility the fulcrum of his candidacy. "My greatest single asset is truth-telling," he said at a campaign event, adding, perhaps with a certain amount of hubris, "I don't duck issues and I'm not capable of deception."[17] McGovern was positioning himself not as the most qualified man for the job but as a Moses or an Amos who would lead America out of its stupor.

McGovern's religious language nearly always applied to broad issues of national character; he hesitated to talk much about his faith in personal terms. Yet as his friend, Robert Duffett, a long-time president of Dakota Wesleyan, explained, "he was clear and vocal about the intersection of Christian faith and politics. Christians were obligated to live out the universal imperatives of Christianity in the public square."[18] McGovern cared little for metaphysics in his practice of Christianity. To him, they were unknowable and abstract to the point of irrelevance. He felt that the significance of any religion lay in how it could govern relationships among the living. Throughout his life, he frequently revealed an agnosticism toward the afterlife that signaled a belief in Christ as primarily an ethical teacher rather than a divine savior. "Wherever I am in the world beyond, if such there be," he wrote late in his life, "when my fellow humans are finally emancipated from hunger, I'm going to lead a chorus of celebration."[19]

Many of McGovern's campaign proposals and positions emanated from these beliefs. Like his position on Vietnam, his tax policy was influenced by liberal Christianity. With help from a crack team of Ivy League economists, he proposed cutting Nixon's military budget by $32 billion, with the savings redirected to social resources in the United States.[20] Other proposals included restoring corporate tax rates to their Eisenhower-era levels and implementing a much steeper estate tax that would cap nontaxable inheritances at half a million dollars. His most controversial suggestion was to award a demogrant—that is, a grant based solely on demographic and age factors—to every American (although, in the case of higher earners, it would ultimately be returned via taxes). To McGovern, these plans were an extension of economic justice in the social gospel tradition. "Wealth is to a nation what manure is to a farm," Walter Rauschenbusch had written at the turn of the twentieth century. "If the farmer spreads it evenly over the soil, it enriches the whole. If he should leave it in heaps, the land would be impoverished."[21]

In 1971, a National Council of Churches resolution had also endorsed the idea of a guaranteed minimum income. But here again the NCC was out of sync with the rank-and-file congregants of its member churches. Although the demogrant bore similarities to Nixon's Family Assistance Plan, its advocates explained the concept poorly, making it seem like froth-at-the-mouth radicalism and reinforcing public skepticism of McGovern. As his adviser Ted Van Dyk put it, the policy made the senator look like an "economic innocent prepared to give federal checks to every man, woman, and child in the country."[22] The campaign retooled its stand on the demogrant before the California primary, just after a disastrous televised debate with Humphrey in which McGovern struggled mightily to explain his own economic policy. His advisers convinced him to instead back a version that expanded the welfare state rather than remade it, so his revised plan highlighted property tax relief and guaranteed a job to every adult. Trying to argue that this plan was not radical, McGovern insisted in a television address that "I like hard work, and I love this nation," before justifying the grant by quoting Isaiah: "The people shall be righteous and they shall inherit the land."[23] Nonetheless, even though he saw his economic policy as practical Christianity applied in a liberal framework, the wider public saw it as a plan that doled out money carelessly without expecting any work in return.

In 1972, the closest McGovern came to disclosing his almost wholly practical and policy-based approach to Christianity was in an interview with Charles Henderson, the chaplain of Princeton University, for the Catholic journal *Commonweal*. In a moment of theological candor, he told Henderson that he rarely prayed, "at least in any conscious sense," although he frequently attended church, usually Chevy Chase Methodist or Foundry Methodist in Washington, DC.[24] The journalist Lou Cassels, after reading this interview, concluded that McGovern rated "the social applications of Christianity" higher than "the personal relationship of an individual to God." Although Cassels's summary was correct, he was also inadvertently laying out the contrast between McGovern and the Democrats' next nominee, the openly evangelical Jimmy Carter.[25]

In an Atlanta church, McGovern outlined how applied Christianity could reanimate the American conscience by restoring and reforming its moribund social institutions: "The true role of Christianity, I would suggest, is neither to ignore these issues nor to duplicate the politicians. Rather, it is to infuse into the solution of public problems the distinctive values, insights, and convictions that Christianity as such has to offer."[26] His ethos was most clearly expressed in an essay that he fine-tuned throughout the frantic campaign season. Intended for inclusion in an edited volume in honor of the Boston personalist theologian, Walter George Muelder, the essay argued that Judeo-Christian religions were linked directly to a tradition that began with the Old Testament prophets and descended through Christ, the Reformation, and the social gospel—an argument that John Herman Randall Jr.'s *The Making of the Modern Mind* had made decades earlier. Each figure or movement shared a common emphasis on "aiding the dispossessed, striving for justice, and improving the human condition through political channels." Yet America was in danger of losing these qualities. Its citizens needed to think deeply and judge wisely, for "in a Christian perspective, the most serious threat to ethical sensitivity in politics is self-righteousness and the blindness it induces." Ultimately, he argued, men and women of good faith had an obligation to reform public life. "There is nothing," he concluded, "to prevent persons of Christian faith joining with one another or with persons of other religious and moral convictions to achieve any legal purpose."[27] The essay offered what may have been McGovern's clearest explanation of a progressive commonwealth, perhaps because his intended audience was tiny and unlikely to take offense or misread his words.

When he discussed US war policy in Vietnam, McGovern continued to criticize it as inhumane and immoral, much as he had done as a senator. By this time, Nixon had transformed the conflict into an aerial war chiefly fought with chemical weapons, and McGovern would often share grizzly descriptions of the damage wreaked by American bombings. Virtually all of his speech "They, Too, Are Created in the Image of God" was devoted to delineating the physical toll of the bombardment on Vietnamese civilians, whose agony was, for the most part, invisible to the American public. The speech's details were shockingly graphic, and the senator's goal was to shake his listeners out of complacency. "We have steel fleshettes [flechettes]," he told an audience in Los Angeles, "that penetrate the skin and cannot be removed. We have napalm—jellied gasoline that sticks to the skin as it burns. We have white phosphorous that cannot be extinguished until it burns itself out." Referring to the famous photograph of Kim Phúc, a young Vietnamese girl who is running naked after her clothing has been burned away by chemicals, he concluded, "I want to say to my fellow Americans that that picture ought to break the heart of the people of America. . . . Can we ever comprehend such horror?"[28]

McGovern's words indicted the Nixon administration but also, by implication, indicted all Americans who uncritically permitted Nixon's policy to take effect. As his speech demonstrated, he believed that the country would not improve unless its citizens acknowledged and repented for the collective sins of the Cold War. This pattern—of condemning America's leaders, revealing their acts of destruction, and then pointing the way toward political salvation—became a hallmark of his campaign. He tied the nation's destiny to the quality of its leadership, just as the Old Testament prophets had condemned Israel and Judah when their kings succumbed to idolatry and cruelty. Recalling his 1965 and 1971 trips to Vietnam, he told a New Hampshire audience, "I saw people whose faces were gone—burned off by globs of napalm jelly. I saw little children one, two and three years of age—without legs, without arms and one of the news photographers who was with me tried to take a picture of a little child completely wrapped in bandages—you couldn't even see where the front of the child was."[29] In his youth, McGovern had hated evangelists who used grisly scenes of hellfire to warn sinners, but in 1972, he was telling a similarly lurid story to the American public, with the goal of hastening a political conversion.

Civil and Uncivil Religions

As McGovern pressed his attacks on Nixon, Nixon was also campaigning, albeit in a different way: by seeming not to run at all. In his bid for reelection, the president made few large-scale speeches and public appearances. Yet despite the appearance of inertia, he was hardly idle. Behind the scenes he was scheming to thwart the Democrats, as the Watergate scandal eventually revealed, as did the so-called Canuck letter directed at Maine senator Edmund Muskie.[30] Nixon rarely referred to McGovern specifically but treated him as an opponent who would combust on his own. He rebuffed the idea of a debate, which might have framed the two as equals, as out of the question. Charles Colson, an evangelical leader who served as Nixon's special counsel, was the administration's unofficial liaison to blue-collar workers and union members, and he spent much of the campaign season hinting that the Democrats had forsaken these traditional supporters and were now beholden to long-hairs, feminists, radicals, and Black Power activists.[31]

But Nixon and McGovern shared an unlikely similarity: both used religious symbols and language to give an aura of sanctity to their candidacies. McGovern relied on what religion scholars often call *prophetic* civil religion, whereas Nixon applied *priestly* civil religion.[32] As the church historian

Martin Marty has explained, priestly civil religion affirms a nation and its people by evoking common symbols.[33] A president who uses this approach serves as the celebrant within a shared cult of nationhood, delivering ritualized assurances that reinforce a belief that the country has been blessed by God. Each time a leader ends an address with the phrase "God bless America," invokes the sacrificial death of soldiers on Memorial Day, or refers to America as a shining city on a hill with a unique role to play in world affairs, he or she invokes this tradition.[34] In the 1970s, the historian Richard Pierard, who was also a member of Evangelicals for McGovern, defined priestly civil religion as "the use of consensus religious sentiments, concepts, and symbols by the state, either directly or indirectly, consciously or unconsciously, for its own political purposes."[35]

In contrast, prophetic civil religion is deeply critical and judgmental, and leaders who use it often argue that a nation has departed from the path of righteousness and must correct itself. Unlike priestly civil religion, which "comforts the afflicted," prophetic civil religion "afflicts the comfortable."[36] McGovern was aware, to some degree, of his use of prophetic civil religion—for instance, when he explained his perception of theologically potent words such as *redeem* during an interview for *Commonweal*. "Such words can be used in two ways," he said, "either in a political or a religious sense. It is important to use words like that to enlist basic feelings and values for legitimate social purposes. I am conscious of borrowing religious phrases for political purposes."[37] There's no doubt that he infused his campaign speeches with resonant religious metaphors, imagery, and cadences because he believed that using this authoritative language would be the best way of explicating the moral shortcomings of the Nixon administration.

Throughout his presidency, Nixon's use of priestly civil religion was well documented and often roundly criticized. Robert Bellah, the first modern scholar of civil religion, initially treated it as a benign feature of public life when he first addressed the topic in 1967, capable of uniting a disparate people by making a common appeal to the Judeo-Christian ethos.[38] But by the 1970s, most academics had come to see Nixon's use of religious language as manipulative and self-serving. Bellah himself observed that Nixon "proclaimed an American innocence that is awe-inspiring, stupefying, in its simplicity."[39] Other critics included Charles Henderson, who condemned the practice in his 1972 book *The Nixon Theology*. He described a figure who was perpetually invoking banal prayers and blessings—at his inauguration, on the safe return of the Apollo astronauts, during the new public ritual of the prayer breakfast—to cover his own faults.[40] Henderson noted that Nixon had called for a day of prayer for prisoners of war on the same day that he began his incursion into Cambodia, thus giving a kind of religious blessing to an act forbidden by international law.[41]

Nixon employed well-known pastors such as Billy Graham to help him perform these ceremonial roles and lend spiritual legitimacy to his political programs. This was particularly clear in the patriotic pageantry of Honor America Day. Held in Washington, DC, on July 4, 1970, this massive event, arranged and funded by Nixon's supporters, was promoted as a tonic to the Mobilization demonstration of 1969. Graham, as a featured speaker, extravagantly praised the nation's commitment to democracy, its generosity abroad, and its transparency in government, using terms that mingled patriotism with Christian faith. He shared the platform with the actor Bob Hope and Hobart Lewis, the head of *Reader's Digest,* and together they represented a kind of holy trinity of Middle America. Graham exhorted listeners to remember that the American experiment had been founded on the Bible, and Kate Smith reinforced his words by singing "God Bless America." The gathering functioned as both a religious service and a Nixon rally, even as once and future Nixon opponents Humphrey and McGovern both felt obliged to attend, lest they appear to dishonor America.[42]

Nixon's version of priestly civil religion tended to divide Americans into two groups: Nixon supporters and an unpatriotic rabble. In contrast, prophetic civil religion could be ruthlessly critical of the nation's shortcomings. Yet in the jeremiad tradition of the Puritans, it held out the possibility that the nation could overcome its faults and sins. Its purpose was not to damn but to offer a lifeline of redemption. Marty has conceptualized prophetic civil religion as an "ecumenical" discourse of "national self-transcendence" that uses religious language in ways that are broad enough to confront political problems but can be commonly understood among the public.[43] The political scientist Brent Gilchrist has described it as a means of communication that "continually strives to . . . recover [a nation's] original moment of 'innocence' "—which was evident when McGovern portrayed the country's Cold War militarism as a historical aberration.[44]

Although he was probably unaware of such academic discussions, McGovern consistently signaled his disapproval of Nixon's conspicuous acts of public worship. As he told an Atlanta audience in 1971, "the story of Christianity is repeatedly stained by this confusion of the cross with the sword and the flag."[45] During his 1972 interview with Henderson, he said,

"Any time the presidential seal moves far out front in an act of worship, I get nervous."[46] He pledged to Henderson that, as president, he would not attend prayer breakfasts or appoint an adviser on religious affairs, as Nixon had done. But that did not mean that religious concern would play no role in McGovern's hypothetical administration.

"Come Home, America"

Unlike many presidential candidates during the 1960s and 1970s, McGovern was closely involved in crafting his speeches. As he'd learned from his days on debate teams, speechwriting was too important a task to fully delegate to his aides. John Holum, Bob Shrum, and Gordon Weil usually worked together to create an early draft of each speech, which McGovern would then heavily edit during a plane trip from one event to the next.[47] Accordingly, many of these public addresses revealed his desire to transform his listeners and awaken their consciences.[48] Speaking at a service in Stanford University's Memorial Church in 1970, he had tied prophetic civil religion to a nationalist vision in ways that would anticipate his language on the campaign trail. He bade his audience to "do our nation the high honor of serving not her power, but condemning her evil and giving her the truth," noting the words to the hymn chosen for the service:

> Send down the truth, O God;
> Too long the shadows frown!
> Too long the darkened ways we've trod:
> Thy truth, O Lord, send down.[49]

Such imagery and language became indelible parts of McGovern's stump speeches, infusing nearly every address he gave in 1972. For example, in a speech to the clergy in Grand Rapids, Michigan, he warned that the United States had broken its covenant as a model democracy, that it was suffering from "a sense of lost purpose, of challenges unmet and greatness unfulfilled." "An election," he said, "is, in a sense, a day of reckoning, a day of taking stock of what we are and what we want to be. It is judgment day for America, not so much of two candidates, but of ourselves." McGovern's conception of this day of atonement was civic in character: that is, he imagined the American public, rather than the Judeo-Christian God, sitting in judgment. Invoking a prophet's abhorrence of hoarding riches at the expense of the poor, he continued, "The Scriptures tell us that none can be content until all are made whole. For if one man is hungry and without food, how can another enjoy his supper? If one man is sick and without care, how can another enjoy his health? If one man is poor and without help, how can another enjoy his riches? We must have a fundamental stirring of conscience that will awaken our compassion and restore the commitment of our hearts."[50]

Grand Rapids was a Republican enclave, but more sympathetic audiences corroborated McGovern's words, particularly those in black churches, which historically favored prophetic language. During a visit to an Atlanta church that had been closely connected to the civil rights movement, the senator was generously introduced as "Senator George McGovern, Ph.D., United States Senator, Advocate for Peace, Friend of the Poor, Methodist Layman, Herald of Justice."[51] In an African American Methodist Church in Harlem, the pastor, William M. James, virtually anointed the senator during the service, as he implored the congregation to join him in singing "The Voice of God Is Calling," from the Methodist hymnal:

> The voice of God is calling
> It summons unto men;
> As once he spake in Zion
> So now he speaks again:
> Whom shall I send to succor
> My people in their need?
> Whom shall I send to loosen
> The bonds of shame and greed?[52]

It was clear to Reverend James that God had sent McGovern to loosen these bonds.

When called to speak before the Harlem congregation, the senator chose language that both reinforced his prophetic role and echoed the tone of the civil rights movement: "I am reminded of an Old Testament Scripture, a favorite of my father before me and of mine. 'The spirit of the Lord is upon me, because he has anointed me to preach good news to the poor. He has sent me to proclaim release to the captives and recovering sight to the blind, to set at liberty those who are oppressed, to proclaim the acceptable year of the Lord.'"[53] In New England, he again cited Isaiah, whose collective judgment of Israel resonated strongly with the tenor of his campaign: "Open ye the gates that the righteous nation receiving truth may enter in."[54]

Nearly every politician in American history has used scriptural allusions in some way, but McGovern was noteworthy because he used prophetic language to reveal the value of mutual responsibility as professed by the social gospel and to suggest that a renewal of America's vision was tied to the outcome of his campaign. This theme of restoration resonated most famously in his campaign slogan "come home, America." Alfred F. Young, one of McGovern's classmates at Northwestern, had encouraged him to "appeal in particular to the shared traditions that can unite Americans of diverse political points of view. There are a good many traditions which bring 'left' and 'right' together."[55] The senator had, in fact, been trying to do precisely that for some time, through the use of this phrase. As Gary Hart recalled in his memoir of the 1972 campaign, "McGovern ended almost every formal speech . . . with an exhortation to the country to return to the traditional values which made it great, the respect for personal liberty, the right not to be harassed by one's government, the appreciation for the worth and rights of the individual, the guarantees of freedom of speech and the press."[56]

McGovern had tried out versions of "come home, America," even before he became an official candidate. In a 1970 address at Colby College in Maine, delivered after the Kent State shootings, he said, "Come home, prodigal America, to the land of your fathers, where we can rebuild our cities, revitalize our farms and towns, reclaim our rivers and streams."[57] The draft of a November 1971 speech reworks the phrase: "I would call America home from the hunger of little children, from the loneliness of the aging poor, the despair of the homeless, the jobless, the un-cared-for sick, to a society that cherishes the human spirit."[58]

The cadences of "come home, America," added a liturgical quality to McGovern's speeches; they functioned as a *kyrie eleison* through which a congregation could profess its collective guilt and pray for its collective redemption. Although he later said that he had borrowed the phrase from King's landmark sermon at Riverside Church in 1967, it also echoes the lyrics of William Lamartine Thompson's late nineteenth-century hymn "Softly and Tenderly," which McGovern may have heard as a child in his father's church in Mitchell:

> Come Home, Come Home
> Ye who are weary come home
> Earnestly, tenderly, Jesus is calling
> Calling, sinner, come home.[59]

Notably, the hymn calls the whole of the congregation to repentance; it speaks to the plural "ye" rather than "you" or "thou."

Pleased with the slogan's public reception, McGovern and his chief advisers directed his speechwriters to include it in the address they were honing for the upcoming Democratic National Convention. At the same time, he was aware that Nixon surrogates were using the phrase to imply that he was an isolationist, so Shrum and Holum polished and refined McGovern's language to make him appear seem less radical. During one television interview, he worked to clarify his use of "come home, America," explaining, "I am not just talking about returning our troops in Vietnam. Nor do I want our country to become isolationist because we are part of the international community but it is really a hunger on my part that I sense on the part of many Americans to get back to the ideals with which this country started."[60]

The 1972 Democratic National Convention opened on July 10 in Miami Beach, Florida, and McGovern stepped to the podium on July 14 to deliver his acceptance speech. It was an electrifying oration, crisp and well-delivered. Almost no one saw it. As a chaotic Democratic National Convention at Miami Beach drew to a close, he arrived at the podium at 2:45 a.m. on the East Coast, long after most Americans had retired to their beds. Only 15 million viewers tuned in, far short of the 70 million the campaign had hoped for. Those who had been watching earlier in the evening had seen crowds of African Americans in afros, feminists in trousers, and shabbily-dressed youths, all of them arguing over controversial minority planks ranging from abortion to marijuana legalization. On live television, some delegates were observed cynically casting vice-presidential votes for Archie Bunker and Chairman Mao. Representative Tip O'Neil, aghast at the lack of control, remarked sarcastically that the convention had been usurped by the cast of the musical *Hair*.[61] Even McGovern's friend and adviser Ted Van Dyk, who had abandoned his long-time mentor, Hubert Humphrey, over the Vietnam issue, recognized that the convention looked more like Woodstock than a respectable and orderly gathering of citizens.[62] The radical youths who had disrupted the Democrats' proceedings in 1968 now seemed to be running the convention. Yet the viewers who stayed awake to watch McGovern were treated to perhaps the finest speech of his career.

After jokingly referring to his address as a "Sunday morning sunrise service," McGovern launched into his prepared remarks. In the speech's most famous passage, he used the phrase "come home, America" as a refrain that punctuated a list of ways in which the nation had deviated from its transcendent higher calling. (Replace the "From" in each opening line with "For" and "Come Home, America" with "Lord, have mercy" and its confessional feel stands out.) The result was prophetic civil religion par excellence.

> From secrecy, and deception in high places, come home, America.
> From military spending so wasteful that it weakens our nation; come home, America
> From the entrenchment of special privilege and tax favoritism—
> From the waste of idle hands to the joy of useful labor—
> From the prejudice of race and sex—
> From the loneliness of the aging poor and the despair of the neglected sick, come home, America.[63]

McGovern's "Come home, America" speech built an American narrative through religious cadences. It evoked a mythic past, one attuned to Jeffersonian equality but glossing over slavery and wars of conquest. In McGovern's idealized America, endemic racism, wealth inequality, and military adventurism were atypical and abnormal. "It is time for this land to become again a witness to the world for what is noble and just in human affairs," he told the cheering but bleary-eyed crowd.[64] By means of the biblical cycle of sin, confession, and reconciliation, he urged the delegates and the nation to commit to a more humanitarian and cooperative vision of the United States.

Nonetheless, in the weeks after the convention, McGovern's prophetic civil religion did little to make his candidacy more palatable to the American electorate. He was often perceived as fault-finding, unpatriotic, and unduly critical, hardly traits one looks for in national leadership. As a friend said, "when he gets angry, it sounds like he is whining," and many voters came to a similar conclusion.[65] In an analysis of the election, the political scientist Kenneth R. Libbey saw McGovern's unwillingness to tone down his prophetic language as a political hindrance: "The real problem . . . was that he couldn't suppress his sense of moral outrage when he talked about the war. Like Kurt Schumacher in postwar Germany, he insisted that instead of escaping from the past, we should repudiate it and purge it from our national soul."[66] Another political scientist, Bernard F. Donahue, agreed: "Nixon wanted the voter to say to himself, 'I am good,' while McGovern was trying to make him say 'I am a sinner.'"[67]

"They know God is a Democrat, but this year they're voting Republican"

McGovern's pensive moralism was particularly problematic among a group of voters who were often labeled *white ethnics:* the working-class, often Catholic, demographic at the center of the Nixonian Thermidor.[68] Many had worked long hours in difficult jobs in order to climb into the middle class, but they were now lumped into the generic category of *privileged whites* whose access to civil service jobs and other advantages were restricted by equal opportunity laws. They declared that the quota system was an attack on merit, and they marched against busing policies aimed at integrating their neighborhood schools. When they watched the actor Clint Eastwood shoot up inner-city criminals on the big screen, many applauded his proactive approach.

Unfortunately for McGovern, many of these voters lived in swing states such as Wisconsin, Illinois, Pennsylvania, Ohio, and Michigan.[69] Moreover, many rank-and-file white Democrats were irate about the convention rules established by his own McGovern-Fraser Commission, which required state delegations to be diversified. In 1972, convention administrators summarily dismissed Chicago mayor Richard Daley's Illinois delegation, with its heavy Irish-, Italian-, and Polish-American labor representation, because it had deliberately flouted commission guidelines on racial, gender, and age balance. Instead, they recognized the delegation led by Reverend Jesse Jackson, whose white contingent was proportional but included few of the working-class Catholics who had historically represented Illinois during the glory days of Roosevelt and Truman.[70] As he complained that his state's delegation now had "no steelworkers, no pipefitters, and worst of all, no plumbers," Daley was also signaling the flight of blue-collar workers from McGovernite liberalism.[71] Many years later, the journalist Amy Sullivan noted the importance of the moment: "The symbolic message was clear to Catholics across the country: they had been kicked out of the Democratic convention" in favor of radicalized identity-politics groups.[72]

Aware of this dilemma, McGovern became inclined to choose a Catholic running mate. But in keeping with the campaign's overall operational chaos, his managers did not allocate enough time or resources to carefully considering the selection of a vice-presidential nominee. Not only were they distracted by Humphrey's legal challenge to their California delegates, but McGovern mistakenly assumed that Massachusetts senator Edward

Kennedy would join the ticket if begged to do so. Kennedy was the only potential running mate who polled well enough to increase McGovern's chances in the general election; but despite the candidate's desperate entreaties, he declined to join the ticket. His reasons were understandable: two of his brothers had been assassinated during the past decade, and he was still dealing with the fallout of his own role in the Chappaquiddick tragedy that left aide Mary Jo Kopechne dead and his reputation in ruins. Moreover, he may have wanted to keep his own options open for 1976 when these crises had simmered down.

After Gaylord Nelson and Walter Mondale also declined McGovern's invitation to join the ticket, he accepted the advice of many of his senatorial colleagues and turned to a rising star in the party, Missouri senator Tom Eagleton.[73] Eagleton was young, urban, friendly to unions, and a Catholic. He had everything a rural Protestant such as McGovern might want for balance on the ticket—at least on paper. From his headquarters, McGovern called Eagleton's hotel room to offer him the vice-presidential spot. Surrounded by a corps of St. Louis reporters, the young senator giddily accepted McGovern's offer. Then the campaign manager Frank Mankiewicz took the phone and asked if there were any "skeletons in his closet."[74] Eagleton crisply replied no.

Despite its haste and its disastrous aftermath, McGovern's choice of Eagleton followed the typical pattern of his day. In 1972, the selection process for running mates was still an agreement among gentlemen colleagues, not the exhaustive, invasive vetting process it has become today. In some ways, Eagleton's selection was actually treated with greater-than-usual care. John Sparkman, the Democrats' vice-presidential candidate in 1952, remarked, "If Adlai Stevenson had asked me the questions that Mankiewicz said he asked Eagleton, I'd have told him to take the nomination and shove it up his ass."[75] In his autobiography, Bob Shrum agreed that McGovern, at worst, failed to challenge a precarious but established method of picking a running mate: "The traditional way of deciding on the vice-presidential nominee was a train wreck waiting to happen, and it was McGovern . . . who got hit by the onrushing locomotive."[76] The incident became a cautionary tale that every subsequent presidential candidate has kept in mind when selecting a running mate.

McGovern and his campaign managers soon learned that their prospective vice-president did have a skeleton in the closet. At several points during the 1960s, Eagleton had checked himself into mental hospitals for depression and nervous exhaustion, and he had twice received electroshock therapy for his illness.[77] As revelations about his medical history trickled out, both campaign insiders and Democratic Party leaders began imploring McGovern to drop Eagleton from the ticket. Initially resisting their pleas, McGovern took part in a heated press conference in which he testily pledged his "1,000 percent" support for his beleaguered running mate. McGovern's initial defense of Eagleton signaled a genuine ethical dilemma. Gordon Weil has suggested that he used such strong language to support Eagleton because he felt that his opponents had "dragged this man's mental history into the public view, and I have to say something affirmative to him. And that was driven by the kind of person McGovern is."[78]

Incidents in McGovern's family life had also influenced the candidate's impulse to keep Eagleton on the ticket. His college-age daughter Terry had shown signs of alcoholism and depression, and his wife, Eleanor, was also enduring a private struggle with depression. Decades later, McGovern wrote, "We reacted as we did in considerable part because Terry had been suffering from a clinical depression not unlike Tom Eagleton's. Despite our concern with Tom's problem . . . I could not in effect punish him for being a victim of depression."[79] Mankiewicz agreed with McGovern's recollection: by rejecting a running mate with a similar affliction, "[McGovern] would in effect be saying to [Terry], 'you're not fit.' "[80]

McGovern's empathy was not returned in kind. Eagleton offered an increasingly disingenuous and duplicitous series of rationales to defend his medical history and his right to remain on the ticket. On *Face the Nation*, he maintained that he had not deceived McGovern's staff, arguing that "a skeleton is something that's dirty, filthy, corrupt, illegal, sinister. There's nothing about having been fatigued and exhausted and being in a state of mild depression that I find sinister, dirty or ugly."[81] Eventually, as the press uncovered more evidence of his medical problems and his concealments, Eagleton agreed to leave the ticket but only if McGovern publicly asserted that he was of sound health. This demand was patently selfish; it made McGovern seem both capricious and insensitive, while rendering Eagleton faultless. In a memo that circulated among his staff, McGovern wrote that the affair was "the worst dilemma of my public career. From that time, the spirit went out of the campaign for both Eleanor and me. We had taken great pride in our credibility and in our candor with the press and the public. Now we were being forced to cover up for a man who had not been fair with us."[82]

After Eagleton agreed to leave the ticket, McGovern replaced him with Sargent Shriver, a former director of the Peace Corps and the husband of the Kennedys' sister Eunice. But the Eagleton affair had already done irremediable damage, in part because it had tarnished one of McGovern's greatest assets, his moral credibility. Prophecy, civil or otherwise, requires trust in the one who delivers the message, and the selection and dismissal of Eagleton compromised that trust. It did not just make McGovern appear incompetent; it made him seem deceitful as well. A poll conducted by *Newsweek* soon after Eagleton's withdrawal found that 25 percent of voters felt less favorable about the Democratic ticket because of the incident.[83] After Labor Day, Haynes Johnson and David Broder surveyed voter opinion in the ten largest states. Their findings were disheartening for McGovern: he not only trailed Nixon, which the pollsters had expected, but fell behind him when participants were asked to compare the candidates on issues of trustworthiness.[84] According to a *Time* magazine poll, voters, by a margin of two to one, believed that Nixon's administration would be more open and honest than McGovern's—despite the fact that Nixon had been labeled "Tricky Dick" since the 1950s. The editors at *Time* were incredulous: "Such results seem to fly in the face of logic," they sputtered. Yet the magazine's poll also found that Nixon outpaced McGovern even in areas in which the Democrat had seemed strongest: concern for the needs of common Americans, tax reform, and the ability to end the war.[85]

As bad as the Eagleton affair had been, matters threatened to get worse. Midway through the campaign season, the McGovern team received a tip that Republican operatives were looking through birth records in Fort Wayne, Indiana. Someone, somewhere, had tipped off Nixon's team about McGovern's illegitimate oldest daughter. Although he handled the matter calmly, he was now forced to reveal her existence to Eleanor, and it added another layer of tension to the campaign.[86] The team was right to worry. As Bob Woodward and Carl Bernstein of the *Washington Post* discovered in 1973, Nixon's aide H. R. Haldeman had concocted a plan to leak the story about McGovern's child to the press and then hint that the administration knew about another damaging matter but was keeping mum about it.[87] This would impugn McGovern's character, while making the Nixon campaign look generous. In the end, McGovern's tanking poll numbers made this tactic unnecessary. Compounding the Eagleton crisis with the issue of McGovern's first daughter would have been excessive, even for Richard Nixon.

Although the scandal was contained for the moment, McGovern

continued to weather difficulties, particularly with Catholic voters. For many, his revivalist language was an unwelcome throwback to an era of Catholic exclusion.[88] To an extent, he recognized this problem. During an annual dinner in support of Catholic charities, sponsored by the Alfred E. Smith Memorial Foundation, he joked that he felt "a little like Al Smith addressing the Baptist League of Eastern Texas."[89] The immigration historian David Gerber has written about how alien and off-putting McGovern's Protestant lexicon could seem to Catholics. As a new professor at the State University of New York at Buffalo, he eagerly campaigned door to door for the candidate. His terrain was home to many of the city's Catholic working-class families, and their visceral reactions against McGovern demonstrated how the Protestant character of the senator's language had damaged his prospects with previously reliable Democrats. According to Gerber, "it conjure[d] up memories of the endless condescension and prejudice their immigrant ancestors had to bear at the hands of American Protestant nativists."[90] No wonder one priest remarked, "They know God is a Democrat, but this year they're voting Republican."[91] An article in *Time* also identified McGovern's problem with this demographic. Quoting one of Mayor Daley's aides, it noted, "McGovern is the classic Methodist—the kind of guy who doesn't sweat. No one is more difficult for an Irish Catholic to get along with than one of those non-sweating Methodists."[92] Nixon had succeeded in convincing urban working-class Catholics that he understood the value of muscular Americanism: hard work and love of country. Like the mainline church leaders, McGovern had mistakenly assumed Protestant guardianship over the American conscience.

So McGovern lost, hemorrhaging support in nearly every demographic and claiming only 41 percent of the Catholic vote, a historic low for the Democratic Party. In the end, there were many causes for his defeat. Nixon's promise that peace was at hand took much of the antiwar wind out of his opponent's sails. The benefits of incumbency, the president's behind-the-scenes machinations, and his considerable breakthroughs in relations with China and the Soviet Union all contributed to a sweeping victory. But Nixon's success owed a debt to McGovern's mistakes. Along with his apparent radicalism and the debacle of his running mate, McGovern's moralism and righteous style alienated many more Americans than it won over. In this respect, the rock on which McGovern stood—his belief in a common good in the social gospel tradition—was also the rock that contributed to his landslide defeat.

On the evening of November 7, speaking from the Holiday Inn in downtown Sioux Falls, McGovern delivered his concession speech. Following the routine pattern of such speeches, he congratulated President Nixon and thanked his own supporters. But as he concluded, he exhorted them to serve as a loyal opposition during the next four years and to steadfastly remind the country of its higher standards. He quoted a passage from Isaiah that he had used often during the election season: "They that wait upon the Lord shall renew their strength. They shall mount up with wings as eagles; they shall run, and not be weary; they shall walk, and not faint."[93] Fittingly, his final words were those of an Old Testament prophet. And with this parting benediction, George McGovern's presidential campaign, conceived and carried out with an ear toward these ancient figures, drew to a close.

McGovern's boyhood was bound by the strictures and deep faith of his Wesleyan Methodist father. The future senator is the elder of the two boys on the floor, the one reading. *Courtesy of Senator George McGovern Collection, Dakota Wesleyan University Archives, Mitchell, South Dakota.*

For several months in 1946 and 1947, McGovern served as a student pastor in Diamond Lake, Illinois, while he was enrolled at Garrett Theological Seminary. Here, he preaches from the pulpit. His wife, Eleanor, is among the singers in the choir. *Courtesy of Senator George McGovern Collection, Dakota Wesleyan University Archives, Mitchell, South Dakota.*

McGovern's tour on behalf of Food for Peace was a diplomatic and humanitarian triumph. He is pictured here during a 1962 visit to Tunisia. *Courtesy of Senator George McGovern Collection, Dakota Wesleyan University Archives, Mitchell, South Dakota.*

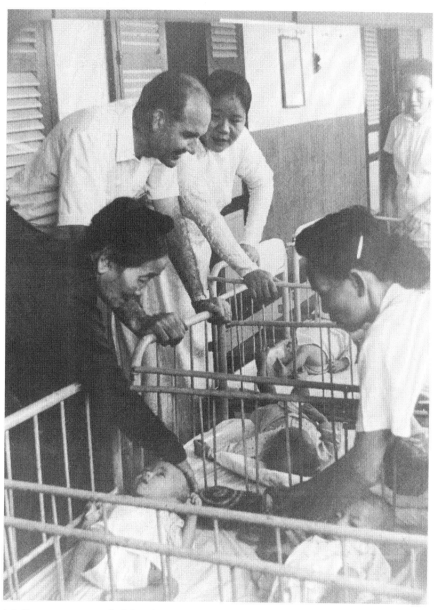

McGovern was appalled by the oppression and devastation he saw during his first trip to Vietnam in 1965. Here, he is visiting a hospital's children's ward. *Courtesy of Senator George McGovern Collection, Dakota Wesleyan University Archives, Mitchell, South Dakota.*

In 1968, the United Methodist Church asked McGovern to serve as a lay representative to the World Council of Churches meeting in Uppsala, Sweden. Here, he is pictured with the Dutch economic development advisor Jan Pronk. *Courtesy of World Council of Churches.*

By the early 1970s, McGovern and Bishop James Armstrong were close confidants and corresponded almost weekly. Armstrong believed in a close partnership between clergy and policymakers, and went on to found Religious Leaders for McGovern. *Courtesy of James Armstrong.*

Eleanor McGovern was not a typical political spouse by the standards of the early 1970s. She had a strong command of the issues and often stood in as a proxy for her husband during news broadcasts. *Copyright © Diana Mara Henry / www.dianamarahenry.com.*

Shortly before his death in 1972, Rabbi Abraham Heschel endorsed McGovern's presidential campaign and joined Religious Leaders for McGovern. Heschel's scholarship on the Old Testament prophets influenced many 1960s social movements. *Copyright © Diana Mara Henry/www.dianamarahenry.com.*

Despite the smiles, McGovern's visit to evangelical Wheaton College was tense and at times confrontational. The visit was coordinated by Evangelicals for McGovern, whose vice-chair, Tom Skinner, is pictured on the right. *Courtesy of Wheaton College, Special Collections, Wheaton, Illinois.*

McGovern's "Come Home, America" address underscored his campaign's use of prophetic civil religion. Here, he delivers that speech as he accepts the presidential nomination during the 1972 Democratic National Convention. *Copyright © Diana Mara Henry / www.dianamarahenry.com.*

6

Religious Leaders
for McGovern

The leaders of the Protestant mainline were facing a serious problem, and they knew it. Church membership was beginning to decline, and congregants who had been receptive to their pastors' social vision in the early 1960s were now resistant to messages about Vietnam and the rights of migrant workers. In the Nixon White House, Republican evangelicals had usurped the liberal leaders' presidential influence. So when a small but prominent group of mainline Protestant clergy (alongside a few Catholic and Jewish leaders) endorsed George McGovern for president, they had little confidence that they would swing many votes. Instead, their coalition, known as Religious Leaders for McGovern (RLFM), was the death rattle of a religious establishment under siege. For decades, church leaders had seen themselves as "guardians of moral treasure," in the words of the historian Edwin Gaustad.[1] During the 1960s, they had spent this treasure on controversial issues of peace, housing, and arms control, not only losing allies in the White House but also angering their congregants. In an age of growing suspicion toward cultural elites and federal solutions to endemic problems, they continued to depend on a top-down bureaucratic style and high-flown pronouncements that few laypeople cared to read. Thus, the mainline leaders failed to win over a public that was not only suspicious of social crusades but also believed that crusading pastors were neglecting their congregations' needs.[2]

In 1972, eight of the eleven largest National Council of Churches denominations had fewer members than they had possessed in 1965.[3] In addition, congregants no longer saw their churches as arbiters of social decency but as heavily politicized actors in a mobilized and divisive era. One NCC poll found that 59 percent of churchgoers believed that churches should not meddle in political controversies or social crises. As a Republican aide derisively told the religion journalist James Adams, "a minister is just another lobbyist. . . . There is a tremendous amount of pressure on Vietnam. But [church leaders] are digging their own graves."[4] The exhaustion and growing impotence of mainline leaders were underscored by President Nixon's open contempt for them. As the political scientist Robert Booth Fowler has said, they became, in less than a decade, "paper tigers in the political process," kingmakers reduced to supplicants.[5]

RLFM was organized partly with the hope of restoring mainstream Protestants' ease of access to the president and influence over the lawmaking process. Breaking postwar expectations of clerical behavior, members formally endorsed a candidate who shared their own upper-middle-class values. Many marginalized groups were attracted to McGovern's candidacy, but this old Protestant vanguard saw the senator as a throwback to the kind of person they could do business with: liberal in theology, progressive and inclusive in outlook, and a churchman with a history of ecumenical engagement. Some may have daydreamed of influence in a McGovern administration after years of being ignored by Johnson and antagonized by Nixon. RLFM was not an act by a confident group of men and women, but an act of desperate hope.

From Protestors to Partisans

Although mainline leadership had long worked fervently for causes that aligned with midcentury liberalism, they had technically remained nonpartisan throughout the 1960s. That changed when Richard Fernandez, the young director of Clergy and Laity Concerned about Vietnam, wrote to McGovern in January 1971, soon after the senator had declared his candidacy, and eagerly offered the organization's help. Up to this point, CALCAV had been the chief route through which Protestant, Catholic, and Jewish clergy had protested the Vietnam War. Yet as their correspondence shows, they recognized the limits of their ability to affect war policy and knew they needed to find a way to influence electoral politics.

Although tax codes did allow churches to address contemporary issues, CALCAV and other religious organizations were constantly aware that excessive politicization might imperil their churches' tax-exempt status. The boundary was murky. An issue of the progressive *New England Churchman* carried both an article about a congressional bill designed to ensure the churches' ability to speak out on social issues and an article lamenting a Tennessee Court of Appeals ruling, which required the Methodist Publishing House to pay taxes on books that did not specifically address religious faith and worship but focused on social concerns.[6] Thus, church leaders knew they needed an organization that was separate from the NCC and CALCAV.

In the meantime, they were trying to figure out how to do more than just speak out against the war; they wanted to help end it by removing Nixon from power. Civil disobedience had been effective during the 1960s civil rights protests, but it was not so effective in antiwar activism. Even as he expressed regret that he had never been jailed for his convictions, Bishop James Armstrong said that, for a pastor, the strategy was counterproductive and would "affect [congregants'] attitudes toward the church."[7] Instead, he and Fernandez argued for working within the system to change the country's leadership; and other notable CALCAV leaders, including Robert McAfee Brown, Abraham Heschel, and William Sloan Coffin Jr. agreed. "The escalation of moral numbness," Brown wrote, "demands the escalation of moral protest."[8] Electioneering became the next stage in this mobilization. As a newspaper article reported, McGovern's supporters among the clergy believed "that ending the Vietnam War [was such] a basic moral imperative that it justified clergy taking sides publicly in the campaign."[9] As both a war critic and McGovern's close friend, Armstrong was a ringleader in bringing together mainline Protestants and other ecumenical leaders who saw their support for the candidate as an extension of their prophetic activity. In the fall of 1971, well before the primaries began, he held a press conference in Charlotte, North Carolina, after being invited to preach at a church in the city. With him were two of his closest allies, Rabbi Joseph Glaser and the Methodist bishop Gerald Kennedy, whom Armstrong had long admired for his progressive views on race relations. Together, the three announced the formation of Religious Leaders for McGovern. At this early stage, Armstrong was using clerical endorsement as a tactic to position McGovern, not yet a household name, as a candidate who would be acceptable to Middle America. He characterized his friend, somewhat disingenuously, as a "moderate," but one who "closely conforms to the ideals of our Judeo-Christian heritage."[10] He also highlighted McGovern's moral leadership and far-sighted courage. Nixon might be improving America's relationship with China, the bishop conceded, but McGovern had been urging the recognition of communist China since the 1950s. "He was a brave and lonely voice," Armstrong told the assemblage.[11] Likewise, he emphasized the senator's ability to create unity among a divided people and argued that he could "help create a new era of confidence" after the divisive 1960s.[12]

At first, the group was known as the National Committee of Religious Leaders for McGovern. The name was later shortened to Religious Leaders for McGovern and, near the end of the campaign, to McGovern-Shriver. Its membership roll read like a directory of liberal Protestant leadership, and in their statements of support, Armstrong and other mainliners worked hard to present McGovern as something more than a candidate. As if to justify their extraordinary partisan endorsement, they often cast him as an unheralded prophet, stressing his truth telling and his willingness to say what was unpopular—traits they also associated with themselves. Coffin wrote that "while others have fought for power, [McGovern] has battled for truth; where others have been pragmatic, he has been prophetic." John Bennett, a founder of *Christianity and Crisis* magazine, declared that McGovern "was one of the first men in public life to see how disastrously mistaken and how cruelly immoral the war in Vietnam is and he continually said so long before this was politically safe."[13] For years, *Christianity and Crisis* had carried the torch for Niebuhr's arguments against pacifist naïveté.[14] Thus, Bennett's endorsement was a strong signal of the war's unpopularity among establishment Protestant intellectuals.

With the election more than a year away, Armstrong identified McGovern's biggest challenge as his obscurity, not his electability. For the moment, the nomination seemed to be Muskie's for the asking; few thought McGovern was a viable candidate. Yet Armstrong's cohort believed that Muskie's measured opposition to the Vietnam War was calculated rather than courageous. He had spoken out, they remembered, only after it had become fashionable to do so.[15] RLFM members knew full well that McGovern's lack of insider support meant that he would have to make his case to voters in the primaries. Thus, as Armstrong wrote to his allies, "We need to provide what help we can before the New Hampshire primary is upon us."[16]

Relying on his growing fame as a prophetic preacher and a Methodist gadfly, Armstrong spent late 1971 and early 1972 contacting friends in the ecumenical movement. In a 1972 press release, he listed twelve of the new organization's most prominent members, including Brooke Mosley, the activist nun Sister Mary Luke Tobin, and Harvey Cox of the Harvard

Divinity School.[17] Heschel, who was one of the most influential American rabbis of the twentieth century, was an especially important luminary on the list. His scholarship on the Old Testament prophets and their affinity for the poor and oppressed was well known in the civil rights and antiwar movements; and in an impassioned editorial to the *New York Times,* he validated McGovern's "call for a revival of our nation's values" as an action in the prophetic tradition.[18] Armstrong told his fellow RLFM members that McGovern had "a decided appeal to religiously committed people. His honesty, his courage, and his creative response to the problems of society make him a natural for us."[19]

At its peak, RLFM included more than two hundred members of the clergy as well as other religious notables. While its prominent members could often find national outlets for their endorsements, the local efforts of less famous pastors were generally quiet and subdued, often limited to press releases. Only occasionally did these provincial efforts stir up interest. For instance, an Ohio clergyman became the subject of an article in the *Dayton Daily News* after he sponsored an antiwar fundraiser involving a lamb auction, which was intended to be a metaphor for the slaughter of soldiers in Vietnam.[20]

Early RLFM publications advocated for McGovern's candidacy as a matter of principle and thus as an appropriate focus for clerical activism. They argued that the Vietnam War, the economy, and government transparency were moral problems, and their tone of lamentation echoed the jeremiad quality of McGovern's speeches. "We have allowed ourselves to become morally anesthetized," Armstrong warned in a mailing. "What in former times would have elicited an indignant outcry from religious people is now widely accepted as 'the way things are.'" He alluded to a mythic American righteousness that McGovern also mentioned in his speeches, and his heading included a quote from the candidate: "I make one pledge above all others, . . . to seek and speak the truth."[21] In this way, RLFM tied itself to McGovern's capacity to speak prophetically and refashion an often undefined Judeo-Christian tradition.

Not since World War II had so many prominent religious figures united to make such an explicit presidential endorsement.[22] Armstrong's assistant, Michael McIntyre, hoped that their praise would be valuable to McGovern, given that so few national politicians had formally endorsed him.[23] Even his closest friends in the Senate, such as Harold Hughes of Iowa, began by endorsing more probable candidates, usually Muskie. The religious leaders saw themselves as valuable proxies, lending an aura of authority and familiarity to a fringe candidate. At the same time, Armstrong struggled to recruit ministers beyond the usual CALCAV contingent. Even some of those who thought favorably of McGovern "didn't want to do it," he recalled, "because they thought it wouldn't be fair to their congregation."[24] He understood such predicaments. In one case, Robert Raines, the pastor of the First Community Church in Columbus, Ohio, headed a predominately Republican congregation that resisted his sermons on ecology, generational poverty, and especially the war.[25] Raines was sympathetic to McGovern's politics but did not wish to further alienate his parishioners, who included the aged John Bricker, a former Republican governor who was on Thomas Dewey's ticket in 1944.[26]

Armstrong and his allies knew they had to focus on defending their unconventional choice to take partisan action. For instance, when speaking at Drew University in early 1972, Armstrong praised the Jesuit priest Robert Drinan, now a congressman, for openly supporting the Democratic Party and the peace movement. As he told his Methodist audience, Drinan was highly respected "by thoughtful social critics for his open, candid partisanship," and he contrasted him with "Billy Graham, who pretends to be above it all, while using his tremendous influence in the most partisan of ways."[27] Clearly, Armstrong's praise for Drinan was also a defense of his own alliance of conscience with the Democratic Party. The bishop framed his support for McGovern as a religiously informed act of personal citizenship, separate from his formal capacity as a bishop. He had made such distinctions before, not only as a campaigner for Eugene McCarthy but also during his work on civic committees in Indianapolis, where he had attempted to balance his work as a city father with his pastoral responsibilities. As he said in 1969, "We will not always agree on issues and candidates," he conceded, "but as individual Christians—*not as a church, but as individual Christians*—we are challenged to enter the rough-and-tumble arena of human activity where the earthbound destiny of a people is determined."[28]

To some observers, however, the RLFM clergy seemed too ready to point out their own offices and titles. In its promotional materials, the organization nearly always paired religious leaders' names and denominations to reinforce the weight of their moral authority. At the same time, to protect their churches from jeopardizing their tax exemption and to emphasize that their denominations and seminaries were nonpartisan, each press release included the explanation "Religious affiliations for identification purposes only." Nonetheless, some readers detected an atmosphere of elitism and self-importance.

Over the years, many members of RLFM had developed personal connections to McGovern, and their endorsements often stressed that relationship. The theology professor Georgia Harkness mentioned that she had been his teacher at Garrett: "I have known him personally for the past twenty-five years and have never seen any fluctuation [in his moral beliefs]."[29] The two had, in fact, stayed in touch since his time at Garrett, and in 1966, he had entered her strong statement against the Vietnam War into the *Congressional Record*.[30] Krister Stendahl, a professor at Harvard Divinity School, wrote, "Ever since I met George McGovern as a fellow delegate at the 1968 Uppsala Assembly of the World Council of Churches, I have been impressed with his sense of urgency and principles."[31] James E. Bell, a Methodist pastor from South Dakota, declared, "During my years of serving church . . . no one else speaking on Christian concerns came close to equaling McGovern on reaching listeners. How I hope your bold and faithful editorial will create chain reactions. The church has never done very well in knowing its prophets."[32] In fact, however, a different kind of chain reaction took place. RLFM's partisanship made it clear that the seminary and the pulpit were, both politically and culturally, at odds with the pew and the church social hall.

James Armstrong and the Partisan Ministry

While Armstrong cajoled well-known clergymen and theologians to join RLFM, his assistant, Michael McIntyre, did much of the heavy lifting—coordinating, recruiting, and organizing on Armstrong's behalf. He visited seminaries, religious conferences, and other places and events frequented by young people who were natural McGovernites. The volunteers he recruited were drawn to the candidate's stance on the Vietnam War but also to his humanitarian work in Food for Peace. One of these young recruits was Rich Eychaner, a twenty-three-year-old lay pastor and seminary student from Kansas City. McIntyre convinced Eychaner to come back to Washington, DC, and work with him at the RLFM offices in a meager workspace provided by Sargent Shriver and shared with other citizens groups, such as Doctors for McGovern.[33] Eychaner was struck by how little grassroots work the operation actually performed; he saw RLFM's strategy as primarily an effort "to get the most names on the letterhead" rather than actively engage with voters of faith.[34]

Eychaner was joined in the office by Dolores Moseke, a former nun who had left her order to marry a priest; both of them part of the mass exodus from religious vocations during the 1960s. She had grown up in South Dakota and, as a close friend of Eleanor McGovern's twin sister, knew the McGoverns well. Moseke was one of the "little folks who did the ground-work," as she recalled. When RLFM received a letter expressing interest in or approval of McGovern, she would write back and ask for further support, often financial. As a Catholic, she was instructed to put her "stamp of theology to all people who were writing in," using whatever religious language they might find appealing.[35] As Moseke saw it, RLFM functioned as an appendage of the campaign, sharing lower-level staff members such as herself. In this sense, it can be best understood as a group that operated on two tiers. There was a higher level of national religious figures offering endorsements and a lower level of volunteers responding to letters and phone calls. Yet neither Eychaner nor Moseke saw the campaign itself mak-ing much of a meaningful outreach to religious voters.

As RLFM's national coordinator, McIntyre supported the mission but was doubtful about its efficacy. He believed that the organization's annex-ation into the machinery of the McGovern campaign had actually hindered its ability to function smoothly. Unsure of how best to use religious volun-teers, the campaign generally put Catholics into the McGovern campaign's Urban Ethnic Affairs Division and Jews into its Issues Division. These generalizations suggest that the organization was handled as if it were just another interest group. The haphazard arrangement also made it difficult for volunteers to communicate and coordinate with one another. McIntyre complained that many of McGovern's aides treated RLFM and other citi-zens' groups as "an afterthought," a striking lack of populism in a campaign that is often remembered for its grassroots activity. He recalled that aides would create bottlenecks whenever his group asked for help with a decision or requested spending money, forcing him to rely on what he called "Yan-kee ingenuity" to keep the organization viable.[36]

Armstrong, however, remained active in the campaign's highest tiers and assumed the task of gathering volunteers and making press statements on McGovern's behalf. "I have tried to stay in fairly close touch with your campaign headquarters," he reported to McGovern in one letter; and in his customary style, he made a beeline for the campaign's leadership. Armstrong and McIntyre arranged a press conference for the campaign manager, Gary Hart, so that he could read aloud statements of endorsement from the clergy. Records also show that Armstrong met with the campaign director, Frank Mankiewicz, and the women's issues coordinator, Amanda Smith, in January 1972. He noted that their headquarters, filled with political novices and operating on a tiny budget, "seem[ed] fractured with sweaty activity—the inevitable byproduct of this sort of effort," and attempted to improve the campaign's efficacy by dispensing frequent, sometimes unsolicited, advice.[37] He often shared the names of young chaplains and religious workers who might be of use. He sent lists of possible supporters, many with Methodist affiliations, whom Hart later acknowledged were "among our greatest strengths."[38] One of his first suggestions was John Adams, a member of the Methodist Board of Christian Social Concerns and a mediator during the Attica prison riots. After McGovern's poor debate performance against Humphrey, Armstrong even sent the prominent theologian Harvey Cox to speak in black churches in California, with the goal of clarifying McGovern's plan for a guaranteed minimum wage before voters went to the polls in the state primary.[39]

Because of his proximity to Mankiewicz, who handled much of the campaign's press, Armstrong served as a media point man whenever questions of religion or spirituality emerged. After *Life* magazine expressed interest in publishing an article about McGovern's pastoral background, Mankiewicz referred its journalists to Armstrong. "The values that McGovern adheres to with remarkable consistency," he told them, "are the values that are both sophisticated and belonging to the later-20th-century mainstream."[40] As he worked to de-radicalize McGovern and rehabilitate the progressive Christian viewpoint, Armstrong filled a necessary role in a campaign whose most conspicuous supporters were Hollywood figures such as Warren Beatty, Shirley MacLaine, and Barbara Streisand.[41] To a wary American public, he vouched for McGovern's personal character and Christian ethos.

Armstrong also used the press proactively, especially the Methodist Church's denominational magazines. Writing in *Engage,* he highlighted McGovern's "decency" and his reputation as "a sincere and honest man." The Democrats, he declared, were the natural party of the thoughtful Methodist. "The moral courage of the McGovern-Shriver ticket is long overdue on the American scene," he wrote, noting the close similarities between the Democratic Party platform and the United Methodist stands on Vietnam, race relations, and other controversies. Armstrong was aware that his words would evoke controversy, but he remained "partisan without apology. I am a bishop of the church. I write, however, not as a spokesman for my denomination, but as a concerned and involved citizen. I write because I believe that the social teachings of my church faithfully reflect the gospel of Jesus Christ, and that they need to be applied to my country and world."[42] Once again, he defended partisanship not as conflicting with his church office but as an outcropping of his rights as a private citizen, even though his prominence as a citizen was tied to his position as a bishop.

On paper, Armstrong's involvement was limited to endorsement and praise, but behind the scenes he used his ecclesiastical clout and political connections to help clear the Democratic field of liberals who might complicate McGovern's primary campaign. In the fall of 1971, he wrote to John Lindsay, the liberal Republican mayor of New York City, who was considering a presidential bid as a Democrat. Armstrong encouraged him to stay out of the primary and give McGovern his support, hoping McGovern would not have to compete for votes within his party's left flank.[43] Lindsay, however, did not know Armstrong well and disregarded this advice, beginning a brief candidacy that ended after a poor performance in the Florida primary. The bishop had more success with Indiana senator Vance Hartke, who announced his candidacy for the Democratic nomination just before the New Hampshire primary. The two had been acquaintances since Armstrong's days as a pastor in Indianapolis. Writing to him on Methodist Church stationary, the bishop reminded the senator that he was crowding the field on the left, and Hartke soon withdrew.[44]

Armstrong also flexed his influence through ecumenical channels. During the campaign, he and Harold Bosley of Christ's United Methodist Church in New York City discussed holding a series of meetings with Jewish leaders to legitimize McGovern's stance on Israel, which contained measured support for a settlement for Palestine.[45] The pair saw this as a crucial means of strengthening the candidate's tentative relationship with Jewish voters, for both Nixon and Humphrey had accused him of supporting Israel insufficiently.[46] "With states like New York, Illinois and California being so strategic for November, hearings like this could render an invaluable service," Armstrong reasoned, echoing the advice for winning the South that Graham had given to Nixon four years earlier.[47] A few weeks before the Miami convention, Armstrong even suggested to McGovern that he might send a religious delegation to Hanoi. But when he asked if such a delegation, or his presence in Miami, would be useful, McGovern's aides politely rebuffed him.[48]

Not all of McGovern's religious coverage depended on Armstrong's public and private support; most of the leading mainline Christian journals covered his candidacy with quiet favoritism. The preeminent *Christian Century*, founded in 1884, had long been a news and opinion source for liberal Protestants, and it regularly covered current issues of social justice. In 1961 and 1962, the magazine had addressed civil rights 155 times, while the evangelical *Christianity Today* had done so just once, preferring to focus instead on anticommunism and defense of free enterprise.[49] The *Christian Century* was a mouthpiece for old-line Protestantism. A great many pastors, church board members, and scholars of religion read it, but few laymen did. In early 1971, when McGovern was still an extreme long shot for the nomination, it was one of the few press organs to take serious notice of his candidacy: "It is time to recognize and celebrate George McGovern as a very brave man who carries into the political arena a powerful authentic testimony to the wholeness of the Christian gospel. As long as there is a George McGovern around, waging a 'campaign of candor and reason' for the highest office in the land, wholesale cynicism about politics and politicians is out of order." He was, the editorial argued, a "human being of increasing stature—both nationally and internationally—who radiates trust and who can speak with an unexcelled moral authority on these issues."[50] Given the backlash the magazine had suffered after trashing Goldwater in 1964, the editors stopped short of an endorsement, but their effusive praise left little doubt about their preferences.[51] At a time when McGovern's recognition was still nationally low and many pundits were dismissing his candidacy as a stalking horse for a more viable liberal such as Ted Kennedy, the editors' language demonstrated their familiarity with McGovern. The years he'd spent accruing goodwill through his ecumenical service and his work with Food for Peace were paying off among the mainline Protestant powers, and this recognition was crucial in helping him to stand out in a crowded Democratic field.

The Mainline Decline and the Crisis of Liberal Protestantism

McGovern did not get the same warm support from members of mainline Protestant congregations. Although congregants were unaware of Armstrong's political machinations, the mere act of endorsement raised concerns. "For the first time in the annuals [*sic*] of modern elections, some prominent churchmen have formed a cross-country interfaith network [to support a candidate]," marveled one account.[52] Many Methodists felt that it was unseemly for a bishop to intervene in electoral politics, especially on behalf of a man so widely disliked by the denomination's southern and evangelical wings. Skeen Smith, the editor of the small *Texas Methodist* magazine, wrote that Armstrong could not "engage in this activity without inferring support of the Methodist Church."[53] Smith believed that Armstrong should resign from his office rather than endorse a politician while serving as bishop.

Smith's unhappiness was indicative of larger tremors within Methodism. In 1972, Armstrong's political activism and social liberalism paralleled lay members' increasing distress about the political statements of clergy and ecumenical groups. One congregant, George M. Ricker, complained in a letter to the editor of the family-oriented *Together* magazine, "I must confess that in recent years, church bodies have seemed to me a little too ready to make public statements on thorny questions that require much thought and expertise, and on certain political matters to come down predictably on one side of the fence." Methodism had become increasingly divided between its social activist leadership and a lay base that believed that pastoral responsibilities must come first. Ricker saw a schism involving praxis, a developing rift between "pietists" and "activists." He feared a clash between those who wished to be left alone and those who wished to fling Methodism into perpetual controversy.[54]

In other words, many of the problems facing the Democratic Party in 1972 were also confronting United Methodism.[55] At the Methodists' disorderly quadrennial meeting in Atlanta, traditionalists and reformists butted heads over control of the church's future.[56] Various members submitted a total of 21,000 petitions on topics informed by the race, gender, and sexual politics that also challenged white male headship at the Democratic National Convention that year. Each faction supported its own resolutions and put forth its own candidates for prestigious church boards and offices. "Many expected 1972 to be the year of the caucus and indeed there was a proliferation of formal and informal interest groups in Atlanta," one observer noted dryly.[57] Mainline Protestantism, like the Democratic Party, was grappling with the politics of quotas as historically marginalized peoples demanded a voice in public affairs. Church leadership had already begun instituting quotas so that young people, women, and racial minorities would have adequate representation in NCC organizations, and many older, more con-servative congregations were upset.[58] The cultural backlash against quotas was affecting not only jobs and political delegations but also church boards and annual meetings.

Like the Democratic Party, the mainline was developing a reputation for being both elitist and radical, and its white working-class congregants felt they were being treated unfairly. As *Engage* magazine reported grimly, "United Methodism is now facing political chaos, compounded by its basic commitment to Jesus Christ."[59] Albert Wildrick, a church member from Indiana, sent a scathing letter to the editor of *Together:*

> I am a tired Methodist. Tired of being blamed for the social ills of the country. Tired of paying taxes while able-bodied persons refuse to work. Tired of supporting illegitimate children while being told I do not under-stand the culture of these people. Tired of crime on our streets because our courts turn the criminal back onto the street. Tired because our churches no longer believe in the Bible. We no longer have ministers with the con-victions to stand up for moral values. I am tired of giving money to the church and seeing a portion of it given to the World Council of Churches to spend on tearing down our country. Tired of watching a church try to solve the world problems while letting their own neighborhoods become jungles.[60]

Wildrick's letter is a textbook example of the coded language of the so-called silent majority, filled with racially loaded terms such as "jungles" and "these people" to describe city neighborhoods and their black residents. In writ-ing it, he borrowed heavily from examples that appeared in a 1971 *Reader's Digest* article, "Must Our Churches Finance Revolution?," that condemned the World Council of Churches for donating money to socialist organiza-tions in the developing world.[61] The article was one in a series of attempts, backed by the conservative businessman J. Howard Pew, to scrutinize the NCC's efforts to send money to foreign countries, where, he believed, it ended up in the hands of Marxist insurrectionists.

The crisis of liberal Protestantism was compounded by dwindling congregations. After the early 1970s, it was no longer possible to discuss the mainline churches institutionally without referring to their vanishing parishioners and their aging membership. Between 1970 and 1980, Meth-odists lost 10 percent of their congregants, Episcopalians lost 15 percent, and United Presbyterians lost 21 percent, and these trends were already apparent by 1972.[62] Americans were losing trust in many of their great institutions:

the presidency, the military, the free market, and mainline churches, especially those that were bound by hierarchies, bureaucracy, and boards. A 1974 study alleged that the mainline churches "appear to be among the hardest hit by the new public mood and the worsening economic situation. . . . Laymen are more vocal in expressing their dissatisfaction with the churches' liberal policies, and they are demanding a stronger voice in church affairs and a return to more traditional religious concerns." According to the study, 46 percent of the clergy thought that the churches' stands on social issues should be decided by a general conference. In contrast, 56 percent of the laity thought that churches should not take stands at all; individuals should decide for themselves.[63]

In *Why Conservative Churches Are Growing*, Dean M. Kelley identified other factors that were contributing to this decline. He believed that the mainline churches were too tolerant for their own good and that they failed to offer concrete, satisfying answers to basic questions about the meaning of life and the purpose of faith. Their ecumenism signaled mushiness and implied that no sect had a monopoly on truth. Worse, he argued, they lacked the discipline, accountability, and solidarity that characterized the successful conservative evangelical churches.[64] Episcopal parents, for example, might not pressure their college-age children to attend services because they might find answers elsewhere that worked better for them. But in an evangelical family, the social consequences—indeed, the consequences for one's soul—of apostasy were far more serious. These changes contributed to a striking dropoff in mainline church attendance and participation. In her recent book on the *Christian Century* and its role in ecumenical culture in the twentieth century, Elesha Coffman notes that "mainline and decline have been joined ever since [these demographic factors manifested]"[65] As they staggered toward an uncertain future, the mainline churches had to juggle their prophetic mission with damage control.

Post-Election Decompression

George McGovern's defeat might have been interpreted as a sign that churchgoers did not care about supporting their pastors' preferences. But most of the people involved in RLFM came to the opposite conclusion: pastors urgently needed to take prophetic action. Even though he was frustrated by McGovern's defeat, Michael McIntyre found heart in the fight, hoping that it signaled a new progressive Christian engagement in politics. In a lengthy piece in the *Christian Century*, he wrote, "We are scarcely done with the McGovern era of social concern, great mandates notwithstanding." Moreover, the experience confirmed what he had long suspected: RLFM had not politicized the churches; civil religion, prayer breakfasts, and Nixon's courtship of evangelical leaders had already done that work. The difference, McIntyre asserted, was that McGovern had used his relationship with the churches for less exploitative and more constructive purposes. He created dialogues with them and was informed by their missions. Nixon, in contrast, merely used his ministerial friends for political leverage. "We did not hesitate," McIntyre argued, "to identify publicly what we thought were the common interests of this campaign and of the church."[66] Thus, he continued to cling to liberal Christianity's optimism that men and women of good conscience and vision might restore a fallen society through the use of wise governance.

Armstrong interpreted McGovern's defeat as one more sign that Middle Americans were turning down a dangerous path that required prophetic and pastoral correction. In a book on the nature of failure and loss, he somewhat melodramatically equated McGovern's defeat to Martin Luther's excommunication, Dietrich Bonhoeffer's sacrificial death, and Roger Williams's exile, which "did not . . . negate their righteous witness." To him, McGovern was a prophet who was not honored at home. Armstrong concluded, "Christian hope is not theological obscurantism, nor is it naïve optimism. It is the other side of political realism. It recognizes and accepts the frailties and inconsistencies of legislative programs and public leaders."[67] A setback was just a moment of time in the divine plan, and public rejection meant only that the Christian minister should continue to speak prophetically and strive for social justice. As the 1970s ran their course, Armstrong kept faith with this commitment, taking part in the American Indian Movement, exploring international liberation theology, and counterattacking the rising religious Right. For the rest of his life he continued to entwine his strong progressive Christianity with his active participation in politics.

As Watergate dominated the headlines in 1973 and 1974, Armstrong saw the scandal as affirming his warnings about Nixon and validating his critiques of Middle America. Given how misguided the electorate had become, he averred that a prophetic body of believers was necessary to set the American people aright and draw them from the wayward path. Such prophets, he said, "have 'seen the light' but are sometimes convinced that their people still dwell in darkness."[68] For Armstrong, McGovern's defeat confirmed his observation that American Christendom was now beholden to a bunker mentality and empty, self-congratulatory patriotism. He did not yet suspect that an unlikely group of young evangelicals would soon come to agree with him.

7

Evangelicals for McGovern

Evangelicals for McGovern: it sounds like an absurd name for a serious political endeavor, as if a character on the cover of *National Lampoon* were slyly winking at the reader. The idea that evangelical Christians, whom many Americans instinctively associate with rightwing political values, might have supported George McGovern seems strange, given his long association with the American Left. But what made McGovern so pivotal to the development of progressive Christianity was his ability to foster religious support beyond the usual suspects of ecumenical clergy in Religious Leaders for McGovern. He also attracted a small but persistently influential group of evangelicals who shared his opposition to the war in Vietnam and were dismayed by the rightward drift of Bible-believing Christians. While many mainline figures dismissed the evangelicals as reactionaries not worth the bother of persuading, McGovern welcomed their support.

McGovern's presidential campaign was the first occasion on which these young activists and academics banded together as expressly evangelical political actors, but their interest in reform had deep roots in the social movements of the 1960s. For them, the New Left, the freedom struggle, and the peace movement had been critical life experiences that had sharpened their ability to critique American social structures. In their view, the evangelical mainstream had neglected the scriptures' clear emphasis on human uplift and equal dignity. What set the progressive evangelicals apart from both their forebears in the New Left and their eventual rivals in the religious Right was their embrace of the prophetic tradition. They cried out against the evangelical community's singular focus on individual sin at the expense of social injustice as well as its embrace of Cold War militarism. Fighting against the rightist instincts that had been present among evangelicals for

decades, these progressives urged their brothers and sisters in Christ to recognize that their political priorities were grotesquely misaligned in favor of
the powerful and the privileged.

At first, the nascent evangelical Left toiled in small groups, with little
coordination among its far-flung branches, which stretched from inner-city
Philadelphia to intellectual nerve centers at Wheaton College in Illinois and
staunchly Calvinist Grand Rapids, Michigan. The group's adherents saw the
national attention that McGovern was receiving and admired his forthright
stands against the war and the Nixon administration. In their first act as a
cohesive movement, they endorsed his candidacy, citing it as an example of
prophetic urgency in the face of injustice. But McGovern's ties to his evangelical supporters were often tenuous and complicated. While they celebrated
his compassion and his courage in opposing the war, they were careful to
keep their distance from his practice of Christianity. They saw him as a man
who was correct on the issues but whose theology was much too liberal for
comfort; that is, they recognized him as a humanist, not a biblicist.

For McGovern and many other liberal Protestants, the theology of the
cross was secondary to putting their religion to work on earth. For progressive evangelicals, their New Left politics were inseparable from the truth
of the Bible and the historic reality of Christ's redemptive death and resurrection. This disparity was important because these youths defined themselves partly in contrast to the mainliners who had heretofore dominated
the Protestant conversation on social justice. Yet even though they founded
Evangelicals for McGovern (EFM) as a campaign-year exercise to make
evangelicals rethink their habitually conservative politics, it developed an
accidental significance by the time the election was over. In the end, it
established its participants' identity as socially conscious evangelicals: active
in the world and following the scriptures' imperative to live with empathy
and engagement among those who suffer from war, hunger, and prejudice.

The Neo-Evangelical Divorce

The young men and women of EFM had been born into an American
evangelicalism that had suddenly become much more visible while remaining an insular subculture. For youth who had grown up in the 1950s and
1960s, there was no denying the fundamental fact of religious culture in the
United States: the old-line Protestants of the institutional churches were
the hegemon. Unlike the evangelicals, they expected and received more

prestige, more respectability, and easier access to society's most powerful decision makers.[1] Tony Campolo, the future leader of the Red Letter Christians movement, recalled moving to suburban Philadelphia in the 1950s and encountering a religious environment in which "mainline denominations had been endowed with a self-assurance that bordered on arrogance."[2] The evangelical community viewed the mainline's posturing with a mixture of jealousy and contempt and treated their liberal theology as apostasy. Randall Balmer, a prominent historian of American religion, was eighteen years old when McGovern ran for president. As the child of a staunchly evangelical family, he remembered with some bitterness that "we were the outsiders, the religious insurgents engaged in a hopeless struggle against the Protestant mainline, which had the wealth, the influence, the status that we simultaneously resented and coveted. They belonged to the Rotary Club and sipped whiskey sours at the country club outside of town; they sat on the school board and the city council."[3] His description illustrates how the chasm between evangelical and mainliner was as much social and cultural as it was theological.

During the late nineteenth and early twentieth centuries, a fundamentalist-modernist controversy had split American Protestantism; and since then, each camp had viewed the other with suspicion.[4] In the aftermath of that split, two pyrrhic victories had become public relations disasters for Bible-believing Protestants: the Scopes trial and Prohibition. For decades, the historical consensus was that fundamentalists had withdrawn into a rich private Christianity, although recent scholarship persuasively complicates this picture.[5] But early Cold War events and the apocalyptic and existential crises of the nuclear age had ushered them back into public view. In the early 1950s the newspaper mogul William Hearst gave fabled instructions to his media aides to "puff [Billy] Graham," and the charismatic Baptist quickly became the most widely respected evangelical of his time. A sublimely talented public speaker, he served as counselor to multiple presidents; and by 1972, he had long been the unofficial figurehead of a movement often called neo-evangelicalism. He and his contemporaries gave evangelicalism a new vitality, infusing it with richer educational opportunities, establishing a vibrant print culture centered around the magazine *Christianity Today,* and distancing themselves from visceral extremists such as Bob Jones who threatened their credibility.[6] Institutionally, they were not bound together by their denominations but through the National Association of Evangelicals (NAE), a looser affiliation that was more of a network than a policymaking body—an intentional choice, given their historically chilly relations with the National Council of Churches and the World Council of Churches.[7]

Neo-evangelical salvation was both shared and intensely personal. Thus, it fit neatly into an age that prioritized insular nuclear families in the sanctuary of the suburban home. In this context, evangelicals often assumed the cloak of free-market conservatism, a position reinforced by the wealthy businesspeople who backed the NAE and *Christianity Today*.[8] Graham and other evangelical figureheads warned that Americans had become too materialistic, yet they hesitated to condemn the accumulation of wealth or the excesses of capitalism that made this possible.[9] Graham frowned on the Jim Crow system and even insisted on integrating his revivals. But as a North Carolinian, he maintained that federal legislation was not the antidote for poisoned race relations. Only a sense of brotherhood among the redeemed could do that work.

Graham led neo-evangelical support for American involvement in the Cold War, often portraying the United States as a messianic entity fighting the forces of Soviet evil.[10] He did not deny the need for reform but declared that only through Christ's sacrifice could humans be reconciled to God; government programs and structural reform could never improve society on their own. "There is one Gospel and one Gospel only, and that Gospel is the dynamic of God to change the individual and, through the individual, society," he told a revival crowd.[11] In Graham's view, any change to the status quo would depend on a revolution of personal conversions of the heart rather than on marches in the street, an idea that the historian Steven P. Miller calls his "politics of decency."[12]

While Graham was skeptical of the gospel of social activism, *Christianity Today*, read by nearly every major evangelical figure, was often openly hostile toward it. One contributor, writing in the fall of 1964 after an intense summer of urban race riots, directly blamed the chaos on the mainline Protestants who had emboldened such behavior. The violence had demonstrated the failings of liberal theology, which "has downgraded individual initiative and responsibility before man and a theology that has failed to stress man's personal responsibility before God."[13] In other words, the evangelical establishment blamed the welfare state and its high-church enablers for allowing blacks to trash their own neighborhoods.

Still, pockets of younger evangelicals in communion with the social movements of the 1960s were questioning this orthodoxy. They did not believe that their activism conflicted with their faith. Compelled to action by the civil rights movement and its message that race and poverty were interlinked, a group of Wheaton College alumni now living in Philadelphia began publishing *The Other Side,* a small journal about evangelical social engagement. Its very title emphasized the invisible poor, who simultaneously had become the subject of new scholarship by Michael Harrington and Harry Caudill.[14] Led by John Alexander, these young activists critiqued the evangelical consensus that saw laissez-faire capitalism as a meritocracy that rewarded hard work with prosperity. Judy Alexander, who was married to John, argued, "When a Christian talks about politics (whether it's busing, unemployment, inflation, welfare reform, Vietnam, South Africa, or Russia), he must give special emphasis to how it affects the helpless, the little ones, the other side."[15] The Alexanders and their allies could not reconcile their awareness of dire inner-city needs with Graham's argument that real social change could only take place after America had turned toward Christ. Fred Alexander, John's father and his chief partner in *The Other Side,* reflected, "Perhaps I am naïve, but it has always seemed to me that after our massive evangelistic campaigns you should be able to see more change. Racial prejudice should diminish, husbands and wives should like each other more, people should worry less about their lawns and more about those who are hungry. . . . Our evangelism is not the gospel. Our evangelism is a revision of the gospel based on a careful selection of Scripture that systematically ignores vast sections of it."[16] In short, their work in the forgotten corners of America impressed on them that saved men were not saving society, as the neo-evangelicals had claimed.

The Alexanders represented Christians who had moved from suburban Wheaton into the wider world. Calvinists connected to the Reformed Church were another branch of evangelicalism's family tree; and many of them worked and studied at Calvin College in Grand Rapids.[17] These Reformed evangelicals were also committed to engagement in the world but tended to idealize a usable past to guide contemporary society, premised on the teachings of John Calvin, Johannes Althusius, and Guillaume Groen von Prinsterer. The Reformed Church had a magazine, the *Reformed Journal,* which reached both its scholars and its laity; and like other evangelicals, its adherents were convinced of the veracity of scripture. This would later complicate their relationship to McGovern and liberal Christianity more generally. One member of the group, Richard Mouw, remembered that, in his youth, McGovern's hero, the mainline pastor Harry Emerson Fosdick, was often invoked as a liberal bogeyman, "a symbol of all that was evil about modernist theology."[18]

The *Reformed Journal* was a testing ground for ideas that deviated from the evangelical orthodoxy of *Christianity Today*, Wheaton College, and Billy Graham. Although it was founded at roughly the same time as *Christianity Today*, the journal often positioned itself as a Calvinist foil, "a voice for more alternatives to mainstream evangelicalism," as a frequent contributor, Richard Pierard, explained.[19] By the 1960s, its aging founders had passed the baton to a younger generation of editors, Mouw and Nicholas Wolterstorff, both of whom taught at Calvin College. The new editors shifted the magazine away from denominational commentary toward national social issues. Under their leadership, the journal turned cautiously toward social justice, and it became a rare and tentative middle ground between the business-friendly conservatism of *Christianity Today* and the establishment-skewering perspectives of *The Other Side* and, later, Jim Wallis's *Post-American*.[20] The editors of the *Reformed Journal* drew a model for the righteous society from John Calvin's view of the state. Some contributors focused on sixteenth-century Geneva, where Calvin's government had overseen a prosperous silk industry and used the profits for public medicine, a hospital for the poor, and subsidized prices for bread, meat, and wine. One suggested that a system of government support comparable to the Tennessee Valley Authority's dominated Calvin's Geneva.[21]

As undergraduates, graduate students, and seminarians, many evangelical New Leftists had taken part in protests against Jim Crow and the Vietnam War. Informed by those movements, they began to conclude that US structural problems could not be reduced to the simple Cold War dichotomies they had grown up hearing from evangelical pulpits. Mouw remembered, "The heroes of my childhood were very skeptical of the civil rights movement. They suggested that if King wasn't a communist, he was certainly helping them out."[22] Resisting such equivocations, he began marching for civil rights; and as a graduate student at the University of Chicago, he joined Students for a Democratic Society (SDS) and occupied school buildings to protest the war. Yet Mouw, who also participated in the 1969 Moratorium, was coming to see that the New Left was rudderless without a religious ethos.[23] His fellow student radical, Jim Wallis, believed that SDS saw the poor as merely a "constituency," the means to an existential and political end.[24] In the dense bureaucratic thicket of government programs and the strident posturing of the student Left, neither social workers nor street protesters could focus on the compassion and the humanity that ought to accompany a thirst for justice. People such as Mouw and Wallis recognized that many of these activists had no true desire to work with the marginalized but preferred to champion causes on their behalf. Frustrated by this disconnect, John Alexander wrote, "Surely Moses has more to say to today's issues than [Marshall] McLuhan and [Herbert] Marcuse combined. And Amos has more to say than Abby Hoffman."[25] In this way he deliberately downplayed the importance of these icons of the New Left in favor of the Old Testament prophets.

Alexander's reservations illustrate the dilemma that faced these evangelical Christians. They saw racial, social, and sexual hierarchies as cancerous growths and, like many of their generation, believed that the ongoing war in Vietnam was the greatest spiritual crisis of their time. Using the history of Anabaptist separatism from the state as his rationale, the peace activist Arthur Gish urged his fellow evangelicals to refuse to pay taxes during the war, maintaining that "the issue is not personal moral purity, but rather the clarity of the witness."[26] The theologian Lewis Smedes wrote in the *Reformed Journal* about the complicit role of evangelicals in their failure to oppose the Cold War state. "What if our national honor really means, in this case, our national pride?" he asked. "What, in short, if this is an unjust war? Must the Christian community then give its blank check to the president? . . . This is why we endorse the national moratorium on the war, we endorse it as the only way of pressing the anti-war conscience on the president."[27] For these evangelicals, Vietnam signaled not only the limits of American power but also the failure of prominent evangelical leaders to bear witness against its senseless destruction.

Instead, most of those prominent leaders strongly supported government actions in Vietnam and harangued the war's countercultural opponents. In the dismissive words of one editorial in *Christianity Today*, "We cannot Christianize their utopias for they have made their own inner logic, and it tends inevitably toward the world of 1984."[28] In like fashion, Billy Graham defended the war until the bitter end. He never expressly condemned the actions of Lieutenant William Calley, whom the Left saw as a war criminal responsible for dozens of civilian deaths, but presented him as an unfairly maligned young man who was just doing his job: "We have all had our My Lais in one way or another. Perhaps not with guns, but we have hurt others with a thoughtless word, an arrogant act, or a selfish deed."[29] For young antiwar evangelicals, Graham's failure to censure a wanton massacre of civilians emblematized his complicity in a sick system. "While condemning personal sin," Joe Roos accused in *Post-American*, "he refuses to take a stand on the corporate nature of American involvement in Vietnam."[30]

Young evangelicals began to explore more radical means of witness, but no figure encapsulated their righteous furor more than Jim Wallis, the editor of the radical evangelical journal *Post-American*. Wallis had grown up in Detroit's suburbs among many middle-class families who had fled from the inner city. During the Detroit race riots in the summer of 1967, his church leaders condemned urban lawlessness but did not address the discrimination, racial antagonism, underemployment, and limited opportunities behind the violence. Wallis took to spending time in the city, talking with black co-workers and, unlike so many of his contemporaries, listening to their perspectives. They shared their frustrations, many of which stemmed from generations of poverty and widespread police abuse. He later wrote, "My forays into the inner city became a spiritual journey for me, putting me into relationship with new realities and friends that my protected white middle-class culture had tried to keep me from ever encountering. But once you cross over to the 'other side,' it is almost impossible to ever go back."[31]

Wallis concluded that evangelicals had become a prosperous, homogenous enclave insulated from the very people to whom Christ had called them to minister. While attending Michigan State University, he became involved in SDS and anti-Vietnam activism, taking part in teach-ins and protests after learning that Ngo Dinh Diem's lieutenants had actually been trained at his college.[32] After graduating, he pursued a degree at Trinity Evangelical Divinity School in Deerfield, Illinois, where he met other seminarians who shared his disgust about the war and the military-industrial complex. Together, they formed a community similar to the Alexanders' but more overtly radical, and they founded *Post-American*, choosing the title as a way to critique the alliance between American militarism and American Christianity.[33] Provocative from the start, the first issue featured a picture of Jesus wrapped in the Stars and Stripes and wearing a bloody crown of thorns. Underneath, a caption read: "And they crucified him." The picture sent a clear message: American evangelicals had rejected the authentic Christ.

Civil Religion and the Nixon Theology

Demonstrating the editors' sympathy with New Left principles, the inaugural issue of *Post-American* decried the "systematic injustice, militarism, and the imperialism of a 'power elite.'" At the same time, its evangelical perspectives challenged "a technocratic society and a materialistic profit culture where human values are out of place."[34] Wallis and his allies voiced not only their opposition to the managerial state but also the militarized forms of patriotism they saw in both the churches and Washington, DC. From the start, the magazine took a confrontational tone. Articles accused the evangelical establishment of abetting a political system that had devalued human life in Vietnam. "The American Church," Wallis wrote, "languishes in conformity and accommodation. Crippled with prophetic impotence, it cannot make the choice between the cross and the flag, while it renders unto Caesar all that Caesar asks." Such complacency among the faithful led him to declare that the solution to the social unrest of the early 1970s lay in "a radical Christian faith" that would be "a liberating force which has radical consequences for human life and society."[35] His disgust and anger increased after Nixon exchanged troops on the ground for an emphasis on bloody and indiscriminate air strikes. The situation, Wallis insisted, "demands prophetic Christian response" because keeping American serviceman out of danger while incurring Vietnamese civilian casualties was not consonant with Christianity's equal value for all life.[36]

Many of the academics involved in the evangelical Left believed that the problem was rooted in civil religion: neo-evangelicals had confused love of country with the worship of God. One egregious example they cited was Graham's 1970 role as the master of ceremonies for the patriotic pageantry of Honor America Day, which they saw as a worship service for the Nixon administration.[37] Others derided Explo '72, a massive gathering of young evangelicals in Dallas's Cotton Bowl, organized by Campus Crusade's leader Bill Bright. Attendees cheered as the South Vietnamese flag was brought out and put their hands on their hearts as the general of the Continental Army led them in the Pledge of Allegiance.[38] To progressive evangelicals, these public gatherings were idolatrous revivals which made the authentic gospel beholden to the military-industrial complex. Joe Roos of *Post-American* wrote angrily that Graham had failed to "distinguish between the God of American civil religion, and the God of American Christianity."[39] The progressive evangelical historians Richard Pierard and Robert Linder saw civil religion as a pervasive and malignant influence on American public life. In 1970, Pierard wrote that evangelicals were captives of a patriotism that overlooked Americans' faults. Their conservatism "misrepresents Christianity by advancing a doctrine which mixes with alien elements those aspects of the New Testament that relate to personal salvation and those of the Old Testament that stress Israel's uniqueness."[40] The broad and generous salvation of the gospels had become an intensely individualized and nationalized faith, and Israel's covenant with God had become a form of American exceptionalism.

Despite their shared outrage, the different branches of this internecine rebellion were in contact only intermittently. Yet each honed in on the prophets as a biblical model for confronting and challenging leaders who had abandoned the social teachings of the gospels. If their goal was to prove the biblicism of their social concern, those ancient figures and their harsh words against hoarded wealth and rapaciousness in war gave them plenty of ammunition. A contributor to the *Reformed Journal* noted that the prophet Jeremiah had "referred to the past history of God's dealing with his people, but he tied it to the prophetic theme of judgment [on a people and their government]."[41] The Christian journalist Wes Pippert wrote, "In recent years, we have reclaimed the prophets from the obscurity of many decades, and in them we have found a starkly contemporary commentary about our world."[42]

In their understanding of Christian praxis, these evangelicals viewed prophetic behavior as a collective and participatory act of dissent. By emulating the prophets' example, they could directly accost both religious and political leaders who confused cross and flag or held the poor in contempt. In particular, the prophet Amos seemed to be tailor-made for this task. Activists took note of how, as an ordinary shepherd, he became a spokesman for the Lord. He denounced rich women as "cows," confronted kings for their neglect of the poor, and condemned fellow Israelites who worshipped false idols.[43] A contributor to *The Other Side* reminded readers that "Amos objected to those who trod down on the poor and perverted justice by bribery (Amos 5:11–12), [and those] who kept the garments of the poor overnight for collateral (Amos 2:8)."[44] Speaking many years later, Nicholas Wolterstorff recalled, "It was the essence of the prophets to be speaking about justice—justice for the little people. The quartet of the vulnerable— widows, orphans, aliens (sojourners), and the impoverished—over and over, they go into that. When I thought about justice, it was this that came to mind—it was that prophetic vision of justice in the land."[45]

Writing in *The Other Side*, John Alexander demonstrated his systematic understanding of prophecy: "The Bible provides endless examples of men who spoke their whole minds and spoke them bluntly no matter how people reacted. Christ's attacks on the Pharisees were certainly not designed to win friends or influence people." Nevertheless, he was concerned that some evangelicals were assuming the prophetic mantle too freely and casually. Because the modern Christian "does not have direct communication with God the way Elijah and Paul did," a degree of humility and introspection was required. Christians were "more likely to be mistaken" now that the age of divine revelation had passed. Like Wolterstorff, Alexander believed that a true prophet is concerned about widows, orphans, immigrants, and others with no advocate: "The prophet who is careful about what he says to large financial contributors but is blunt with the poor is no man of God. The man in public office who compromises black children while pleasing powerful business interests must be thrown out of office."[46]

Why, these young evangelicals wondered, were liberal Christians the only ones challenging these attitudes when Bible-believing Christians should be taking the prophets most seriously? David Moberg, a sociologist at Marquette University and an influential member of the group, wrote, "We, the People of the Book, must be at the 'Prophetic forefront of society.' If we are truly filled with the compassionate love of Christ, we ought to be the first to seek means of alleviating the suffering of the masses."[47] Accordingly, the young evangelicals were disappointed when Nixon co-opted neo-evangelical leaders into his circle. During White House–sponsored prayer breakfasts and Sunday services, guest ministers such as Graham, Elton Trueblood, and Harold Ockenga would focus on personal sin and upright behavior, never daring to critique the president's programs in his presence. "Our prophets," Wallis concluded sadly, "are no longer stoned. They are invited to the White House to praise the Nixon Theology."[48] Pierard was even more direct: "I am particularly outraged at Nixon's shameless exploitation of evangelicals in general and Mr. Graham in particular."[49] Moberg agreed, arguing that evangelical acquiescence to conservative policies had given observers the inaccurate impression that "the only Christian position on key issues is one that coincides with the vested interest of the wealthy." In his view, that position served to "alienate conscientious youth, the laboring classes, racial minorities and poor people."[50] As a result, conservatism wasn't just unbiblical. It was bad evangelism.

Nixon had come to symbolize the callousness and neglect of God's laws that had once roused the ire of the prophets. "Richard Nixon," Wallis thundered, "is an apostle of a self-righteous American piety which even takes on a certain religious mystique. This national self-righteousness is one of aggressiveness . . . and an imperial spirit."[51] Among evangelicals concerned about social justice, it became almost a rite of passage to rail against Nixon's center-right policies and his appropriation of religious language. H. H. Claassen, a physics professor at Wheaton College, contended, "It was an indifference to the poor, I think, that led Nixon to veto bills for better education, better health care, and for day care centers."[52] Pierard made a similar argument in *The Other Side,* noting that Nixon had vetoed bills that would have funded housing and hospitals while bailing out large firms with federal funds. It was, he charged, "socialism for the rich, . . . welfare for the affluent."[53] Moberg believed that the "linkage of the power structures in the Republican Party" worked "at the expense of the lower class."[54] These young evangelicals shared the student Left's hostility toward the president, but their anger sprouted from their conclusion that Nixon was a manipulative, pharisaical priest using the language of Christianity for his own machinations. He was not a crook but a cynical idolater.

Forming Evangelicals for McGovern

By demonstrating that the liberal McGovern embodied historical Christian teachings in a more meaningful way than Nixon did, many young evangelicals hoped to jolt other American evangelicals out of their complacency and present a radically different way of living out the gospels. To a striking degree, McGovern's political program aligned with their own priorities for a more Christian commonwealth. They shared a moral revulsion regarding the war, a sense that the economic system was weighted unjustly in favor of the wealthy, and a penchant for using prophetic language to tie their dissent to a credible spiritual tradition. Just as they had yearned for a New Left style of politics in which everyone could share power, they longed for a platform that would bring their Christian ideals closer to reality. Thus, McGovern's somewhat countercultural reputation gave him credibility in their eyes. They probably would not have supported a Democratic candidate with stronger ties to the party establishment (for instance, Humphrey) or the defense industries (such as Henry "Scoop" Jackson).

McGovern's presidential campaign was an opportunity for young evangelicals to speak boldly about how their generation might change society for the better. Their visceral hatred of Nixon's presidency compelled them to work toward his defeat, yet they also saw considerable strengths in his Democratic opponent. McGovern embodied an admirable, if imperfect, mixture of compassion and prophetic challenge, and they admired his sincere use of scripture in public discourse. Their affinity for him rarely arose from any partisan preference for the Democratic Party. Most had grown up as suburban Republicans, and many were enamored of the antiwar senator Mark Hatfield, a moderate Republican from Oregon. Through his aide Wes Michaelson, Hatfield was connected to progressive evangelicals, and by 1972 he had even contributed guest editorials to *Post-American*.[55] They were delighted when Hatfield lambasted the hypocritical piety of Nixon's prayer breakfasts in full view of the president, but the senator was not seeking higher office.[56]

Other than this connection to Hatfield, the people who organized into Evangelicals for McGovern lacked access and proximity to America's political elites. In this they were very different from their mainline counterparts in Religious Leaders for McGovern. Wes Pippert was virtually the only member of the cohort who had known McGovern personally before the campaign, and he saw the senator as "an ideal candidate."[57] Although Pippert often conjectured that McGovern's foundational influence had been his thoroughly evangelical father, most EFM members understood that the senator was on record as a *former* evangelical and were aware that he was a Methodist whose religious sensibilities were chiefly concerned with social ethics. Wolterstorff, one of McGovern's strongest supporters, judged that the senator "fails fully to discern the radicalness and the realism of the gospel. He comes too close to reducing the scripture to a moral message and a social program."[58] Those words telegraphed to Wolterstorff's readers that McGovern was a theological liberal and, for all his virtues, not really one of them. Yet even though McGovern viewed the Bible principally as a social creed, he lacked the arrogance and anti-evangelical bias they saw in politically liberal circles and mainline Protestant ecumenism. Wolterstorff later recalled, "I suppose it was clear to me [that] he was a member of the liberal wing of the church; it struck me that he did not have any disdain for evangelicals. In fact, McGovern was a great human being—he didn't have disdain for many people! He was wide open to cooperation with all sorts of people. He didn't think you had to be a liberal to be authentic."[59]

While faulting McGovern's social gospel theology, Wolterstorff praised the discipleship inherent in his humanitarian work. By pursuing peace and battling worldwide hunger, he had answered the call to identify with and work for the downtrodden. If he wasn't fully biblical in his theology, then at least he came close in his praxis. "How many of us," Wolterstorff asked his skeptical evangelical colleagues, "have taken that yoke upon our shoulders. . . . How many of us have borne the scorn of working for that?"[60] Robert Webber, a professor of religion at Wheaton, agreed. He told *Newsweek*, "We like the way McGovern is getting his feet dirty. He's concerned about hunger, war, poverty and ecology."[61] Pierard believed that "McGovern had a broader social vision" and felt that his embrace of the marginalized was worthy of thoughtful evangelical support.[62] He was, these evangelicals declared, the only viable presidential candidate whose priorities mirrored their own.

EFM was the first truly collaborative effort among these diverse branches of progressive evangelicals. The organization was the brainchild of Ronald Sider, who had been active in peace issues and racial reconciliation but had heretofore played only a minimal role in this evangelical movement. Born into a lower-middle-class farm family in Ontario, he had grown up as a member of the Brethren in Christ, a small denomination that fused a Wesleyan stress on holiness with a Mennonite emphasis on discipleship. Sider was a promising scholar, and in the late 1960s he earned a Ph.D. at Yale, where his studies of church history influenced his approach to the role of religion in public life. Much of his early work concerned Andreas Bodenstein von Karlstadt, who had radically broken away from Martin Luther's Reformation on the grounds that it would not sufficiently reform the church.[63] Sider saw parallels in his own era, identifying a similar unreformed evangelical Christianity that was breaking away from liberal theological heresies but not following through on its transformative promise.

While studying at Yale, Sider became keenly interested in justice for African Americans and the poor, and he joined the NAACP and the Intervarsity Christian Fellowship. After earning his degree, he was hired by Messiah College to teach at its campus in inner-city Philadelphia, and he took notice of the Alexanders' *Other Side* community there. During his time in the city, his awareness of the issues afflicting the poor—inadequate housing, poor family structure, and low-paying jobs—heightened considerably.[64] Trying to reconcile these concerns with his faith, Sider began reading the various publications of socially concerned evangelicals but recognized that there wasn't much of an organizational apparatus binding them together. He believed that a coordinated national effort could unite these disparate evangelical groups. As he later recalled, "I . . . understood my working for McGovern as a practical outworking of what I thought the scriptures were telling me about economic justice and racial justice."[65]

One of Sider's first tasks after forming EFM was to find a group of better-known evangelicals to serve as its board. Although he was functionally in charge of the group's operations, he contented himself with the position of secretary. He invited Walden Howard, the editor of *Faith at Work* magazine, to serve as chair. Howard was aligned with relational Christianity, an evangelical movement that emphasized group spiritual exercises.[66] He was in no way associated with radical evangelicalism, and he served primarily as a figurehead for EFM, lending a reassuring, recognizable name to an organization dominated by lesser-known academics.

For vice-chair, Sider turned to Thomas Skinner. By nearly any definition, Skinner stood out from most of the other Christians in this movement: he was an outspoken black man in a group that was still primarily white. During his rebellious and troubled youth, he had risen to leadership in the Harlem Lords gang, before listening by chance to a sermon on the radio that led to his conversion. Throughout his life, he kept a knife with twenty-two notches, one for each person he had stabbed as a gang member, as a remembrance of the violent, directionless life he had led before his conversion.[67]

With Skinner and Howard on board, Sider sought a broader network, and the eventually the EFM letterhead listed the names of many prominent socially concerned evangelicals. They included seminary professors such as Lewis Smedes of Fuller Seminary and Gilbert James of Asbury Seminary; magazine editors such as Roger Dewey of *Inside* and John Alexander of *The Other Side;* Calvin College professors aligned with the *Reformed Journal,* such as Richard Mouw, Nick Wolterstorff, and Stephen Monsma; and Christian historians such as Richard Pierard and Robert Linder. The organization's goal was to persuade fellow Bible-believing Christians that McGovern's politics aligned with biblical teachings on social justice, which in EFM's view meant solidarity with the poor and active peacemaking. "The richest 10% of Americans make more than the poorest 50%," the first mailing declared. "That is true even after one takes the income tax (with all its loopholes) into account. If Amos is right in declaring that God disapproves when the rich live in luxury at the expense of the poor, then surely Christians should help McGovern close the loopholes and make the rich pay their fair share."[68]

EFM members argued with conservative evangelicals on their own ground, claiming that a politics that identified with the marginalized reflected the proper evangelical approach to scripture. Yet their unfamiliarity with partisan politics often created problems. Sider made a novice's error when he listed his Messiah College phone number as a way to reach EFM, thereby using a nonprofit institution's resources for political purposes. A number of Republican critics urged the school's board of trustees to formally reprimand him, but Messiah's president decided that Sider had simply made a mistake and told him to acquire a different phone number.[69] Nonetheless, the episode highlights the degree to which EFM's effectiveness was limited by both its amateurism and the fact that progressive evangelicals had never before banded together for a common cause. The group's activities could be disorganized, haphazard, and occasionally counter-productive. For instance, Monsma, who was then teaching at Gordon College in Massachusetts, volunteered to drive a group of elderly voters to the polls, only to find that all of them were voting for Nixon.[70] As one member, William Harper, later recalled, the group's efforts "dropped like a stone in a deep lake."[71] Pierard lamented, "We didn't even have the tools to do grassroots work."[72]

EFM's influence, then, was largely limited to the circulation of evangelical magazines that urged social action. But in Jim Wallis's case, his pro-EFM work at *Post-American* was his ticket into the machinery of the McGovern campaign. After Wallis and McGovern met at Wheaton College, the senator's aides invited the young editor to oversee the campaign's groundwork in Evanston. He took a leave of absence from his seminary classes at Trinity and began calling on his experiences in organizing peace protests as a way to get out the vote for McGovern. He recruited heavily among students at Garrett Seminary and Northwestern University, who were as idealistic and leftist in the 1970s as they had been in the late 1940s. "I ran it like an antiwar campaign," Wallis remembered, and he used this cohort of the student Left to canvass the Chicago suburbs in a style reminiscent of the 1968 "Clean for Gene" campaign in New Hampshire.[73]

The novelty and apparent paradox of McGovern-supporting evangelicals attracted some press interest. In the week before the election, *Newsweek* ran a piece on evangelical voters, which gave EFM its first and only taste of mainstream press attention. *Christianity Today* also took notice of the group but dismissed its ability to sway conservative Christians with wildly different views about Vietnam and the nature of the free market. Most evangelicals, the editors confidently predicted, would emulate Graham by casting a vote for Nixon. As early as 1971, *Christianity Today* had suggested that "if evangelical Billy Graham's millions of religious followers take his advice, the result should be an electoral bonanza for President Nixon."[74] Shortly before the election, its editors reiterated their prediction, saying that the voters in America's evangelical community would "probably follow the lead of evangelist Billy Graham."[75]

Sider hoped to challenge this instinct, and he wanted to use EFM to make a statement about the nature of evangelical discipleship. In a mailing, he argued that the organization sought to "end the outdated stereotype that evangelical theology automatically means a politics unconcerned about the poor, minorities and unnecessary military adventures."[76] He and his colleagues pointedly challenged the leadership of American evangelicals. "In the past," Walden Howard told *Newsweek,* "evangelicals have let Graham do their thinking for them. . . . Our organization is the message that Billy Graham does not speak for all the nation's evangelicals."[77] Pierard conceived of the group as "a counterweight to the unabashed support which was being given to Mr. Nixon by Billy Graham and many other prominent evangelicals."[78]

As Mouw later said, EFM was not just a campaign for social justice but for *evangelical* social justice. "It was very important," he recalled, "that we stake out a space where we can say, 'We're not liberals, this isn't the social gospel,' [because] this is what it means to be a radical follower of Jesus Christ, who is a savior, not just one who calls us to peace and justice." EFM gave these young evangelicals room to articulate an identity and to define themselves against their neo-evangelical forebears. Campaigning for McGovern, Mouw remembered, "was an opportunity for us to say, as evangelical Christians, we don't just automatically support the government. . . . We'd been protesting against the war, and here was a candidate who spoke clearly and said, 'This is an unjust war.' It was a unique opportunity to get involved in a national campaign while maintaining our conscience."[79]

In this sense, EFM bore some resemblance to the feminist and gay political groups that supported George McGovern in 1972.[80] However much their members may have admired McGovern, these organizations were not so much concerned with the candidate himself but were consciously using electoral politics to forge an identity that depended on a common set of values. For EFM organizers, it was important that the money they raised be donated collectively, as a demonstration of the strength inherent in the evangelical vote. "By contributing a significant amount," said one mailing, "we evangelicals can both gain a voice and also declare publicly that orthodox theology does not necessarily mean a politics unconcerned about poverty, minorities and inflated military budgets."[81]

EFM sought to reframe modern evangelicalism rather than ensure McGovern's success. The young evangelicals took pains to clarify that they, not the senator, stood resolutely in the prophetic tradition. James Daane argued in the *Reformed Journal* that prophecy necessitated the utterance of God-breathed truths. In his view, the candidate did not fit this criterion because "what Senator McGovern preached on the campaign trail, after all, was not Jesus Christ, but at most a liberal, ethical version of Christianity."[82] John Alexander argued that politicians cannot serve as prophets because successful statesmanship requires subtlety, tact, and guile, all of which compromise the prophetic mission. He concluded that "some Christians should be prophets, and some politicians," neatly bifurcating the roles and implying that prophecy is best left to those outside government office who can freely speak the truth.[83] While RLFM members had no qualms about characterizing a man from their own religious milieu as a prophet, evangelicals were not so willing to give him that designation.

By acquiring the subscription rolls of the various journals published by socially active evangelicals, Sider eventually developed a list of 8,000 potential donors. He sent a mass mailing to all subscribers of *Eternity, The Other Side, Post-American, Inside,* and the *Reformed Journal.* While he did receive a few affirmations and some meager contributions, he also received a flood of negative, even hostile, responses. A review of those negative responses suggests that, at least when judging candidates, the fundamentalist emphasis on individual rather than social and collective sin was most relevant. Many respondents cited McGovern's personal peccadilloes and misbehaviors. For instance, W. T. Miller, a conservative New Testament scholar, told Howard that he opposed McGovern because he had told a young heckler in Michigan to "kiss his ass"; apparently he was unaware of Nixon's more prolific use of foul language.[84] A number of respondents critiqued McGovern's handling of the Eagleton controversy, referring to it as two-faced conduct unbecoming of a Christian. Others were shocked that a group of evangelicals had taken the decidedly worldly step of endorsing and fundraising for a presidential candidate. "I am surprised," marveled one woman, "that there are men of your status and calling concerning yourself with the business of political moneylenders."[85] William Coray, a missionary and an author, was more direct: "I deplore with all my heart your temerity, in the interest of compassion and social justice, in trying to influence evangelical Christians to support a man who holds views that cut so directly across the Word of God."[86] These rejections were not far different from the national evangelical opinion of McGovern, who in the end earned fewer than one white evangelical vote for every four won by Nixon.[87] Most evangelicals assumed that the senator's leftist politics precluded the faithful from supporting him. An editorial in the *U.S. Farm News,* an agricultural digest for midwesterners, observed, "Here, pious prayer meeting groups think McGovern is a socialist, and therefore godless."[88]

In some cases, the neo-evangelical leaders countered EFM by publicizing their own support for Nixon. Like the mainline church leaders who endorsed McGovern, they based their support on personal acquaintance and trust as much as policy. As in 1968, Graham declared shortly before the election that he had cast an absentee ballot for his friend Nixon. But while Graham's 1968 endorsement was a quiet and understated affair that focused on Nixon's merits, his 1972 statement took McGovern to task for his brazen attacks on the president. McGovern, Graham charged, was "desperate, and he is tired." The pastor vouched for Nixon's character, despite nascent rumors of foul play at the Watergate Hotel: "I have great confidence in his personal honesty. I voted for him because I know what he is made of."[89] Graham would rue those words a few years later.

Harold Ockenga, the president of Gordon-Conwell Theological Seminary, had once presided over a Sunday morning service in the Nixon White House. Now he followed Graham's lead. In his formal endorsement, Ockenga cited the president's "high moral integrity" and his efforts to bring the Vietnam War to a close, while referring to the Watergate situation as a mishap in which the president was not involved. "Nixon," he maintained, "deserved praise for his term in office; 1972 saw far fewer race riots, and student uprisings. He had restored a sense of order to a country being torn at the seams but four years ago."[90] Ockenga's attitude was emblematic of American evangelicals' stance in general. They argued for Nixon's merits on the grounds of outward stability, while EFM centered its case on the persistence of structural injustice. In the meantime, the Nixon administration had invited a number of religious leaders, ranging from William Smith of the African Methodist Episcopal Zion Church, Jess Moody of Palm Beach Atlantic College, and Elton Trueblood of the Society of Friends, for official briefings on how they might help his campaign.[91] Nearly all of them had preached at the White House during Nixon's first term.

Making Sense of the Wreckage

In the short term, EFM labored in vain: Nixon won a staggering 84 percent of the evangelical vote. Almost immediately after McGovern's defeat, the group's organizers began theological postmortems of the campaign. They tended to interpret the import of the senator's defeat in one of two ways. First, many blamed McGovern's failure as a product of his outdated commitment to the social gospel. Daane concluded, "I know that Christian ethics not grounded in Christian doctrine is an optimism with a soft underbelly, vulnerable to the attacks of hard-nosed political realism."[92] Likewise, Mouw warned that when "liberal Protestants hear evangelical Christians denouncing racism or militarism or calling for a 'post-American' lifestyle of obedience to Jesus Christ, they would do well to keep in mind that these evangelical activists are no more comfortable with theological liberalism than is the rest of the evangelical community."[93]

Second, EFM's organizers realized that progressive evangelicals had a place in public discourse but perhaps not in the scuffle of electoral politics. Campaigning for McGovern had created a common platform, but it did little else. The group had attracted only 358 evangelical donors and had cobbled together a fundraising total of only $5,762, comically short of its $100,000 goal. Yet in letters to a number of former group members, Sider pointed out that EFM had succeeded in communicating the idea that politics were part of the all-encompassing jurisdiction of discipleship. In a memo to contributors, he wrote, "If evangelicals are to take Jesus' Lordship seriously, he must be the King of our politics." Sider and many of his allies concluded that EFM had been a poor opening tactic but that the strategy of taking coordinated political action against large-scale social problems was important and doable. He concluded in his memo, "If we are listening to all that biblical revelation says about justice in our society, then our politics must reflect a concern not only for pubs, pot and pornographic literature, but also about racism, poverty and the grossly unjust distribution of wealth."[94] Now he was considering the possibility of "some organized structure for evangelical political action" around issues neglected by mainstream evangelicals, one that would mobilize without the potentially divisive ramifications of partisan politics.[95] In the same vein, the theologian Clark Pinnock wrote in *Post-American* that "costly discipleship is needed now more than ever," a turn of phrase that channeled Bonhoeffer while playing on Nixon's reelection slogan.[96]

EFM's significance lay not in its unimpressive numbers but in its role in bringing together a disparate group of socially conscious evangelicals for a common political purpose. It broadened their focus, shifting it away from localized advocacy or academic musings. Ron Sider moved into the foreground of evangelical debates about the role of the living church in society. He soon became a regular contributor to *The Other Side*, the *Reformed Journal*, *Post-American*, and other mainstays of the dissident evangelicals' literary network. For the next decade, he, more than any other figure in the movement, was the mind behind many of its most ambitious and effective initiatives. Thus, EFM proved to be prophetic in both senses of the word. The organization demonstrated that evangelicals were an untapped vein of political activity. Given the visibility and success of the religious Right later in the decade, there is a certain irony in the fact that the first major postwar candidate to enjoy coordinated evangelical support was the leftist George McGovern. But EFM also exhibited prophecy in the manner that the group more frequently used the word: the deliverance of God's judgment upon unjust social structures. Emboldened and now in regular contact with one another, the activists were ready to spread the prophetic word throughout America, to evangelicals and the unredeemed alike.

8

The Christian Left's
Failure to Launch

In every election season, presidential candidates reach out to historically unreceptive audiences, hoping to broaden and reframe their campaigns. John F. Kennedy's 1960 address to the Protestant conclave at the Greater Houston Ministerial Association changed the focus from his Roman Catholicism to a common American Dream, where merit superseded the particulars of faith. In 1980, Ronald Reagan made a Labor Day visit to New Jersey, where he defended the value of unions, a largely Democratic constituency. In 2012, Mitt Romney's speech to members of the NAACP reached out to a demographic widely considered inaccessible to Republicans. Likewise, George McGovern's address at staunchly evangelical, Republican Wheaton College in the middle of the 1972 election season was designed to pivot the conversation toward a politics of compassionate conscience. It didn't work.

Why was a unified movement toward progressive Christianity so elusive in the 1970s? Why were mainliners and evangelicals so reluctant to work across religious traditions, even when they shared common political goals? As I searched for answers, I looked with special attention at McGovern's speech at Wheaton, his most conspicuous act of outreach to evangelicals. He had hoped that his words would unite religious advocates for social justice under one Democratic banner, but his short visit to the campus instead clarified his indelible liberal Christianity in ways that made even his strongest evangelical supporters uneasy. In an age of identity politics and personal authenticity, progressive evangelicals eschewed a working relationship with liberal politics and theologically liberal church members. Despite their flirtation with Evangelicals for McGovern, they preferred to work for social justice through their own organizations and on their own terms. That mission culminated in the Chicago Declaration of Evangelical Social Concern, released a year after McGovern's ill-starred visit to Wheaton.

The Michaelson Memo

Ron Sider founded Evangelicals for McGovern without much initial encouragement from the McGovern campaign. In contrast, Religious Leaders for McGovern enjoyed from the start a warm, clubby relationship with the candidate. Yet McGovern and his campaign eventually saw EFM as a conduit into the nation's evangelical body, in part thanks to Mark Hatfield's aide Wes Michaelson. Michaelson had been a point man for the proposed McGovern-Hatfield amendment in 1970; and like both senators, he opposed the Vietnam War. Thus, he felt compelled to quietly cross party lines and offer his assistance to McGovern. According to Gordon Weil, one of McGovern's closest campaign aides, Michaelson showed them that the senator's revivalist argot, which "was not put on to achieve a political effect was, in fact, having an effect with evangelicals."[1] Michaelson even covertly wrote a memo detailing how a liberal of McGovern's bent might make inroads into that community. Evangelicals, he argued, were not as lockstep behind Nixon as they seemed to be. Their support for the president was instinctual but not especially deep or loyal. "Because the evangelical community regards a politician's faith as more decisive than his politics," the evangelicals might be won over if they properly understood how McGovern's faith motivated him. In other words, he could challenge religious support for Nixon, a famously unobservant Quaker, among a demographic the president was taking for granted. Michaelson believed that McGovern should either make a public display of affinity with the evangelical community or take part in a "private, informal, candid discussion" with their leaders to test how receptive they might be to his program. He concluded the memo by suggesting that McGovern should speak about his understanding of Christianity and its role in politics at either Wheaton or Calvin College, institutions with strong intellectual reputations that reverberated among evangelicals. He implored McGovern to discuss how a political program alone could not revive the nation, to emphasize that it would take "individual change in one's attitudes, values, and life." This was "the central insight of the gospels," he argued, and it would resonate with McGovern's message of "coming home," and choosing the righteous path.[2]

Unexpectedly, McGovern was invited to Wheaton before he could request a campus visit himself: the student council sent an invitation to both McGovern and Nixon, expecting that neither would accept. Unfortunately, the letters to the candidates were accidentally switched, so the senator received the infelicitous assurance that "all of us here at Wheaton are for you, Mr. President."[3] Perhaps the mix-up was a sign of his difficulties to come. To the students' surprise, however, and quite probably to their consternation, McGovern eagerly accepted their half-hearted invitation.

Wheaton was not only the most widely respected of the nation's evangelical colleges but also Billy Graham's alma mater. Symbolically, this made it an appealing choice. Yet to some, the visit looked like a fool's errand, and they feared that McGovern would squander valuable time speaking to an audience that would be difficult to win over. A prominent communications scholar, Martin Medhurst, later suggested that McGovern went to Wheaton largely to fulfill a psychological need to win approval from his father's people.[4] On the contrary, his expressed intent was to evangelize for liberalism from a religious angle and transform the election into a referendum on values. He was eager to challenge the G.O.P.'s monopoly on evangelical voters.[5] The difficulty was that, aside from Michaelson's advice, his campaign knew little about evangelical subculture. McGovern may not have realized just how far removed he was from the religion of his youth. Although he believed that explaining his own, more liberal faith and his evangelical boyhood would establish points of connection, he still had to overcome evangelicalism's longtime antipathy to mainline theology and culture. The slog would be harder than he anticipated.

Wheaton was decidedly unfriendly to both theological and political liberalism. The invitation that McGovern had accidentally received was true; support for Nixon and the war in Vietnam was something of an article of faith at the college. Its president, Hudson Armerding, was a stalwart Cold Warrior, and he had banned both Hatfield and Jim Wallis from speaking on the campus because of their antiwar views.[6] According to the historian Randall Balmer (who, as an undergraduate, had followed the McGovern visit closely), Armerding also attempted to rescind McGovern's invitation to the campus.[7] The president even pressured Robert Webber, a professor and New Testament scholar who was a member of EFM, to either withdraw his support for the candidate or resign from the faculty. Webber's colleagues at the college quietly but firmly rallied to his side. Although they were largely conservative, they felt that a tenured professor did not deserve such shabby treatment.

In light of this opposition, the logistics of bringing McGovern to Wheaton required collaboration among McGovern's campaign, well-connected mainliners, and socially concerned evangelicals. Their cooperation began when Sider contacted Michael McIntyre, the RLFM coordinator, to ask how EFM might be of service to the campaign. Eager to build ties between mainline and evangelical Christians, McIntyre asked Webber and Wallis to manage McGovern's appearance at Wheaton College. This was EFM's only direct activity with the senator's campaign during the election.[8]

Given their preference for Nixon, Wheaton's administrators agonized over the precise nature of a McGovern visit. If they permitted a partisan political rally, they risked a confrontation with Wheaton's sizable body of Nixonites, one that might mirror a 1964 incident when violence nearly broke out between Johnson and Goldwater supporters.[9] Yet a wholly religious, school-sanctioned chapel service would have implied that Wheaton had endorsed McGovern's policies and would anger the school's heavily Republican donors and trustees. Ultimately, the college found a solution by billing McGovern's address as a convocation service, an opportunity to meditate on Christian life, and scheduled it in Edman Chapel, Wheaton's impressive new worship facility, which could hold 2,500 people. In this way, his visit was framed not as a campaign stop but as an occasion in which a Christian addresses his brethren on matters of spiritual importance.

Recognizing that this speech would be the senator's best chance to make inroads into an untapped religious demographic, the McGovern campaign worked furiously to polish it. Ted Van Dyk told a reporter that "we spent more time talking about and reading that speech than anything [else that] week," except for a national television address on Vietnam.[10] The speechwriters Bob Shrum and John Holum consulted Michaelson for advice.[11] At the time, Michaelson and Holum were housemates, which made it easier for Michaelson to advise the opposition candidate discreetly. The writers developed a pattern: Michaelson would compose a first draft of the speech, and Shrum and Holum would polish it. McGovern would then heavily edit the second draft. As Michaelson recollected, the senator focused on infusing his speech with autobiographical flourishes that stressed his evangelical upbringing and how it had shaped his character.[12] Holum felt that McGovern "[was] trying to say 'I can empathize and identify pretty deeply with you, with what you are because . . . my own pilgrimage has taken me through places that are very much like where you are now."[13] Nonetheless, there were problems. With so many authors, the Wheaton address, now titled "Sources of Our Strength," became a hermeneutical Frankenstein's monster constructed from disparate and ill-matched parts. McGovern's liberal Christianity, Michaelson's deep evangelical faith, and Shrum's lapsed Catholicism mingled in awkward and often contradictory ways. The speech made appeals to Wheaton students, often in evangelistic language, but any educated evangelical would have been able to detect the social gospel heresies in its underlying message. Even so, the McGovern campaign staff was very hopeful for the speech's prospects. According to the journalist Wes Pippert, McGovern's aides believed that the Wheaton speech would be the most significant of the campaign, save perhaps for the "Come Home, America" speech delivered at the Democratic National Convention.[14] As if to accentuate its importance, the senator's press secretary, Dick Dougherty, later took the unusual step of including lengthy excerpts from it in his own campaign memoirs, using it as a chance to ruminate on McGovern's moral vision.[15]

McGovern on Campus

On October 11, McGovern arrived at Wheaton College to deliver his speech and to meet briefly with a select number of evangelical leaders. Unaccustomed to attention of this magnitude, the town of Wheaton closed streets and blocked traffic, rendering the college insular and isolated from the outside. Both literally and figuratively, McGovern was now fully immersed in evangelical Christendom for the first time since his childhood. Yet the college itself scarcely promoted the event. David Moberg, who had driven down from Wisconsin for the proceedings, called the administration's attitude "a terrible disgrace." Wheaton seemed almost embarrassed by McGovern's visit. As Moberg recalled, "It was as if they said that their constituency was so firmly Republican" that the administration was reluctant to admit "a Democratic candidate was on their campus."[16]

The first order of business was a breakfast summit meeting with prominent evangelical leaders, many of whom had traveled long distances to attend the event. EFM had been given the responsibility for choosing which leaders to invite to the convocation, so many of its own members were present, including Sider, Wallis, Mouw, Moberg, and Wolterstorff. It was,

in fact, the first time that Wallis and Sider, two of the era's most important evangelical voices for social justice, met face to face.[17] Years later Wes
Michaelson (now Granberg-Michaelson) marveled at the exciting prospects
of social justice evangelicalism in 1972. "Once in a while, the timing is right
and you get the right people in the room, and you touch on a message that's
really galvanizing—you touch on the right words at the right time. It was a
great group of people who were in the process of discovering one another,
and discovering the common set of reactions that we were having."[18]

When sending out invitations, EMF favored evangelicals who were curious about McGovern rather than mainliners who were already familiar with
him. For the young evangelicals, it was an opportunity to draw men of their
faith tradition (and they were almost entirely men) into a serious conversation about social justice. Conservatives at the event included Rufus Jones,
the general director of the Baptist Home Mission Board, and Clarence
Boomsma, a leader in the Christian Reformed Church. Wallis remembered,
"What became clear was that [McGovern] knew his scriptures. [The conser-
vatives] didn't expect that. He was biblically literate and very articulate."[19]

Donald W. Dayton, a historian of American evangelicalism, asked the
senator a question that was on many minds at Wheaton: Why he had moved
from the evangelical Wesleyan Methodist Church to a mainline church?
McGovern replied that the Wesleyan Methodists seemed to have forsaken
their social responsibilities, although he saw hope that this would change.
Wesleyan Methodism, he observed, had "the notion that to change society
you had to do it one by one by changed individuals. I accept much of that
doctrine. The concept of personal salvation is not an unimportant one. In
recent years, evangelical churchmen have become aware they have a mission
in society. I would like to see them move much further."[20] McGovern's view
of salvation as "not unimportant" did little to reassure the evangelical academics at the gathering.[21] John Warwick Montgomery, a prominent Christian apologist, asked if McGovern's training at the liberal Garrett Seminary
had compromised his understanding of humanity's sinfulness. McGovern
shot back, "So because I don't fully subscribe to the theology of complete
human depravity, and because Richard Nixon practices it, you're going to
vote for him?"[22] The joke triggered some nervous laughter, yet it hit on an
uncomfortable truth. The evangelicals who weren't already in EFM might
have been impressed by McGovern's surprising command of scripture. But
they were going to vote for Nixon anyway.

Accompanied by Wallis and Webber, McGovern was driven to Edman

Chapel to deliver his address before the Wheaton student body. Charged with selecting a man to introduce him, EFM had tapped its vice-chair, the evangelist Tom Skinner, who had spoken at the college on several other occasions. Although he sometimes angered middle-class evangelicals when he intimated that they worshipped a God who was "too white," he was nonetheless a familiar presence.[23] His introduction, however, was an uneasy and maladroit synthesis of McGovern talking points and evangelical doctrine. Using words he'd taken almost verbatim from McGovern's typical stump speech, Skinner condemned Nixon's economic policy, which allows "a man who is a multimillionaire . . . [to] write off a twenty-dollar martini luncheon, when most people in America cannot write off a bologna sandwich." This populist line did not resonate among a group of middle-class evangelicals whose families could afford private college tuition. Skinner then elicited a few jeers when he reminded the audience that McGovern was the son of a preacher: the crowd probably thought he was making a hasty attempt to burnish McGovern's spiritual credentials. There were many more boos and cries of protest when Skinner went on to declare that "Senator McGovern stands in the vein of the prophet Amos."[24] By comparing a liberal, a mainliner, and a Democratic standard bearer to a prophet of the Lord, he had gone too far. Skinner, heretofore a popular evangelical figure, was visibly upset by the audience's negative reaction. "I had never seen [him] so rattled," said Wallis.[25]

Despite his missteps in the introduction, and despite vast differences in race and class, Skinner and the Wheaton students shared a common religious worldview that McGovern did not. During the convocation at Edman Chapel, the senator made a number of small but revealing mistakes that hurt his attempt to reach his listeners and validated their impression that he was not their kind of Christian. Pippert observed that the Wheaton audience was "suspicious of McGovern because of his liberal views and perhaps even more [because] he once was one of them, and in their opinion, he has strayed."[26] The senator did little to assuage those misgivings. Describing his background, he mispronounced the name of his father's alma mater, Houghton College, saying "How-ton" rather than the correct "Hoe-ton," which instigated snickering and illustrated his unfamiliarity with evangelical institutions.[27] For much of his speech, he reminded the evangelicals of their long record of social activism. Often drawing from information he'd learned at Garrett, he referred to key evangelists in Anglo-American history but consistently downplayed their work at winning souls and instead stressed their humanitarianism. He praised John Wesley, not for his preaching but for his work in setting up medical clinics for industrial England's poor. Likewise, when he cited the Puritan minister Jonathan Edwards, he briefly acknowledged his role as a great intellectual light of the Great Awakening but principally commended him for offering himself as a test case for the smallpox vaccine, an "act of charity and love and sacrifice that took his life." McGovern mentioned the prominent abolitionists Charles Finney and William Wilberforce as men of God who were dedicated to the improvement of society. Slavery had been abolished, labor conditions had been improved, and prison reform had been put into law, he affirmed, "because the conscience of the nation had been touched, and enlivened by these religious and spiritual awakenings."[28]

The candidate praised Christianity not for reconciling God and humankind but for improving humanity's material conditions on earth. In contrast, most Wheaton students viewed Christianity as a commitment to Christ. Even for progressive evangelicals, the purpose of faith was to restore a relationship with God broken by sin; any social improvement that came from that faith was ancillary. So when McGovern told his audience that America "must have the fundamental stirring of our moral and spiritual values," he was connecting these values to a series of political ideals that most evangelicals found unpalatable.[29] He went on to associate this moral resurgence with politically progressive platforms such as jobs programs, battles against malnutrition, cuts to the military budget, and pollution controls. Listing these policies was unlikely to win over students who, like their parents, were enjoying many of the privileges that the social movements of the 1960s and 1970s had challenged. McGovern's positions were liberal both politically and theologically. As Arthur Holmes, a professor at the college, noted, his rhetoric "stir[red] ghosts of the theological past; and his conception of personal redemption remain[ed] vague."[30]

McGovern's visit to Wheaton was a pointed reminder that America had two very different versions of Protestantism. It was no accident that the most evangelical line in his speech, "changed men can change society," generated the most applause. Billy Graham also commonly used the phrase in his speeches and revivals. But while the evangelist meant that personal reconciliation with God must come first, McGovern prioritized changing society.[31] As a result, his speech seemed to embody H. Richard Niebuhr's famous jibe that liberal Christianity offered nothing more than "a God without wrath," one who "brought men without sin into a kingdom without judgment through the ministrations of a Christ without a cross."[32] As a Wheaton student told a reporter, McGovern "hadn't come out all the way for Jesus."[33]

Randall Balmer, then a student at a nearby college, said that the senator was "besieged by boos, jeers and catcalls" and recalled that Wheaton students interrupted the proceedings to march through the chapel bearing placards, banners, and photographs of Nixon.[34] Finally, after noticing a banner in the balcony reading "Vote for Jesus," McGovern went off script. "Let me make one thing perfectly clear," he said, mimicking one of Nixon's rhetorical tics. "If Jesus were running, I would withdraw tomorrow and throw my support to Him. But let me make one more thing perfectly clear. Running against Richard Nixon is not like running against Jesus Christ." "And with that," Wallis remembered, "he shut down the booing."[35] The listeners who'd begun by hectoring the candidate gave him polite, if unenthusiastic, applause at the end. As he had done during his morning meeting with the evangelical leaders, McGovern had turned outright hostility into begrudging respect. Although the speech did not go entirely as planned, it did reinforce McGovern's hope that the election could be framed as a contest of moral leadership. In fact, he thought so highly of "Sources of Our Strength" that he included it in the volume of selected campaign speeches released in 1974.[36]

Pippert, who was privately thrilled by McGovern's argument that religious men had obligations to improve society, had hoped to send a lengthy account of the address to UPI. Unfortunately, because of a transmission malfunction, the news desk never received his draft.[37] The loss of Pippert's manuscript may have cost McGovern his opportunity to present his ideas about religious conviction in politics to a larger and less hostile audience. Rather than summarizing his visit to Wheaton, press reports on McGovern's activities focused on his midday visit to Chicago, where he had lunch with Mayor Richard Daley and 1,200 city precinct captains.[38] The tense affair was a necessary gesture if McGovern wanted to retain any hope of winning Illinois after the snubbing of Daley's delegation at the Democratic National Convention. But the end result was that instead of showing McGovern articulating a clear moral vision, the day's press coverage linked him to a man whose name was synonymous with machine politics.

The Mainline-Evangelical Divide

RLFM's coordinator Michael McIntyre hoped that McGovern's appeal would stimulate a more fruitful collaboration between mainliners and evangelicals. He wondered what kind of coalition might develop if the energy of the young evangelicals were to combine with the political savvy and long reach of the ecumenicals. After the election, McGovern himself made a brief attempt to foster cooperation between the groups, arranging a meeting in early December 1972 so that RLFM and EFM members could meet. Sider remembers that someone in the campaign took a photo of all the supporters in attendance, and McGovern later gave him a copy with the inscription "What a contrast to the Watergate gang."[39] To McIntyre, such gestures signaled that "[McGovern] does not mean to abandon the friendship offered him by those evangelicals who cared very much about his candidacy." But in the aftermath of the defeat, McIntyre was nearly alone in puzzling over why the camps were not working together more closely. They were, he reasoned, natural allies with a shared commitment to social justice that arose from their religious faith. He saw their failure to unite as a sad indictment on the divided state of American Protestantism: "The 'establishment' churches' lack of familiarity with their evangelical counterparts was simply astonishing. This or that religious leader would tell me, 'gee, call so-and-so, I heard that he knows some of the evangelicals.' It was almost as though, religiously, we lived in two different countries."[40] As Richard Quebedeaux noted, these two branches were still grappling with the fallout of the fundamentalist-modernist controversy of the 1920s and 1930s over differing means of engaging both scripture and the secular world. "It was that dispute which divided Protestantism in America into two hostile camps and resulted in a factionalism within the church from which it has never fully recovered."[41]

Just as McGovern's religious language rubbed many Catholics the wrong way, his address at Wheaton reinforced many evangelicals' assumption that he was just another mainliner who refused to take their perspective seriously. The Presbyterian pastor Richard Hutcheson Jr. once lamented, "Evangelical writers [tend] to be far more familiar with liberal-ecumenical books, ideas, and theology than most of us are with theirs."[42] Yet in the 1960s and 1970s, mainliners rarely felt any need to be conversant with evangelical ideas, viewing them as marginal and intellectually thin. As the historian James Smylie has noted, mainliners assumed an identity in an increasingly pluralist society as transformers of culture and voices of conscience, and their social prominence and their churches' long history of respectability gave their ideas heft.[43] Liberal Protestants enjoyed the luxury of being taken seriously: they were the culture, and the evangelicals were the subculture.

Mirroring the way in which Protestants had long imagined the Roman Catholic Church, evangelicals saw the ecumenical churches as a "new Babylon"—bloated, corrupt, elitist, and heretical.[44] Equally uncharitably, mainliners often ridiculed evangelicals for their simplistic theology and easy answers to complex social problems. In a 1956 issue of *Christianity and Crisis,* Reinhold Niebuhr himself famously critiqued Billy Graham's stewardship of evangelical Protestantism, calling him an "obscurantist."[45] Niebuhr argued that Graham reduced the practice of Christianity into little more than charismatic preaching and emotional altar calls, making the act of redemption an arbitrary moment of choice. Mainline leaders frequently conflated neo-evangelicals and fundamentalists into a single intellectually suspect subgroup. In an 1965 opinion piece in the *Christian Century,* John Opie Jr. held their biblicism in open contempt. Evangelicals, he wrote, believe that the mainliners "have not reckoned sufficiently with the Bible as an intrinsic reality which is beyond criticism. They consider most unscientific the proposition that Isaiah had more than one author or that Moses did not write the Pentateuch. To them this is like saying fire does not burn and water cannot freeze. To their way of thinking, the Bible's own testimony, like the evidence of the physical world, cannot be contradicted without making it meaningless."[46] More often, the institutional mainline ignored Graham and other evangelicals, treating their books and their conferences as unworthy of their attention, except for the occasional snide editorial. One *Christian Century* segment on the fate of modern Protestantism wondered if the two traditions had "no discernible common denominator" now that their shared anti-Catholicism had abated. The magazine's editors asked a number of religious figures to offer their perspectives on the matter, even inviting Rabbi Heschel to take part, but they did not solicit contributions from any evangelical.[47]

Throughout the twentieth century, mainliners and evangelicals peered at one another suspiciously across a doctrinal no-man's land. Although the social and cultural underpinnings of this divide were real, disagreements often manifested in theological terms. Mainliners accused evangelicals of anti-intellectualism, while evangelicals charged that the mainliners took undue liberties with the revealed truth of scripture. By 1972, each had carved out its own enclave within Christendom. The mainliners read the *Christian Century* and *Christianity and Crisis* and organized around their denominational structure and ecumenical councils. Their promising seminary students went to Emory, Garrett, or Union and monopolized the Ivy League divinity schools. Evangelicals read *Christianity Today* and sent their promising seminary students to Wheaton, Fuller, or Gordon-Conwell. "The things that separate us are partly theological and partly cultural," concluded Stephen Monsma.[48]

Given this historic mistrust, the idea of an enduring leftist coalition among McGovern's religious supporters seemed likely to die after his Wheaton speech. Yet like McIntyre, Marlin Van Eldren, a frequent contributor to the *Christian Century* and *Christianity and Crisis,* wondered after the election if cooperation between liberal Christians and the young evangelicals could be possible, though "any alliances . . . will be uneasy ones."[49] It would be foolhardy, he concluded, to assume that a common passion for social justice and a shared Protestant heritage could overcome their differences. The divide was compounded by serious philosophical differences about how to solve the problems of poverty and inequality. With their New Left background, the McGovern evangelicals were not convinced that government fiat was the best means to promote social justice. Instead, they often favored approaches that privileged personal discipleship or living in communities. Monsma explained that, historically, "mainliners *talk* about solidarity [but] it so quickly translates into advocacy and lobbying government. Social justice becomes a matter of lobbying government to do it. With evangelicals, there's more of a balance between working directly and hands-on, *and* advocacy."[50]

Writing to Sider in the months after McGovern's defeat, David Moberg argued that the young evangelicals should orient their future activism in ways that contrasted with the model of lobbying and bureaucracy that characterized NCC. Evangelicals, he believed, should emphasize "the collective as well as the personal aspects of sin, the need for both evangelism and social reform, salvation and service, changing lives and changing society, proclamation and demonstration, the vertical and horizontal relationships of man, personal piety and social service, faith and works, believing and loving, the inward and the outward journey."[51] In short, they should not divorce their social action from their Christian witness, as they feared the liberal NCC had done.

These evangelicals caricaturized the liberal mainline, sometimes cruelly and unfairly, in order to articulate their own moral vision. They began to view themselves as a group that was addressing two sets of excesses. Liberal Protestants neglected the weight of the scriptures in favor of a humanist gospel that avoided any true recognition of sin, while extreme rightwing evangelicals neglected the Bible's unmistakable social teachings about poverty, peace, and compassion. As Richard Mouw wrote in *Political Evangelism,* "Christians must not choose the political passivity that has often been the posture of a culture-denying fundamentalism, nor must they engage in the mindless activism that has regularly characterized the stance of liberal worshipers at the altar of relevance."[52] By defining themselves against the mainline churches, the progressive evangelicals crafted a narrative of theologically liberal Christianity whose decline sprang from its apostasy. They imagined a future in which evangelical Christians would claim a more powerful role in shaping public affairs by virtue of greater numbers, increasing prominence, and forthright witness. "Everybody recognizes," Sider wrote in an EFM memo, "that at this moment in history, we have a fantastic opportunity and also a heavy responsibility. Liberal theology and politics are in shambles. A conservative religious tide is sweeping the country."[53] He predicted confidently—and accurately: "For better or for worse, evangelicals will be the dominant religious influence in the '70's."[54]

The evangelicals worshipped an active God far removed from the self-limiting deity of personalism. As Mouw recalled with studied understatement, "we were not at all friendly toward liberal Protestants."[55] Notably, the branch of Christian theology that had most inspired McGovern—the social gospel—was the one that the young evangelicals most reviled. Soon after the candidate's defeat, Sider issued a sharp attack on it: "The fact that liberal theologians have reduced Jesus' role to that of [an] example dare not prevent evangelicals from insisting that the disciple of Christ is one who has a passionate, unconditional commitment to his Lord's example."[56] Even many years later, most of them saw the idea as a corruption of Christianity. In 2009, for instance, Wallis wrote, "The social gospel cannot be sustained without a personal experience of Jesus, who brings the good news."[57]

Born in Chicago

Despite their discomforts and disappointments, the McGovern evangelicals were aware that his campaign had given them the opportunity to find one another and create a nascent network. Their first post-election collaboration was the Chicago Declaration of Evangelical Social Concern, an attempt in 1973 to transform their amorphous commitment to social justice into a permanent, active movement. Scholars of American religion often see the declaration as the clarion call of the modern social justice movement among evangelicals, and EFM was a crucial antecedent.[58] Using the networks and religious identity they had forged during the campaign, the former EFM members spent much of the year planning and publicizing the gathering that would highlight the declaration. Yet as happened so often in the 1970s, articulating who they were (and whom they were with) took precedence over effectively solving the problems that had brought them together in the first place.

To be successful, the gathering could not be partisan in the way that EFM had been. Sider, as director, was eager to move away from a caucus sensibility so that "people who disagree[d] politically could be held together and continue learning from each other."[59] He wanted them to feel that peace and empathy were nonpartisan issues. Sider remembered the chilly reception McGovern had received at Wheaton as well as how many evangelicals had flatly told EFM organizers that they would refuse to support a liberal Democrat. It would be better, he reasoned, to avoid parties and candidates altogether. He hoped instead to focus on neighborhoods and ghettos, hunger and war, in ways that defied a neat liberal-conservative dichotomy.

Early in the planning process, Sider proposed the idea of creating small coalitions that would operate locally to address problems particular to their communities.[60] The Mennonite scholar John Yoder agreed, writing that "the primary social structure through which the Gospel works to change other structures is that of the Christian community."[61] In a circular letter to his evangelical friends, Sider declared that "my activities in the past 6 months have confirmed the conviction that a momentous development is taking place within evangelical circles. . . . It is still a minority movement, but it is widespread and growing. This emerging group of evangelical social activists . . . needs direction."[62] He suggested that these activists should unite in an organization he called the National Congress on Biblical Faith and Social Concern. Once again, however, he defined the action in direct contrast to mainline theology. "If at this historic moment of unparalleled influence, evangelicals offer a truncated Gospel concerned only with individual salvation and personal piety, an inevitable revival of theological liberalism will follow," he warned. "And it will have been our fault for having failed to proclaim God's total word for the whole man."[63]

As far as Sider was concerned, the group would be expressly an evangelical form of social action, not a generic movement of the Christian Left. Thus, he and his allies chose to schedule their Chicago gathering on Thanksgiving, a day of prayer and contemplation that had backslid into a civic holiday and an orgy of feasting. To emphasize the need to identify with the poor, he chose a YMCA on South Wabash Street as the gathering's headquarters. McGovern's visit to Wheaton had brought these evangelicals to the comfortable suburbs, but this time they would meet in the middle of a dilapidated cityscape. In a dig at the luxurious settings of the National Association of Evangelicals meetings, one participant recalled, "We were tired of meetings in fancy hotels and retreat centers, especially [when the agenda was] concerned with social involvement."[64] The symbolism of the Chicago conference's setting is itself striking for its historical import. In the nineteenth century, progressive Christians had, after all, founded the YMCA as an effort to reduce the temptations that confronted young men in the city.[65] At the same time, however, the YMCA was a testament to the impact of the social gospel on urban America. These evangelical activists for social justice could not escape the legacy of the social gospel, no matter how much they wished to repudiate it.

By expanding this conversation outward from his small coterie of McGovern supporters, Sider drew in evangelicals who shared some of EFM's concerns but did not identify with the Left. "The amazing thing," marveled Mouw, "was that we were joined by others who weren't opposed to the war."[66] They included Rufus Jones, the Baptist minister who had met McGovern at Wheaton; Paul Rees, who worked for World Vision, a Christian humanitarian lobbying organization; and Frank Gaebelein, a political conservative and a board member of the charity Bread for the World. "We need," Sider told them, "to find ways to effectively carry the biblical message of social concern to middle American Christianity."[67] This meant persuading the greater body of evangelicals that social action was the duty of *all* Christians.

While these well-known figures broadened the workshop's appeal, their involvement made the creation of a cohesive statement on social action far more contentious. Initial drafts contained passages exposing the evangelical tendency to "condemn selected classes of sin and overlook others. They forget that the church must always be about both evangelism and prophetic social criticism."[68] Pierard, ever a sharp critic of civil religion, wrote to Sider hoping to challenge evangelicals' conflation of national pride with religious faith. He suggested a plank that read, "Civil religion, unlike biblical faith, is largely devoid of moral content and can easily be manipulated to serve the needs of national policy."[69] Nancy Hardesty, who would go on to found the evangelical feminist magazine *Daughters of Sarah,* pushed unsuccessfully for the inclusion of a passage affirming the equality of women and men both in and out of marriage and calling for equal pay for equal work. She was one of the only members of the group to broach the issue of abortion, putting forth a plank designating the fetus as a being of "increasing value" from conception but not yet achieving all the intrinsic rights of human life until birth had taken place.[70] Attendees wrangled over proposals calling for a drastic 50 percent cut in the American standard of living and a graduated tithe based on capacity to pay, both of which the voting body ultimately rejected. The organizers even fashioned a worship service at the YMCA, including a makeshift liturgy that affirmed the fallen nature of humankind and its dependence on Christ's grace:

> Leader: Man is not good; but by God's grace, he is capable of good.
> Unison: Man has not fashioned the good society; but through Jesus Christ, who is Lord forever, he has caught an unforgettable glimpse of it.[71]

Even in this earnest liturgy, organizers were attacking the social gospel for its neglect of original sin and framing their hopes in evangelical terms.

Plenary sessions, prayer groups, and discussion groups were incorporated into the Thanksgiving Day workshop. Within these modes of worship, two generations of academic evangelicals, both older conservatives and younger radicals, were able to discuss the wide array of structural problems in the country, including racism, economic imperialism, nationalism, and sexism. The gathering's chief purpose was to craft the foundational document that became the Chicago Declaration of Evangelical Social Concern. This declaration, Sider and the other participants hoped, would guide future efforts to encourage evangelical awareness of structural injustices under the banner of a new organization, Evangelicals for Social Action.

The manifesto resembled the Students for a Democratic Society's Port Huron Statement far more than it did any NCC resolution. Mirroring SDS, a small but intellectually vibrant and countercultural coterie was issuing a ringing challenge to a stale bureaucratic establishment, calling for an end to war, a reconsideration of materialism, and resistance to a dehumanized society. Yet the Chicago Declaration differed from the Port Huron Statement in one crucial respect: it highlighted the participants' own culpability.

In fact, this confessional tendency separated them from both the secular Left and the religious Right. By including such lines as "We have failed to condemn the exploitation of race at home and abroad by our economic system," the signatories confessed their past sins—not as Americans or even Christians but as evangelicals.[72] At the same time, the declaration was calling evangelicals to work toward a more equitable distribution of wealth, a sustainable peace, and a society free of prejudice.

After finalizing the statement, attendees ended the gathering with a ceremony of salt, in which each participant took a pinch from a common bowl as a reminder of Jesus' commission to be salt for the earth, distinct and easily identified. With this simple gesture, they ended their meeting. The next step was to spread word of their activities and to circulate the Chicago Declaration through both the evangelical and the mainstream media. But the group's cohort of professors and theologians was not well connected outside of academia, and they knew it would be difficult to interest media outlets, even evangelical ones. "Most evangelical institutions," said Wallis, "are financially dependent on the rich, and the official evangelical support for American capitalism is well known."[73]

Many group members had hoped that the Chicago Declaration would condemn recent developments in politics, particularly the Watergate scandal and America's apparent involvement in the overthrow of the Chilean president Salvador Allende. These planks might have surfaced in the final document had not the more conservative attendees, who were new to the movement, voted them down. As a result, John Yoder decided not to sign the document, believing that it did not put forward specific recommendations and included too many compromises in order to attract moderate evangelicals. Paul Jewett of the Reformed Church also declined to sign it, explaining his reasoning in the *Reformed Journal*: "The Declaration never commits those who sign it to any specific action to ameliorate these injustices. Nor does it even suggest any specific action that should be taken at some point in the future."[74] In *Christianity Today*, Pippert complained that the proposed solutions assuaged rather than challenged Middle America. The declaration was, he said, "so broad as to lack real meaning."[75]

Nonetheless, it received widespread interest from most other sectors of American Protestantism. *Christianity Today*, whose readership was the organizers' target audience, offered a cold description of the gathering. The Chicago Declaration was not original in its content, the editors concluded, but was unique in eliciting a "broad range of sympathies" from the evangelical community. They noted that never before had such consensus been reached among Calvinists, pacifist Anabaptists, and those with "neo-Marxist" sympathies (an insult directed at Wallis and the *Post-American* community.)[76] In other words, the magazine found the Chicago Declaration newsworthy but not exactly praiseworthy. Yet most other evangelical press organs, including the popular, long-running *Christian Banner,* greeted it enthusiastically. The Chicago organizers had made greater inroads into mainstream evangelical circles than EFM ever had. Even the secular media took note and seemed surprised that evangelicals were tackling social issues. Roy Larsen, covering the gathering for the *Chicago Sun-Times,* boldly predicted that "some day, American church historians may write that the most significant church-related event in 1973 took place last week at the YMCA Hotel on South Wabash."[77] While his words might have been hyperbole at the time, subsequent accounts of the evangelical Left rarely fail to cite the Thanksgiving workshop and the Chicago Declaration as primary points of initiation.[78]

Michael McIntyre of RLFM watched these events from afar. As a liturgical Methodist, he had not been invited to take part, although Sider had consulted him during the planning stages and asked him to help obtain grants from the liberal churches, an intriguing possibility that did not come to fruition. Yet on reading the Chicago Declaration, McIntyre was delighted to see that it had "challenged all forms of humanism and theology which wanted to avoid hard words of Jesus and the meaning of his cross."[79] At long last, he had found a group of social reformers who embraced biblical orthodoxy. But it was James Robert Ross, a close friend of both Sider and Wallis, who most accurately caught the movement's significance and its place in evangelical history.

> In some of the announcements which preceded the workshop and at Chicago itself there was talk of the decline of liberal and radical interpretations of Christianity and thus the possibility that evangelicalism might now become the new "religious majority." There is nothing wrong in being a majority, or more realistically a significant minority. But some of us sensed the subtle pride of power manifesting itself in a manner not becoming the disciples of a crucified Christ.
>
> If power corrupts, then it corrupts evangelicals as well as liberals or fascists or Marxists or anyone else. And if our involvement in social and political action becomes a self-serving means to take the reins of power, then we shall not only have been corrupted personally but the gospel we preach will have been compromised before the world.[80]

Ross perceived that evangelicals were the awakening giant of American politics. The crises of the 1960s and 1970s that had challenged so many traditional American institutions were leading evangelicals to participate in the public sphere in ways not seen since the days of William Jennings Bryan. Yet while Ross assumed that this political engagement would direct evangelicals toward the marginalized and the forgotten, the result was very different. By 1980, the voices of Wallis, Sider, and their allies were urgent whispers under the din of the Moral Majority and other populist religious enterprises. Evangelicals became a force for reshaping American politics; but to progressives' horror, they advocated free enterprise, a hawkish American exceptionalism, and antipathy toward feminism and other social movements of the 1960s. In a shift that was particularly painful to the McGovern evangelicals, the rising religious Right often treated poverty as the result of poor decision making and a lack of initiative, conclusions that rang false among those who, like Sider and the Alexanders, had worked extensively among the poor. Progressive evangelicals, along with their contemporaries in the mainline churches, were preparing for a long exile in the American wilderness.

9

Becoming Sojourners

By 1975, the *Post-American,* the foremost journal of radical evangelical discipleship, was no more. Its publication had not ended, but its leadership had moved the magazine from the Chicago area to Washington, DC, and furnished it with a revitalized identity and philosophy to reflect a new age. Now that America had withdrawn from Vietnam and the editors no longer had Nixon to kick around anymore, they had decided to rechristen the magazine (and their community) as *Sojourners.* A change in outlook accompanied the change in name. In Washington, a city Wallis had once characterized as "colonial"—that is, filled with men and women of color who work as menials for the nation's affluent and powerful—Sojourners established a fellowship where the magazine's staff and their families lived, worked, ministered, and worshipped in the poorest neighborhoods.[1]

Wallis explained that *sojourners* is "one of the central biblical metaphors for the people who are to live in the world as strangers, pilgrims, aliens . . . because of their loyalty to the Kingdom of God, because of their identity as those who have entered into a new order of things. Historically, 'sojourners' was one of the earliest names used to describe the first local Christian congregations."[2] The concept is a useful way to understand how the progressive Christians who had aligned with McGovern responded to the challenges of the 1970s. James Armstrong, for his part, described McGovern's defeat in this way: "In the eyes of many, he appeared to be a nagging, self-righteous moralist during the presidential campaign. It has become increasingly apparent that he was a prophetic voice crying in the wilderness, trying to share hard truths with the electorate, truths they were unwilling to accept."[3] For progressive Christians of all types, the remainder of the decade as well as the Reagan era that followed were analogous to a long walk in the wilderness without much hope of reaching a promised land.

Americans were entering into an age that was suspicious of great reforms and social crusades. Retreat was in the air, literally, when Nixon resigned from the presidency and fled from the White House on a helicopter, when the last helicopter left Saigon to end the only war the United States had ever unambiguously lost. At the same time, Americans were learning how to make do with less.[4] The seemingly endless supply of cheap oil had run dry, and customers waited for hours to buy gasoline at ruinous prices. Inflation and recession ate away at savings, one-income households were forced to transition to two, and the postwar ideal of the male breadwinner was slain. Divorce rates rose, and cohabitation became commonplace. Proud New York City seemed to descend into a hellhole of pornographic sleaze and fiscal insolvency. To cope, some Americans turned inward toward self-help and pop-culture homilies such as Richard Bach's *Jonathan Livingston Seagull*, retreating from neighborhood and community in ways that led the writer Tom Wolfe to label this period the "Me Decade."[5] Others were attracted to sundry new subcultures, from computer programming, to do-it-yourself projects, to punk rock. Some looked backward to a mythic and halcyon 1950s. Others looked outward, affixing blame for these conditions onto liberals, whom they increasingly associated with an urban, elite culture that held the heartland in contempt. The antifeminist crusader Phyllis Schlafly established a grassroots network of Americans concerned about the fate of the traditional family, and its efforts were crucial to the failure of the proposed Equal Rights Amendment. A coup at the 1977 convention of the National Rifle Association transformed the sportsmen's organization into a lobbying group bent on destroying gun control.[6] Whichever path they took, most Middle Americans were in no mood for social crusades on behalf of the marginalized. From their point of view, *they* were the marginalized, and many either tuned out or echoed the sentiments of the disgruntled anchorman from the movie *Network:* they were "mad as hell, and [they weren't] going to take it anymore."[7]

Progressive Christians tried to buck these insular and self-interested trends, but their coalition struggled after McGovern's defeat. Through the remainder of the 1970s, they were resident aliens in a hostile political world. McGovern's senate seat became a target of the religious Right, while Armstrong clung to his prophetic discourse within a Methodism that had grown weary of his politicking. McGovern evangelicals watched with dismay as many of their co-religionists entered politics as conservative foot soldiers, but they also distanced themselves from the Democratic Party and mainstream liberalism as issues such as abortion highlighted their differences. They often resisted being called leftists, and they would never again support a candidate with the ardor they had showered on McGovern.

McGovern Agonistes

In January 1973, when Richard Nixon was sworn into office for the second time, George McGovern was nowhere in sight. He had not only declined to attend the inauguration but had left the country entirely. From Oxford University, he delivered a speech titled "American Politics: A Personal View," a blistering critique of Nixon's foreign policy and peacemaking attempts, which he saw as disingenuous, insincere, and deceptive.

> I had hoped to be occupied elsewhere today. But the American electorate has made it possible for me to spend this time with you. Had my fellow citizens been better acquainted with your history, they might have seen certain parallels between Richard Nixon and his namesakes who sat on the English throne. Like Richard I, Richard Nixon has been celebrated for his foreign journeys while his own land has been troubled and unattended. Like Richard II, who wasted England's wealth in a failing war in Ireland, Richard Nixon has squandered America's good name in Indochina. And like Richard III, if we can believe Tudor historians, Richard Nixon has usurped powers that are not his in law or tradition. You have been spared a King Richard IV. We seem to have him—for four more years.[8]

McGovern was hurt and disappointed. Nonetheless, the speech was a mistake, earning him wide criticism as a sore loser who was ungracious in defeat. Anyone who had voted against him might have felt some vindication as they read his words. In England's greatest city of erudition, McGovern must have wondered, in the light of an overwhelming mandate against him, how things could have gone so lamentably wrong. Why had Americans rejected his vision?

In a society that is often contemptuous of failure, the losers of presidential elections have often had trouble figuring out a follow-up act.[9] Some, like Alf Landon, who lost to Roosevelt in 1936, have stayed out of history's way and drifted into obscurity, but most have continued to contribute to public life, rehabilitating their legacy in some way. Wendell Willkie, who lost to Roosevelt in 1940, graciously offered his service as an international envoy during World War II. James Blaine, Charles Evan Hughes, William Jennings Bryan, and John Kerry all served as secretary of state after their defeats. Thomas Dewey was an informal adviser to Eisenhower, and Adlai Stevenson was a U.N. ambassador. McGovern's situation, however, was different. Having led his party to an Election Day rout, he could not expect a prize appointment in his immediate future. Instead, like Barry Goldwater, McGovern chose to become an ideological standard bearer in the Senate.[10] Despite their political divisions, the two men were friends; and Goldwater tried, in his own rough way, to assuage McGovern's disappointment by sending him a framed political cartoon showing the two of them as the couple in Grant Wood's painting *American Gothic*. In the margin, Goldwater wrote, "If you must lose, lose big."[11]

One of the first substantive interviews McGovern gave after his defeat appeared in the *Christian Century*. He was friendly with the editor, James Wall, who had served as a McGovern delegate from Illinois and had been an unsuccessful candidate for Congress in a district representing the Chicago suburbs. Wall's article captured McGovern's rudderless state. Chastened and disheartened, the senator uncharacteristically asked the editor if the ethical questions he had raised as a candidate had a place in American politics. He mused, "If you are really concerned about property valuation, social prestige, and the like, you may be intelligent and moral enough to know you should not support programs that might segregate a neighborhood, but you may be uncomfortable with and angry at anyone who reminds you of that fact. I think the presidential candidate who draws issues in terms of moral imperatives is on very shaky ground in terms of putting together a majority coalition." McGovern seemed frustrated with the electorate for turning away from social concerns, yet he also said to Wall, "It is uncomfortable to be reminded that the bombing we are carrying on is barbaric and that we are slaughtering tens of thousands of innocent people."[12] This was as close as McGovern came to admitting that his moralist tone had not suited the politics of 1972. He had realized too late that, in his prophetic zeal, he had sounded angry at and ashamed of the United States and had failed to offer most voters a real incentive to vote for him.

Throughout 1973 and 1974, the journalists Bob Woodward and Carl Bernstein exposed the White House's involvement in the Watergate scandal, and Nixon subsequently resigned from office. Although the events did not bring McGovern much satisfaction, they did affirm his criticisms of the president. Armstrong and McGovern were together at the senator's house in Washington, DC, when Nixon shocked the country by announcing his resignation. Armstrong recalled, thirty-five years later, that the television watchers in the living room were boisterous and rowdy throughout the announcement and that the McGovern children cheered. But McGovern calmed them down, saying, "None of us can know the depths of the hurt that Nixon is going through."[13]

Although he carried the burden of the electorate's rejection, McGovern eventually began making peace with old adversaries. After Gerald Ford took over as president, McGovern was invited to the White House for the first time since his break with Lyndon Johnson over the Vietnam War. McGovern even discussed Middle East policy during a cordial luncheon with Henry Kissinger, a meeting that would certainly never have taken place in the previous administration.[14] Just as Richard Pierard, among others, was wondering if Billy Graham's reputation could "survive Richard Nixon," the evangelist also reached out to McGovern.[15] After a successful crusade in Soviet-dominated Poland, Graham dined in Washington with the Polish ambassador, who invited him to bring any two guests he wanted. Graham selected George and Eleanor McGovern. At the dinner, Graham lamented his endorsement for Nixon and his harsh words for McGovern during the election season. The senator remembered:

> I told him "George McGovern appeared to you as a tired and desperate man—that was exactly right! I was exhausted during that campaign—and to campaign against Mr. Nixon. I was exhausted! So was my entire staff, and we were desperate to win because we thought we had to end this war. You had it right; I was tired and desperate!" I had a slight smile as I said that; I didn't want him to think I took his endorsement too grimly. That was the only exchange we ever had—it was quite clear he was trying to make amends.[16]

McGovern also had to reconcile with South Dakota voters, many of whom felt that he had abandoned the state's interests while pursuing a higher office. He was fortunate to run for reelection in 1974, a midterm year when anti-Republican sentiment was at a fever pitch. South Dakota has historically tended to vote out senators who become "too Washington" (as Larry Pressler and Tom Daschle have also discovered), and McGovern's campaign for the presidency had been a consummate Washington move.[17] He later described his Senate reelection strategy as "bending over and letting everyone kick me in the ass."[18] Nevertheless, South Dakota voters had long memories. Even in a post-Watergate environment, when liberals were easily winning offices, McGovern won by a scant five-point margin over a former Vietnam prisoner-of-war named Leo Thorsness, who had never held elective office.

McGovern's landslide failure in 1972 meant that the Democrats would almost certainly not nominate him again in 1976. Yet he was still ambitious, and throughout the decade he pondered about whether or not to try for the presidency again. His closest friends and family members gently but consistently discouraged him. Henry Kimelman, a long-time friend and campaign donor, told McGovern that he "did not want to see you and Eleanor exposed to the kind of personal agony you would both suffer."[19] Still, McGovern even talked with his old neighbor and rival, Hubert Humphrey, about the possibility of a Humphrey-McGovern ticket that would unite traditional lunchpail Democrats with McGovern's youthful supporters. Humphrey, however, was weary of rejection and sick with terminal cancer, and he turned McGovern down.[20]

Instead, McGovern watched from the sidelines as a candidate from Georgia rose from obscurity to sweep through the primary states and claim the nomination. Although he had previously made few accommodations to his party's liberal base, Governor Jimmy Carter was able to attract many of McGovern's allies and staffers. Jim Wall of the *Christian Century* supported his fellow southerner, and Carter also recruited the direct-mail mastermind Morris Dees, the young pollster Pat Caddell, and (briefly) the speechwriter Bob Shrum.[21] "Each time an old friend from '72 makes one of these decisions, I feel a slight twinge," McGovern confessed in a letter to Armstrong.[22] McGovern saw Carter's success as a product of opportunistic timing rather than core conviction. He did not forget that, in an effort to secure a less radical candidate, Carter had led the "Anybody but McGovern" effort during the lead-up to the 1972 convention. Moreover, he saw Carter adapting his grassroots strategy to win the nomination but ignoring his desire for social transformation. In McGovern's view, Carter's Christianity began and ended with his own born-again experience and was devoid of larger social responsibilities. Whereas Carter talked with ease about his personal faith on the campaign trail, McGovern had rarely discussed his inner spiritual life. Carter's faith, at least in 1976, was inward and personally transformative; McGovern's was outward and socially transformative. Because he thought Carter was a cynic who was exploiting his faith, McGovern voted for Ford. Only four years after being the Democrats' standard bearer, he had turned to a Republican.[23] Ford had his grudging respect, stemming from their years together in Congress and his thoughtful invitation to the White House. Ford, though moderately conservative, was at least the devil he knew.

Throughout the 1970s, McGovern stayed true to his liberal Christian humanism. As a senator, he still led the Nutrition and Human Needs subcommittee, and he strengthened food stamp programs. He even visited Cuba in 1977, an act that drew the ire of Cold Warriors. But his hopes for the decade were never realized. Far from undergoing a humanistic rejuvenation, the country was demonstrating the banality of empty patriotism and historical whitewashing. As the United States geared up to celebrate its bicentennial, McGovern declared in an editorial in the *Christian Century* that he would "like to see people oriented events, rather than elaborately staged productions" that celebrated a hollow, purposeless nationalism.[24]

McGovern had hoped for a lengthy career as the conscience of the Senate, but his time in the chamber was ended by a new religious coalition that was taking shape in American politics. His 1980 reelection bid took place amid a wave of conservative alliances and new grassroots efforts to raise money, spread messages, and corral voters into envisioning a smaller government, freer economics, and a more proactive approach to the Cold War. Using loopholes in the Federal Election Campaign Act, organizations such as the National Conservative Political Action Committee (NCPAC) could spend money with impunity. NCPAC focused its attacks on McGovern and other long-established liberal senators who were up for reelection, such as Birch Bayh, Frank Church, and John Culver. Explaining the negative tone of the group's activism, its chair, Terry Dolan, asserted, "There is no question about it—we are a negative organization. . . . We're not interested in respectability. We're going to beat [these senators] and send a shiver down the spine" of each liberal seeking reelection. His insurgent politics were marked by a distrust of G.O.P. leadership and a desire to select the party's candidates. He maintained that the Republican Party was "a fraud. It's a social club where the rich people go to pick their noses."[25] Yet even though Dolan would have been loath to admit it, his insurgent philosophy was indebted to McGovern's own path to the Democratic nomination. McGovern's grassroots mobilization had proven to be so influential that it was now being used to unseat him from the Senate.

In South Dakota, candidates had traditionally met constituents in person, often crisscrossing the state, visiting one small town after another to secure votes. Now, in 1980, newly formed organizations inundated South Dakota with advertisements and mailings in ways that were altering the state's sense of itself as a prairie republic. Two of the most persistent were NCPAC and the Life Amendment Political Action Committee. One LAPAC mailing charged that McGovern "oppose[d] traditional family values" and listed a series of "facts" that included exaggerations ("McGovern's money comes from the super rich—Jackie Kennedy, Norman Lear . . .") and conjecture ("will vote for tax-funded abortions").[26] Current election laws allowed nearly limitless money to be spent on independent groups, even though direct contributions to the candidate were limited. In other words, these organizations couldn't explicitly support McGovern's Republican opponent, Representative James Abdnor, but they could issue plenty of negative press about McGovern.

NCPAC materials flooded the cheap South Dakota media markets. In 1979, the organization spent more than $100,000 on radio, television, and newspaper ads against McGovern, a staggering total for a South Dakota race at the time.[27] One flyer declared that "a true Christian must take his faith into the voting booth," echoing a sentiment that McGovern himself had promoted for years. It listed the senator's deviations from Christian principles, alleging his socialism and softness on drugs. A political action committee called Americans for Life used his previous activism against him, issuing an inflammatory pamphlet titled "Stop the Baby Killers," which included assertions such as "Recall during the Vietnam War when hypocrites like McGovern and these others piously wrung their hands and denounced the brutal slayings of Vietnamese children" and went on to accuse him of not defending young lives in the United States.[28] An LAPAC mailing portrayed McGovern, Bayh, the liberal Republican Jacob Javits, and others as "devils incarnate" because they not only supported abortion but also federal funding for it.[29] In a telling display of how far the mainline's reputation had fallen, even the senator's bona fides as a Methodist churchman were used against him. "[McGovern] has a history of left-wing religious liberalism," another mailing claimed, tying him to the perceived excesses of the NCC and the WCC.[30]

The political action committees' strategy of portraying McGovern as a man at odds with religious values worked all too well. "What really hurt me the most," McGovern reflected in an interview in the *Harvard Crimson*, "were people who I knew, who'd supported me in the past, old friends coming up and saying, 'I just can't go with you this time.' And they wouldn't say why."[31] He remembered an encounter with a pair of elderly women in a South Dakota supermarket, who informed him that they could not vote for him because he was too far to the left and then proceeded to use food stamps, one of his signature programs in Congress, to pay for their groceries.[32] The ground had shifted in his state. Now that the religious Right had altered so many voters' priorities, old-fashioned republican politics based on personal familiarity and a shared currency of churchmanship could no longer secure victory.

The religious mobilization against McGovern in South Dakota was exemplified in a terse exchange between the senator and a Roman Catholic priest, Leonard Nemmers, who served a parish in the town of Hoven. Nemmers was strongly opposed to McGovern's reelection. He had repeatedly spoken out against abortion from the pulpit and had allowed LAPAC operatives to insert their literature under his parishioners' windshield wipers while they were inside attending mass. McGovern volunteers retaliated, leaving windshield flyers that included Pope John XXIII's praise of McGovern's humanitarian work when he was the director of Food for Peace. Nemmers was irate, and after the election he wrote to McGovern's headquarters and demanded an apology. McGovern refused. "Far from giving you an apology," he wrote to the priest, "I want to say that if I had to pick the Number One candidate for the biggest horse's ass in South Dakota in 1980, you would win hands down. I think you are a disgrace, both to the church and decent politics."[33] Nemmers forwarded the letter to his local newspaper, which promptly published it, as did several other South Dakota newspapers.

The Nemmers incident was not McGovern's finest or most charitable hour, and his ire was reminiscent of his reaction to losing to Nixon. But it also highlighted a metamorphosis in prairie politics. In 1960, South Dakota Republicans had defeated McGovern by slyly intimating that he was Catholic. In 1980, evangelicals and Catholics had worked together to defeat him by focusing on his liberalism. The electorate that swept Reagan into office swept McGovern out, and he lost by a margin almost equal to his national defeat in 1972. On Election Day, he won a paltry 39.4 percent of the vote compared to Abdnor's 58.2 percent, an immense loss, larger than any incumbent senator had suffered for the past thirty years. But he was not alone: many of the Senate liberals first elected in 1956, 1962, and 1974 were also defeated, and Republicans gained control of the Senate for the first time since the Eisenhower administration. Along with McGovern, the chamber lost Bayh, Church, Culver, Javits, Gaylord Nelson, and Warren Magnuson. A former congressional staffer called it "the greatest exodus of talent and experience in Senate history."[34]

Armstrong and the Lonely Mainline

Throughout the 1970s, Armstrong continued to defend his belief that the mainline denominations could be both politically progressive and politically savvy. At the same time, as he traveled abroad and delved into the liberation theology that was challenging the despotic governments of Latin America, he was envisioning a more globally attuned Christendom. Nonetheless, like McGovern, he had to spend much time after the 1972 election mending fences with South Dakotans who were unhappy with liberals and ecumenicists. His efforts were not always successful. In 1974, a group of displeased Methodist ministers and laypeople met at First United Methodist Church in Sioux Falls, one of the largest churches in the bishop's diocese. Armstrong was not present; he was attending a peace conference in Belgium (which some saw as a misplaced priority). In his absence, the group passed a resolution reprimanding him for "participation in political and other secular affairs outside the normal pattern of church believers" and pointing specifically to his appearance in a television advertisement for McGovern's 1974 Senate reelection. The resolution stated that Armstrong's brazen partisanship had been "very counterproductive to the purposes of the United Methodist Church."[35] In fact, South Dakotans were not necessarily opposed to their religious leaders' participation in politics, as the Nemmers incident demonstrates. But when Armstrong challenged his parishioners' law-abiding prairie republicanism (which often doubled as white privilege), they rose up against ministerial meddling.

The Sioux Falls synod was probably triggered by Armstrong's role in mediating the American Indian Movement's 1973 occupation (or reclamation, depending on one's point of view) of Wounded Knee, located on the Pine Ridge Reservation in southwestern South Dakota.[36] Tensions between activists and government forces erupted after about two hundred members of AIM took control of 1890 massacre site, which had since become a macabre tourist destination. The Nixon administration, showing remarkable indifference to the historical significations linking them to the first Wounded Knee siege, called in the proverbial cavalry. At the peak of the confrontation, one hundred police officers, two hundred federal marshals, and representatives from the Justice Department, the Central Intelligence Agency, the Federal Bureau of Investigation, the Secret Service, and the Bureau of Indian Affairs had gathered to deal with the standstill.

To help mitigate the crisis, the NCC sent more than forty representatives to South Dakota to observe the negotiations and transport food and other supplies to AIM throughout the siege. The organization's long-standing work on civil rights and peace issues made it a logical intermediary: it understood the needs of disenfranchised groups as well as the nuances of law enforcement. Because Armstrong had enjoyed good relations with the region's Sioux population, council leaders asked him to serve as one of their observers. But the bishop soon expanded his role to negotiator and convinced John P. Adams, a seasoned mediator and fellow Methodist clergyman, to join him.[37] On March 11, a protestor shot an FBI agent, and negotiations broke down. At this point, Adams stepped in and subsequently played a crucial role in facilitating talks between the feds and AIM.[38] As the government was preparing to use military force to expel the protestors, Adams, on Armstrong's recommendation, was able to craft a last-minute cease-fire agreement.

After the standoff, Armstrong boasted that the NCC had served as a fair arbiter, but the historian Rolland Dewing disputes that claim, writing that "no one close to Adams during the Wounded Knee crisis doubted that his sympathies were with AIM."[39] According to Armstrong, one NCC observer asked a marshal, "Yours or ours?" after hearing that someone had been shot. Such a question, he noted wryly, is "not the language of a mediator."[40] Whatever their private sympathies, however, Adams and Armstrong helped to achieve a relatively peaceful resolution. By averting a second Wounded Knee massacre, they secured a brief triumph for liberal Christianity in one of its most tenuous hours. At the same time, the NCC was able to make use its history of reconciliation as leverage to defuse violence between two deeply hostile parties.

Nonetheless, Wounded Knee became a public relations nightmare for the mainline churches in South Dakota. Nearly all of the state's major newspapers criticized the NCC's role during the standoff. They disclosed the amount of money that mainline churches had given to AIM, not only through the NCC itself but also through local American Lutheran, United Methodist, and Episcopal churches.[41] South Dakotans interpreted the NCC's activity at Wounded Knee as interference that favored renegades over law-abiding Americans. As Adams later said, "A scapegoat was needed," and the NCC served that function.[42] While he and Armstrong had seen their work as an act of prophetic peacemaking, many South Dakotans saw AIM's actions as a threat to both their safety and their livelihood, given western South Dakota's profitable tourism industry. The *Sturgis Tribune,* one of the newspapers operating closest to the site, was particularly unrelenting in its criticism of the churches. One editorial argued, "Church support of AIM has been an embarrassment to local pastors who generally share the views of their parishioners on such questionable spending practices by denominational hierarchies. One of the major reasons some denominations have remained out of the National Council of Churches membership is its proclivity for financing questionable causes."[43]

In response, Armstrong published his own editorial. "I am frank to confess," he wrote, "that the nature of some of the criticism frightens me. I served churches in the southeast during Civil Rights days. The irrational intolerance, uninformed racism and vigilante mind-set, common in the rural South during those days, is present on our doorstep."[44] Russell Dilley, his executive assistant, told the *Christian Century* that South Dakota newspapers showed concern only for how the occupation would affect the tourist season. Meanwhile, "poverty on the reservations remains an inescapable reality" that white Dakotans chose to ignore.[45]

Armstrong's and Dilley's lack of sympathy unnerved white residents who believed "that South Dakota was being victimized by outside forces."[46] Many could tolerate NCC's prophetic social action when it applied to distant places and causes—Vietnamese villagers, the urban poor, African Americans in the Jim Crow South. But the council's interference at Wounded Knee seemed tantamount to giving legitimacy to insurgent lawlessness. Writing in the 1980s, one critic accused mainline leaders of becoming "insulated from the grassroots, . . . pioneer[ing] a new form of prophecy which engineer[ed] budgetary victories in bureaucratic in-fighting and steer[ed] pronouncements through the jungle of church conventions."[47]

Such animus deepened when Armstrong visited Cuba in the late 1970s. After his visit, the bishop acknowledged that the nation lacked many basic freedoms but gave it measured praise as "the least repressive communist state" in the Cold War binary. Its revolution, he believed, was "developing guidelines that will lead toward a near utopian Third World State," which, he predicted, would eschew the corruption and elitism of its neighboring countries. His conclusions were partly influenced by his growing familiarity with a liberation theology that, he argued, arose from and demonstrated the "outrage of people long impoverished and oppressed because of callous, greedy economic systems and cruel police states."[48] In Armstrong's view, Cuba's regime under Fidel Castro was a manifestation of this discontent, although he naïvely insisted that the government did not jail political dissidents and suggested that a fair investigation into the island's prisons "might well be answered in Cuba's favor."[49] For worried congregants who believed that the Soviet Union was gaining an upper hand in the Cold War, a Methodist bishop's defense of communism's human rights record was a chilling indication of their church's leftward drift.

In 1980, Armstrong was appointed bishop of Indiana, just as the state was shifting hard to the right.[50] Given the power of the Moral Majority in Indiana, he found himself in a dilemma. He could not easily denounce clerical involvement in politics, having blazed that trail himself throughout his career. Yet as he wrote in the *Christian Century*, the Moral Majority represented "moral and spiritual arrogance and . . . distortion of the gospel," and it imposed a retributive version of the Christian ethos on a diverse population. A week before the 1980 election, Armstrong tried to counter the Moral Majority, signing a statement with twenty-three Protestant, Catholic, and Jewish leaders regarding the rights of religious minorities, but the electorate was in no mood for another ecumenical resolution that would tell them how to act.[51]

Like McGovern, Armstrong was blindsided by a newly cohesive Right that was growing more adept at using the tools of grassroots organizing for conservative ends. John Brademas, an Indianapolis-area congressman who was voted out office in 1980, had told him that the ecumenicals were well positioned to parry the religious Right. According to Armstrong, Brademas had said, "Politicians can't take on the religious extremists as effectively as the church can. It's up to people like you . . . or the nuts will take over."[52] In the bishop's eyes, the religious Right was a clear danger to progressive Christianity, and he spent much of the early 1980s defending the mainline's obligation to serve as a social witness. He gained a broader platform in November 1981, when the NCC elected him as its president. He remembered, "I was on the roof of my house in a flannel shirt, sweeping leaves off into oblivion," when he received an unexpected call from the nominating committee offering him the position.[53]

Armstrong was pleased to step into the role, but his tenure as president was brief and tempestuous. The Institute for Religion and Democracy, a conservative think tank supported by generous corporate funding, had made the NCC one of its primary targets. Often, it would frame the council's prophetic social witness as frittering away parishioners' donations on dubious causes. The IRD's media offensive angered many liberal clergy

because it uncritically brought rightwing perspectives into mainstream outlets that pretended to be objective. For instance, in 1982 the *Reader's Digest*,
a staple of conservative Middle America, published an article that reiterated
many of the IRD's talking points against the mainline churches—primarily,
that they were taking funds from pious churchgoers and funneling them to
radical regimes while criticizing their own country. The article's first page
suggested a lurid choice between "Karl Marx or Jesus Christ." The piece also
portrayed David Jessup and Edmund Robb, two IRD leaders, as everyday
parishioners who were raising concerns about suspicious church donations
rather than as the seasoned political activists they really were. The article
parroted the IRD line about the NCC, even ending with a section on "what
you can do to stop this," which included options such as starting a grassroots watchdog group and refusing to give money to church collections that
would go to the NCC.[54] Under the guise of investigative journalism, the
article had deepened the chasm between liberal, seminary-trained pastors
and their conservative grassroots congregants.

In January 1983, *60 Minutes* aired an investigative segment titled "The
Gospel According to Whom?" As NCC's president, Armstrong had agreed
to be interviewed for the piece, but "we weren't into it five minutes before
I realized it was a booby trap; there was no question, the jury was out."[55]
The host, Morley Safer, peppered him with questions about the NCC's
awareness of its parishioners' outrage but never asked about the validity of
the IRD's charges. When challenged about NCC's donations to Nicara-
guan groups that supported the Sandinistas, Armstrong tried to frame that
decision within the context of the council's larger humanitarian vision: "I
don't understand why we're never asked about international Sunday school
lessons. I don't understand why we're never asked about 5 billion pounds of
clothing and foodstuffs and medicine that have gone to every part of the
world to relieve every form of human misery. These are things that don't
come into these conversations."[56]

When Safer interviewed Richard Nehaus and Edmund Robb of the IRD,
he was far less aggressive, merely asking them for examples of unethical
NCC donations, an inquiry they were well prepared to answer. Armstrong
was incensed. "It appears to me that the thrust of the program ha[d] been
determined before the cameras did their selective work," he complained
to the press soon before the program aired.[57] Safer had gotten most of his
information about the NCC directly from Robb and had repeated much of
it uncritically. Armstrong also bitterly noted that the program focused on a

North Indiana Methodist Conference resolution requesting that the United Methodist Church withdraw from the NCC but not on how and why the conference had rejected the motion by a ten-to-one ratio.[58]

Thus, the IRD, one of the dimmer stars in the conservative firmament, was able to successfully represent itself as a champion of the Protestant faithful. James Wall complained in a *Christian Century* editorial that "a small band of neoconservative clergymen has convinced both CBS-TV and *Reader's Digest* (a historically anticommunist enterprise that needed little convincing) that it represent[s] a large, responsible portion of American Protestantism."[59] Armstrong, speaking in Seattle, chided the media outlets for not taking measures to correct the "uninformed sensationalism" that had driven these pieces.[60]

The bishop endeavored in these years to serve as mainline Christianity's spokesman for progressive politics. In 1982, shortly before the *Reader's Digest* and *60 Minutes* pieces appeared, he was already working hard to refute the IRD's criticism of the NCC. During an appearance on *Firing Line,* the program's host, the iconic conservative William F. Buckley Jr., implored him to defend the Vietnam withdrawal that he had advocated in the 1970s, a course that Buckley believed had resulted in hundreds of thousands of deaths in southeast Asia. Armstrong conceded the truth of that "frightful waste of life."[61] But as the conversation continued, he urged Buckley to remember "the primary mass of oppressed people in the world, those of the Third World," on whose behalf the WCC and the NCC were working. That, Armstrong believed, was the crux of the gospel message, and one that could not be abrogated.

In the midst of these public debates, the most private of mistakes brought Armstrong's ecclesial career to an abrupt end. In November 1983 he issued a press release announcing his resignation from both the NCC's presidency and the bishopric of Indiana. The underlying cause was his affair with a woman he had counseled, brought to light when his wife found their correspondence. Armstrong had planned to make a full confession in his press release, but other NCC leaders convinced him to avoid mentioning it directly and so adding to the scandals they were already handling.[62] In the end, the bishop chose to split the difference: he wrote that he was "physically and emotionally exhausted" by his work schedule and explained that this fatigue had caused him to fail "many persons, as well as the gospel. I deeply regret what I have done to my loved ones."[63] In this way, one of ecumenical Protestantism's most persistent advocates for a conscientious liberalism abruptly withdrew from public affairs. Like his old friend George McGovern, he became an outsider looking in.

The Years of the Evangelical

Evangelicals were big news in the bicentennial year of 1976. They graced the cover of *Newsweek* under the headline "The Year of the Evangelical."[64] Record numbers of Americans claimed that they were born-again Christians, including the president-elect. Their growing media savvy was apparent in the growing popularity of television programs such as *Hour of Power* and *The 700 Club*.

The McGovern evangelicals treated this unexpected turn of events with optimistic caution. "Evangelicals," Jim Wallis wrote, have "come out of their closets and into everybody's living rooms."[65] Many saw their hope of a religious awakening coming to fruition. The tricky part was to move this momentum in the direction of social justice and avoid allowing themselves to become bureaucratized and intoxicated with power, as the mainliners had done. By this time, four years after the senator's candidacy, nearly a dozen former members of Evangelicals for McGovern had published books urging the wider evangelical community to follow a more progressive route toward social justice. These books included Robert Linder and Richard Pierard's *Politics: A Case for Christian Action* (1973), Paul B. Henry's *Politics for Evangelicals* (1974), Richard Mouw's *Political Evangelism* (1973), and Ron Sider's masterpiece, *Rich Christians in an Age of Hunger: A Biblical Study* (1977).[66] Each laid out the case for more focused, organized, and thoughtful evangelical engagement in politics, whether one worked as a volunteer, an activist, a voter, a neighbor, or a thinker. The books constructed a biblical framework for social action and challenged other evangelicals' proclivities for personal morality and American nationalism. In doing so, they created what the historian Brantley Gasaway has called a "public theology of community."[67]

The progressive evangelicals kept their distance from political power to preserve their prophetic authenticity. They lobbied and engaged in public protest selectively and focused on their discipleship. They lived simply, established relationships with the marginalized communities on whose behalf they spoke, and tried to exercise wise environmental stewardship. One emblem of this movement was the *More-with-Less Cookbook,* compiled by a Mennonite named Doris Longacre and widely used by the members of

Evangelists for Social Action and Sojourners. Its recipes called for simple, affordable ingredients available even to very poor families while avoiding meat and dairy products as a way to better preserve the earth's resources.[68]

Like many veterans of the student Left, these evangelicals struggled as they dealt with historic injustices and grievances. Whenever socially conscious evangelicals gathered, Nancy Hardesty grew frustrated as women's initiatives were shot down or sent to languish in subcommittees, always in the interest of unity.[69] During this period, she began to channel her activism into the evangelical feminist magazine *Daughters of Sarah,* which encouraged equal responsibilities in marriage and challenged the rampant sexism in evangelical culture.[70] A follow-up workshop in 1975 clarified the diverse frustrations within the Evangelicals for Social Action movement and was an acrimonious disaster. Divisions arose among frustrated feminists, black participants who saw only a lukewarm commitment to racial justice, and the many white males who listened sympathetically but wanted an agenda that would not scare off less radical evangelicals. In what *Christianity Today* mocked as a "rip-roaring business session," the meeting degenerated into arguments over quotas, and most attendees left Chicago without much to show for their work.[71] After this gathering, the evangelical Left never again operated under a single banner.

The conservative Moral Majority's intense desire to take control of the country dominated the public conversation on religion and politics, much to the chagrin of progressive evangelicals. Led by such figures as Jerry Falwell, the organization used direct mail, radio, and television to reach disaffected Americans distressed by a lack of patriotism, secularization, and the decline of the traditional family.[72] The organization's embrace of free enterprise, its disgust toward the welfare system, and its indifference about racial and sexual equality threatened the progressives' hopes for American evangelicalism. Nonetheless, they did not respond by running to the Democratic Party. Now that reformers such as McGovern had lost control of the party, they saw the Democrats' liberalism as stale, secular, and statist. These radical evangelicals (and most of them would have been comfortable with that terminology) were stringently opposed to bureaucratic, paternalist forms of liberalism. "The modern state is the great power, the great seducer, the great captor and destroyer of human life," wrote Wallis.[73] Clearly, his days of electioneering were over.

Abortion had become the primary issue that separated these evangelists from the Democrats, and progressive mainliners and evangelicals generally came down on different sides of that divide. Pierard, who had been a committed antiwar radical, reflected, "I felt isolated by my stance, viewed by liberals as hopelessly reactionary, anti-feminist, and ideologically in league with the far right."[74] Wallis, now living in the ghetto but still suspicious of statist overreach, called abortion "a brutal substitute for social justice and even . . . white society's way of controlling the population of racial minorities."[75] While members of the NCC generally supported a woman's right to choose, most progressive evangelicals saw abortion as a tragedy.

To frame their critique while remaining distinct from the militarism, poor shaming, and corporatism of the religious Right, many progressive evangelicals adopted Sider's philosophy of being "completely pro-life."[76] In this way, they fashioned themselves as challengers of both evangelicalism and political liberalism. The stance meant speaking out against abortion but also against nuclear proliferation. It meant opposing the death penalty but also being slow to affirm same-sex relationships.[77] It meant caring for the environment while standing resolutely against pornography. This ethos made the progressive evangelicals sojourners indeed, for their positions did not fit neatly into either Reagan conservatism or 1980s liberalism. They were becoming less and less welcome in a Democratic Party dominated by social liberals, the high-tech suburbanites known as the Atari Democrats, and the moderates of the Democratic Leadership Council. Likewise, the religious Right often doubted their faith in the gospel because of their fierce opposition to militarism and nationalism.

Yet a number of mainline leaders saw the dynamic potential in this budding evangelical movement. In 1975, the NCC reached out to veterans of the Chicago workshops, and Sider, Wallis, and Yoder traveled to Nairobi to take part in a WCC meeting. That same year, dozens of progressive evangelicals met with members of the United Methodist Board of Church and Society, who were eager to discuss how to link social witness to their biblical roots.[78] Despite these promising interactions, however, there was little meaningful dialogue between the groups, and they seldom worked together—with a few important exceptions. In 1982, Sojourners spearheaded a Peace Pentecost gathering in Washington, DC, that attracted members of the mainline in addition to the evangelicals tied to Wallis and Sider. An ecumenical service was held at the National Cathedral in which ten thousand churches across the country took part in solidarity. Even Clergy and Laity Concerned, a descendant of the antiwar Clergy and Laymen Concerned about Vietnam, was there. Together, united as Christ's body, participants sang hymns and prayed for nuclear disarmament. The Sojourners community joyfully reflected that "barriers of creed were overcome by the power of the Spirit to unite all believers in common opposition to the gathering storm clouds of nuclear holocaust."[79]

So, once again, progressive Christians were uniting awkwardly and intermittently in a moment of great moral crisis during a presidency that was hostile to their aims. Their meetings were rare, but they continued on, despite the unresolved division between their mainline and evangelical factions. Politics can be strong, but culture, social conditioning, and theology are often stronger. The progressives' love for peace and their concern for the poor could not always overcome the social forces that separated them, but they shared their sojourning together. As conservative movements calcified into the networks and organizations of Ronald Reagan's America, these Christians continued to preach uncomfortable truths as they saw them. Wanderers and prophets on the political landscape, they believed it was their vocation to speak and live out God's message of good news to the poor.

Yet it would be wrong to say that they were never discouraged. One day in the mid-1980s, a dejected Walter Mondale spotted George McGovern across a Washington, DC, street. Mondale, another failed candidate for president, had recently been trounced by President Reagan, winning only Minnesota and the District of Columbia and earning even fewer electoral votes than McGovern had. Now he ran to catch up with his old Senate colleague. How long, he asked McGovern, did it take to overcome the sense of sadness and despair that came with being rejected by the American public on that scale? McGovern, battle-scarred but fiercely idealistic, still convinced he had fought the good fight, looked wearily at his friend. "I'll let you know when I get there."[80]

Conclusion

George McGovern was a complex man, and his complexities could often appear to be contradictions. He was a decorated bomber pilot who abhorred war. His self-assurance, and sometimes arrogance, seemed at odds with his slow, deliberate, high-pitched voice. He advocated for hungry children across the world, but his relationship with his own illegitimate daughter was distant and indirect. He was a Democrat who won five elections in one of the most Republican states in the country. He was a progressive humanist whose sense of justice arose from the Judeo-Christian tradition. "American democracy at its best," he explained during his brief pursuit of the Democratic presidential nomination in 1984, "has been undergirded by the insights of the Hebrew prophets and the Christian gospel."[1]

McGovern's relationship to progressive Protestant Christianity in America was also complex and nuanced. He was inspired by it, he shaped it, and he was a reflection of its challenges. His advocacy for peace and food equality owed much to his youthful fealty to the social gospel and was strengthened by his strong partnership with ecumenical church leaders throughout his adult life. Unlike any other in recent memory, his presidential campaign was subtly but deeply religious, beginning in solidarity with the mainline but eventually triggering the rise of the evangelical Left and giving biblicist and kerygmatic support to the cause of social justice.

But McGovern's failure to resonate with the wider American electorate highlighted its own set of hard, uncomfortable truths. Prophetic and progressive Christianity needs a place in American political discourse, but it will be most effective when it casts aside the belligerence and coalition politics modeled by the religious Right. Moreover, prophetic action and presidential elections do not mix well; even erudite, incisive criticisms of the United States will seem discordant amid the pageantry and patriotism that characterizes those events. McGovern called on Americans to remember the poor and the neglected; he asked them to focus on the greatest victims of the war in Indochina, the Vietnamese people, at a time when self-interested concerns such as busing, the draft, and a fear of quotas were dominating American thinking. There is a role for such remonstration in civic life, but it is probably outside of electoral politics. McGovern's colleague, Senator Herman Talmadge, spoke for much of the public when he said, "if you get up there and preach day and night against America, you're not going to be elected."[2]

Many religious men and women who believe in social justice see a cautionary tale in the religious Right's absorption into the Republican Party, and they remain determined to stay independent. Unlike the Moral Majority, progressive evangelicals will never be good soldiers or reliable partisan warhorses. Nonetheless, few of them believe that the Democrats will enthusiastically embrace religious voters any time soon. The situation does not disturb them. "I believe in a prophetic role, not becoming a sect of the party," Jim Wallis told me. "Democrats wanted myself and others to serve as the religious chaplains of their party, and I said, 'No. We're going to hold you accountable.'"[3]

The United Methodist Building in Washington, DC, is still a center for mainline church lobbying, but James Armstrong's dream of an alliance of conscience between ecumenical churchmen and politicians has long since evaporated. Liberal ministers and laypeople are now mere supplicants. The progressive activists working for the National Council of Churches focus on damage control when conservative budget cuts threaten social services. Their mantra is "Remember who you are serving, listen to the word of God. Resist believing that God prefers your political party."[4] They are committed to being progressivism's conscience but not its voting base. In the hard world of politics, there is no such thing as a caucus of prophets.

Prophets, as always, have been consigned to the role of outsider. They rarely achieve an undiluted victory and are rarely welcome at home. Yet they know that the rejection of a message does not mean that the message was wrong. Listeners have hard hearts, and one must, like Amos, tirelessly call the people to the righteous path. A prophet's commission is marked by patience. Sometimes vindication arrives years, even generations, later;

but with perseverance and faith, the prophet soldiers on. As McGovern's favorite verse in the gospel of Matthew exhorts: "Whosoever will save his life will lose it: and whosoever will lose his life for my sake will find it."[5]

As Jim Wallis, Richard Mouw, and Ron Sider grow older, a new generation of evangelical activists has taken up the call. Shane Claiborne, who was once Tony Campolo's protégé, now works and evangelizes among the poor, coiffed in a set of dreadlocks that signifies a passing of the generational torch. Donald Miller's book *Blue Like Jazz,* which became a best seller when I was a student at Houghton College, mixes thoughtful ruminations on Christian life with barbed criticism of former president George W. Bush.[6] The InterVarsity Christian Fellowship, a ministry of collegiate evangelicals with more than 40,000 members, recently endorsed the Black Lives Matter movement as part of a great racial reconciliation. Joe Ho, the group's director of Asian outreach, explained that the endorsement was a way to show members' repentance for the organization's silence during the civil rights movement.[7]

While their attendance statistics still look grim, the mainline churches are showing signs of vitality for the first time in decades. They are attracting people such as Rachel Held Evans, a prominent Christian blogger, who grew up in a fundamentalist church in Dayton, Tennessee, most famous at the setting of the 1925 Scopes Trial. Evans began her writing career as a questioning evangelical but after years of wrestling with her faith joined the Episcopal Church. At the core of her unhappiness was a deep disagreement over social and economic issues; and rather than unite with the social justice evangelicals, she chose to attend a church institutionally committed to those causes. While acknowledging that the mainline needs to find a way to authentically reach out to young Christians, Evans "also hear[s] from a lot of evangelicals who have begun attending mainline churches precisely because they welcome LGBT people, accept scientific findings regarding climate change and evolution, practice traditional worship, preach from the lectionary, [and] affirm women in ministry."[8] Given the large number of religious young people who favor same-sex marriage and even see it as a moral issue, the Episcopal Church's recent decision to perform these marriages may work to its benefit. Still, disagreement between liberal denominations in the United States and their conservative counterparts in other parts of the world will complicate these commitments.

The number of nonbelievers in America continues to rise, but the historian Diana Butler Bass argues that mainline Christianity will be prepared because it has learned to adapt as a countercultural force. Its travails in the 1970s were, she writes, a "more sustained opportunity to explore what faith might mean to twenty-first century people." For her, such a faith "maintains the historic liberal passion for serving others but embraces Jesus' injunction that a vibrant love for God is the basis for a meaningful life."[9] In contrast, evangelicalism, even within its social justice wing, seems somewhat conflicted. For example, Sider and Mouw remain opposed to same-sex marriage, while Wallis and Campolo support it. At the core of such divisions are unresolved tensions involving religious liberty and social justice and questions about whether organized Christianity is the persecutor or the persecuted.[10]

Perhaps the labels *mainline* and *evangelical* may soon cease to be useful ways to categorize American Protestants. The members of Wallis's Sojourners, a doggedly evangelical enterprise in its early days, are now about one-third evangelical, one-third liberal Protestant, and one-third Catholic.[11] In an era when evangelicals enjoy greater public visibility and outnumber liberal Protestants by nearly two to one, calling the established denominations *mainline* seems silly. Unconventional churches are thriving—among them, the House for All Sinners and Saints in Denver, a congregation of outcasts and hipsters led by tattooed, foul-mouthed pastrix Nadia Bolz-Weber, who touts a personal encounter with Jesus while using the Lutheran lectionary. The old boundaries that divided and defined American Protestantism have blurred and changed.

McGovern might have appreciated this outcome. He himself lived out many different lives during retirement. He ran for president again in 1984 and formed Americans for Common Sense, a short-lived progressive think tank, in 1981. He taught at a handful of universities and ran a hotel in Bridgeport, Connecticut, managing it so poorly that one wonders how he might have performed the more demanding administrative duties of commander in chief. In the 1990s, President Bill Clinton, who had coordinated the Texas branch of McGovern's 1972 campaign, named him US ambassador for food and agriculture, a position that eventually led to service as a roving ambassador charged with addressing world hunger.[12] In 2008, McGovern and his former Senate colleague, Bob Dole, shared the World Food Prize for their work on an international school lunch program that fed 22 million children in more than forty developing countries.[13] In 1994, he endured the tragic loss of his daughter Terry to alcoholism and channeled his agony into research for his best-selling book *Terry*, in which he struggled to understand the nature of the disease and wrestled with his own demons of guilt and depression.[14] During his final years, death became a constant companion. McGovern lost his son Steven, his wife Eleanor, all three of his siblings, both of his running mates, several long-serving members of his staff, and most of his closest friends in the Senate. Only Dole, Gary Hart, and Walter Mondale, all three of them also unsuccessful presidential candidates, lived long enough to eulogize him.

Despite changes in his roles and shifts in his focus, George McGovern remained faithful to his commitments, both as a private citizen and as a public advocate. Even after deaths and defeats, he found the strength to return to the fray. The evangelist Matthew's admonition, that one who loses his life shall find it, kept him engaged in the activism and intellectual pursuits that characterized his old age. In an interview, the conservative columnist Cal Thomas asked him archly if, in the midst of his humanitarian work, he was neglecting a fundamental truth of the gospels: that one is saved by faith and not by works. McGovern insisted that his questioner was missing the point. He explained that if he were speaking to God as his own soul stood in judgment, he would say, "Well, God, I wasn't quite sure what you were like, or how best to communicate with you, but I've tried to be a decent human being."[15] In McGovern's view, the best moments of our time on earth are marked by love, compassion, and life-giving service. Doctrine and Christology are arbitrary. The commission to help others is not.

In the second of my two interviews with Senator McGovern, he spent an hour carefully and thoroughly answering my questions about his time at Northwestern and Garrett and his navigation of the mainline and evangelical worlds. As our interview wound down, he politely excused himself. He was speaking on world hunger at Dakota Wesleyan University before a large international audience that afternoon, and he couldn't keep them waiting too long for his arrival. Even in his late eighties, in the winter of his life, George McGovern had promises to keep.

Notes

Abbreviations

AJA   James Armstrong, personal papers, Casselberry, FL.

ALC   Arthur Link Collection, Seeley Mudd Manuscript Library, Princeton University, Princeton, NJ.

ESAP   Evangelicals for Social Action files, Palmer Theological Seminary, Philadelphia, PA.

ESAW   Evangelicals for Social Action Collection (Collection 37), Billy Graham Center Archives, Wheaton College, Wheaton, IL.

GMCD   Senator George McGovern Collection, Dakota Wesleyan University Archives, Dakota Wesleyan University, Mitchell, SD.

GMCP   George McGovern Collection, Seeley Mudd Manuscript Library, Princeton University, Princeton, NJ.

RPC   Robert Pennington Collection, Dakota Wesleyan University Archives, Dakota Wesleyan University, Mitchell, SD.

WCA   Wheaton College Archives, Wheaton, IL.

WPP   Wesley Pippert Papers, Wheaton College Archives, Wheaton College, Wheaton, IL.

Introduction

1. "George McGovern, Patriot and Hero," *Washington Post,* October 21, 2012; David Jackson, "Obama: McGovern a 'Statesman of Great Conscience," *USA Today,* October 21, 2012.

2. Biden omitted the lengths he took to distance himself from McGovern when running in 1972 as a senator from Delaware, which President Nixon carried by twenty points. See Jules Witcover, *Joe Biden: A Life of Trial and Redemption* (New York: HarperCollins, 2010), 71–86.

3. Bob Dole, "George McGovern, the Man Who Never Gave Up," *Washington Post,* October 21, 2012; "State of the Union with Candy Crowley," *CNN,* October 21, 2012, www.cnn.com.

4. Ruy Teixeira, "The Emerging Democratic Majority Turns 10," *Atlantic,* November 9, 2012.

5. Henry Kissinger, October 26, 1972, Washington, DC, press conference.

6. L. Brent Bozell III invited McGovern to Colorado to personally endorse Tim Wirth during his 1986 campaign for the Senate, going so far as to send him airline tickets in the mail. McGovern demurred because the travel date conflicted with scheduled surgery in Washington. See "National Conservative Political Action Committee," GMCD, box 6, folder "July 16, 1986."

7. "Three Hundred Big Boys," *Futurama,* directed by Swinton O. Scott III (2003; Los Angeles: 20th Century Fox Home Entertainment, 2010, DVD).

8. Contemporaries who viewed McGovern's campaign as a disruption include Theodore White, *The Making of the President, 1972* (New York: Atheneum, 1973); Jeane Kirkpatrick, *The New Presidential Elite: Men and Women in National Politics* (New York: Russell Sage Foundation, 1976); Robert Novak, *The Prince of Darkness: 50 Years of Reporting in Washington* (New York: Crown Forum, 2007); and Kristi Witker, *How to Lose Everything in Politics Except Massachusetts* (Chicago: Academy Publishers Chicago, 1988). Similar historical and political assessments appear in Ronald Radosh, *Divided They Fell: The Demise of the Democratic Party, 1964–1996* (New York: Free Press, 1996); Kenneth Baer, *Reinventing Democrats: The Politics of Liberalism from Reagan to Clinton* (Lawrence: University of Kansas Press, 2000), 22–26; Dominic Sandbrook, *Eugene McCarthy and the Rise and Fall of Postwar American Liberalism* (New York: Anchor, 2005); and Thomas Ferguson and Joel Rogers, *Right Turn: The Decline of the Democrats and the Future of American Politics* (New York: Hill and Wang, 1986).

9. John B. Judis and Ruy Teixeira, *The Emerging Democratic Majority* (New York: Scribner, 2002), 37.

10. Doug Mataconis, "Mitch Daniels: Social Issues Truce is Necessary to Keep the GOP United," *Outside the Beltway,* March 12, 2011, www.outsidethebeltway.com.

11. Ross Douthat, *Bad Religion: How We Became a Nation of Heretics* (New York: Free Press, 2012), 141.

12. Cal Thomas and Ed Dobson, *Blinded by Might: Why the Religious Right Can't Save America* (Grand Rapids, MI: Zondervan, 1999), 23.

13. David Kinnaman and Gabe Lyons, *unChristian: What a New Generation Really Thinks about Christianity* (Grand Rapids, MI: Baker, 2007), 34.

14. "America's Changing Religious Landscape," *Pew Research Center,* May 12, 2015, http://religions.pewforum.org.

15. John S. Dickerson, "The Decline of Evangelical America," *New York Times,* December 15, 2012.

16. Francis Schaeffer Jr., "Why I Still Talk to Jesus—in Spite of Everything," *Patheos,* July 11, 2014, www.patheos.com.

17. Pam Chamberlain, "Young Evangelicals Are Rejecting the Christian Right's Bigoted Agenda," *Alternet,* March 5, 2009, www.alternet.org.

18. Amy Sullivan, *The Party Faithful: How and Why Democrats Are Closing the God Gap* (New York: Scribner, 2008), 4.

19. Jim Wallis, *God's Politics: Why the Right Is Wrong and the Left Doesn't Get It* (New York: HarperCollins, 2005),.

20. Richard Nixon, "Address to the Nation on the War in Vietnam," speech, Washington, DC, November 3, 1969, www.nixonlibrary.gov.

21. Thomas Reeves, *The Empty Church: The Suicide of Liberal Christianity* (New York: Simon and Schuster, 1996), 1.

22. David Hollinger, "After Cloven Tongues of Fire: Ecumenical Protestantism and the Modern American Encounter with Diversity," *Journal of American History* 97 (June 2011): 21.

23. These relationships are recounted, generally favorably, in Nancy Gibbs and Michael Duffy, *The Preacher and the Presidents: Billy Graham in the White House* (New York: Center Street, 2007).

24. Quoted in Patricia Sullivan, "George S. McGovern, Democratic Nominee Who Lost to Nixon, Dies at 90," *Washington Post,* October 21, 2012.

25. David R. Swartz, *Moral Minority: The Evangelical Left in an Age of Conservatism* (Philadelphia: University of Pennsylvania Press, 2011), 9.

26. Wallis, *God's Politics*, 75.

27. Jill K. Gill, *Embattled Ecumenism: The National Council of Churches, the Vietnam War, and the Trials of the Protestant Left* (DeKalb: Northern Illinois University Press, 2011), 8.

28. Quoted in Bruce Miroff, *The Liberals' Moment: The McGovern Insurgency and the Identity Crisis of the Democratic Party* (Lawrence: University of Kansas Press, 2007), 125.

29. The rise of populist critiques of liberalism is a major historiographic theme that dominates early twenty-first-century histories of the 1960s and 1970s. Prominent examples include Dominic Sandbrook, *Mad as Hell: The Crisis of the 1970s and the Rise of the Populist Right* (New York: Knopf, 2011); Kevin Kruse, *White Flight: Atlanta and the Making of Modern Conservatism* (Princeton: Princeton University Press, 2005); and Darren Dochuk, *From Bible Belt to Sun Belt: Plain-Folk Religion, Grassroots Politics, and the Rise of Evangelical Conservatism* (New York: Norton, 2012). Also see Lisa McGirr, *Suburban Warriors: The Origins of the New American Right* (Princeton: Princeton University Press, 2001); and Jefferson Cowie, *Stayin' Alive: The 1970s and the Last Days of the Working Class* (New York: New Press, 2011).

30. See Swartz, *Moral Minority*, as well as Brantley W. Gasaway, *Progressive Evangelicals and the Pursuit of Social Justice* (Chapel Hill: University of North Carolina Press, 2014).

31. In addition to Gill, *Embattled Ecumenism*, see David Hollinger, *After Cloven Tongues of Fire: Protestant Liberalism in Modern American History* (Princeton: Princeton University Press, 2013); Elesha Coffman, *The Christian Century and the Rise of the Protestant Mainline* (New York: Oxford University Press, 2013); Matthew Hedstrom, *The Rise of Liberal Religion: Book Culture and American Spirituality in the Twentieth Century* (New York: Oxford University Press, 2013); and Bryan Dubose Perry, "John Coleman Bennett, Robert McAfee Brown, and the Push for Religious Pluralism," paper presented at the Organization of American Historians' annual meeting, April 7–10, 2010, Washington, DC.

32. Elesha Coffman, comment, on Paul Harvey, "The Mainline Protestant Moment? Or Embattled Ecumenists?," *Religion in American History*, December 12, 2011, http://usreligion.blogspot.com.

33. This philosophy is most fully delineated in Ronald J. Sider, *Completely Pro-Life: Building a Consistent Stance* (Downers Grove, IL: InterVarsity Press, 1987).

34. For the evangelical case for same-sex relationships, see especially Matthew Vine, *God and the Gay Christian* (New York: Convergent, 2014). Also see Mark Achtemier, *The Bible's Yes to Same-Sex Marriage* (Louisville, KY: Westminster John Knox Press, 2014); and Justin Lee, *Torn: Rescuing the Gospel from the Gays vs. Christians Debate* (New York: Jericho, 2012).

35. Micah 6:8, King James Version.

1. George McGovern's Soul

1. See George Marsden, *Fundamentalism and American Culture: The Shaping of Twentieth Century Evangelicalism, 1870–1925* (New York: Oxford University Press, 1980). For a peculiarly midwestern strand of fundamentalism, see William Vance Trollinger Jr., *God's Empire: William Bell Riley and Midwestern Fundamentalism* (Madison: University of Wisconsin Press, 1990). Reverend McGovern did not seem to be in contact with these men or others like them, which inclines me to believe that he did not belong to any fundamentalist camp.

2. See Timothy L. Smith, *Revivalism and Social Reform in Mid-Nineteenth Century America* (New York: Harper and Row, 1957); Melvin Dieter, *The Holiness Revival of the Nineteenth Century* (Metuchen, NJ: Scarecrow, 1996); Donald Dayton, *Discovering an Evangelical Heritage* (New York: Harper and Row, 1976); and Lee Haines, *An Outline History of the Wesleyan Church* (Indianapolis: Wesleyan Press, 1985).

3. McGovern traced his family's struggles with the disease in *Terry: My Daughter's Life and Death Struggle with Alcoholism* (New York: Villard, 1996), 193.

4. See Robert Sam Anson, *McGovern: A Biography* (New York: Holt, Rinehart, and Winston, 1972), 12–20. Anson drew on interviews from McGovern's now-deceased siblings and other Mitchell residents, and it remains an excellent source of information about Joseph McGovern's life. For an account that includes archival research, see Thomas J. Knock, *The Rise of a Prairie Statesman: The Life and Times of George McGovern* (Princeton: Princeton University Press, 2016), 1–15.

5. On the link between baseball and American Christianity, see the essays in Christopher H. Evans and William Herzog, *The Faith of Fifty Million: Baseball, Religion and American Culture* (Louisville, KY: John Knox Press, 2002), which make a strong case for the primacy of baseball in creating American civil religion.

6. On the abiding influence of utopian thinking in New York State after the Second Great Awakening, see Arthur E. Bestor, "American Phalanxes: The Study of Fourierist Socialism in the United States, with Special References to the Movement in Western New York" (Ph.D. diss., Yale University, 1938).

7. For an academic assessment of Houghton's founding mission, see Timothy J. Nichols, "For the Good of the World: Education and Salvation at the Houghton Wesleyan Methodist Seminary and Oberlin Collegiate Institute" (Ph.D. diss., State University of New York at Buffalo, 1996).

8. George McGovern, telephone interview by author, July 28, 2009.

9. "Genealogy: McGovern Family," GMCD, box 5A, folder "Genealogy: McGovern Family."

10. Christopher Lydon, "McGovern Sisters Recall Hopes," *New York Times,* October 8, 1972.

11. "South Dakota Resources," GMCD, box 5A, folder "Genealogy: McGovern Family."

12. "50 Years of Profiles in Faith" (typescript), 1966, GMCD, box 5A, folder "Genealogy."

13. George McGovern, interview by author, September 22, 2008, Mitchell, SD.

14. G. D. Lillibridge, "Small-Town Boys: Growing up in Mitchell in the 1920s and 1930s," *South Dakota History* 25 (Spring 1995): 1–36. Lillibridge expanded the article into a more personal narrative in his *The Innocent Years: Growing Up in a Small Town in the 1920s and 1930s* (Huron, SD: East Eagle Company, 1994).

15. Charles Barlett, "McGovern's Solid Hometown," *Washington Evening Star,* May 25 1972.

16. Anson, *McGovern,* 20.

17. George McGovern, "Remarks at the McGovern Library Dedication," speech delivered in Mitchell, SD, October 7, 2006.

18. George McGovern, *What It Means to Be a Democrat* (New York: Blue Rider, 2011), 20.

19. George McGovern, *Grassroots: The Autobiography of George McGovern* (New York: Random House, 1977), 4.

20. Richard Meryman, "I Have Earned the Nomination," *Life,* July 7, 1972, 36.

21. McGovern, *Grassroots,* 8.

22. John E. Miller, "Restrained, Respectable Radicals: The South Dakota Farm Holiday," *Agricultural History* 59 (July 1985): 429–47. See also Robert S. Thompson, "The History of the South Dakota Farmer's Union" (M.A. thesis, University of South Dakota, 1985); and Allan Mathews, "Agrarian Radicals: The United Farmer's League of South Dakota," *South Dakota History* 3 (Fall 1973): 408–21.

23. "*Zion's Herald* Interviews George McGovern," *Zion's Herald,* March–April 2004, 17.

24. McGovern interview, 2008.

25. Meryman, "I Have Earned the Nomination," 37.

26. Barlett, "McGovern's Solid Hometown."

27. McGovern interview, 2008.

28. Harry Emerson Fosdick, *The Modern Use of the Bible* (New York: Macmillan, 1924), 93, 61.

29. Harry Emerson Fosdick, *Adventurous Religion and Other Essays* (New York: Grosset and Dunlap, 1946), 265.

30. When McGovern was running for Congress in 1958, South Dakota Republicans corralled

Pearson into denouncing his former student's foreign policy of "appeasement." Pearson, who was in desperate financial circumstances, had been promised a postmastership for his efforts. For more about this bizarre episode, see Anson, *McGovern,* 82–84.

31. McGovern spoke about the role of debate in his life in Michael Leahy, "What Might Have Been: In Which George McGovern, the Senior Member of a Rare and Burdened Tribe, Reveals Just How Long It Takes to Get Over Losing the Presidency," *Washington Post,* February 20, 2005.

32. Clifford W. Brown Jr., *Jaws of Victory: The Game-Plan Politics of 1972, the Crisis of the Republican Party, and the Future of the Constitution* (Boston: Little, Brown, 1973), 117.

33. George McGovern, "Sources of Our Strength," speech at Wheaton College, Wheaton, IL, October 13, 1972, Wheaton College Archives, CD-29.

34. For an official history of the college, see Violet Miller Goering, *Dakota Wesleyan University: Century I* (Freeman, SD: Pine Hill, 1996).

35. *Tumbleweed* (Dakota Wesleyan University yearbook), 1942, 16.

36. McGovern kept the pregnancy incident a closely guarded secret for many years but eventually revealed it to the historian Thomas Knock (*The Rise of a Prairie Statesman,* 27–28).

37. Justin William Moyer, "In Confession to Historian, McGovern Reveals He Had a Secret Child," *Washington Post,* July 30, 2015.

38. Eleanor McGovern and Mary Finch Hoyt, *Uphill: A Personal Story* (Boston: Houghton Mifflin, 1974), 70.

39. George McGovern, letter to Bob Pennington, July 5, 1943, RPC, folder "George McGovern Letters."

40. In *The Wild Blue: The Men and Boys Who Flew the B-24s over Germany* (New York: Simon and Schuster, 2001), Stephen E. Ambrose retells much of McGovern's wartime history, so I will include only a few incidents here, choosing those that shed light on the development of his social vision.

41. George McGovern, Robert Dole, and Donald Messer, *Ending Hunger Now: A Challenge to Persons of Faith* (Minneapolis: Augsburg Fortress, 2005), 22.

42. George McGovern, letter to Bob Pennington, November 4, 1944, RPC, folder "George McGovern Letters."

43. George McGovern, letter to Bob Pennington, November 15, 1943, ibid.

44. Ambrose, *The Wild Blue,* 233, 189.

45. McGovern and Hoyt, *Uphill,* 75.

46. McGovern interview, 2009.

47. Ibid.

48. On Brightman's theology, see Randall E. Auxier and Mark Y. A. Davies, *Hartshorne and Brightman on God, Process and Persons: The Correspondence, 1922–1945* (Nashville, TN: Vanderbilt University Press, 2001); James John McLarney, *The Theism of Edgar Sheffield Brightman* (Washington, DC: Catholic University of America, 1936); Paul Deats and Charles Robb, eds., *The Boston Personalist Tradition in Philosophy, Social Ethics and Theology* (Macon, GA: Mercer University Press, 1986); and Arthur P. Gleason, "The Conception of God in the Thought of Edgar Sheffield Brightman" (Th.D. thesis, Northern Baptist Theological Seminary, 1950).

49. McGovern interview, 2008.

50. John Herman Randall, *The Making of the Modern Mind: A Survey of the Intellectual Background of the Present Age* (Cambridge, MA: Riverside, 1954), 40, 563.

51. McGovern, *Grassroots,* 34.

52. On Rauschenbusch, see Paul M. Minus, *Walter Rauschenbusch: American Reformer* (New York: Macmillan, 1988); Christopher H. Evans, *The Kingdom Is Always but Coming: A Life of Walter Rauschenbusch* (Grand Rapids, MI: Eerdmans, 2004); and Gary Scott Smith, "To Reconstruct the World: Walter Rauschenbusch and Social Change," *Fides et Historia* 23 (Summer 1991): 40–63. Janet Forsyth Fishburn stresses how Rauschenbusch worked within the gendered contours of middle-class respectability; see her *The Fatherhood of God*

and the Victorian Family (Philadelphia: Fortress, 1981), which is among the first accounts of the social gospel written from a feminist perspective.

53. Walter Rauschenbusch, *Christianity and the Social Order* (New York: Macmillan, 1912), 51.

54. Walter Rauschenbusch, *Christianity and the Social Crisis* (New York: Macmillan, 1907), 360.

55. On the development of Rauschenbusch's theology, particularly its Germanic strands, see Donovan Smucker, *The Origins of Walter Rauschenbusch's Social Ethics* (Montreal: McGill–Queen's University Press, 1994), 39.

56. "*Zion's Herald* Interviews George McGovern," 16.

57. Rauschenbusch, *Christianity and the Social Order*, 431.

58. McGovern interview, 2009.

59. Ibid., 2008.

60. Wesley Pippert, "UPI Writing, Not Transmitted," October 12, 1972, WPP, box 4BII, folder "McGovern Religious."

61. Charles P. Henderson, "The [Social] Gospel of George McGovern, Richard Nixon," *Commonweal*, September 29, 1972, 520.

62. "From Cave to Cave," GMCD, box 5A, folder "From Cave to Cave, 1946 Oration."

63. Rauschenbush, *Christianity and the Social Crisis*, 44–92.

64. This school of Cold War realism began with Reinhold Niebuhr, *The Nature and Destiny of Man: A Christian Interpretation* (New York: Charles Scribners' Sons, 1941, 1943). The larger implications of this movement, and some its secondary lights, are discussed in Robin W. Lovin, *Reinhold Niebuhr and Christian Realism* (Cambridge: Cambridge University Press, 1995).

2. For-Prophet Education

1. For a set of recollections, see Murray Leiffer and Dorothy Leiffer, *Enter the Old Portals. Reminiscences: Fifty Years on a Seminary Campus* (Evanston, IL: Garrett Theological Seminary, Bureau of Social and Religious Research, 1987). For a more official version, see Frederick A. Norwood, *Dawn to Midday at Garrett* (Evanston, IL: Garrett Theological Seminary, 1978).

2. Norwood, *Dawn to Midday at Garrett*, 150.

3. Oxnam's hearing is detailed in Angela Lahr, "The Censure of a Bishop: Church and State in the McCarthy Era," *Methodist History* 44 (October 2005): 29–42.

4. The term comes from Stanley High's the controversial article "Methodism's Pink Fringe," *Reader's Digest*, February 1950, 134–38.

5. This shift is discussed in Doug Rossinow, "The Radicalization of the Social Gospel: Harry F. Ward and The Search for a New Social Order, 1898–1936," *Religion and American Culture* 15 (Winter 2005): 64. In "The Emergence of Social Gospel Radicalism: The Methodist Case," *Church History* 50 (December 1981): 436–49, William McGuire King argues that the strident language of Christian reformers in the 1930s did not originate with the economic ruin of the Great Depression but had deep roots in the social gospel during World War I. See also James V. Heidinger II, "The Impact of the Social Gospel on Methodist Thought, 1890–1918" (M.Div. thesis, Wesley Seminary, 1973).

6. Ernest Tittle, "A God-Centered Ministry," *Christian Century*, June 21, 1939, 797.

7. Quoted in Floyd Cunningham, "Pacifism and Perfectionism in the Preaching of Ernest F. Tittle," *Methodist History* 31 (October 1992): 34.

8. Quoted in Robert Moats Miller, *How Shall They Hear Without a Preacher? The Life of Ernest Fremont Tittle* (Chapel Hill: University of North Carolina Press, 1971), ix.

9. See Christopher H. Evans, *Social Gospel Liberalism and the Ministry of Ernest Fremont Tittle: A Theology for the Middle Class* (Lewiston, NY: Mellen University Press, 1996), 2.

10. Niebuhr frequently characterized the social gospel Protestants as yoked to naïve utopian ideas that misjudged the inherent sin in human nature. For an argument that Niebuhr

mischaracterized both the social gospel and Rauschenbusch, see Harlan Beckley, *Passion for Justice: Retrieving the Legacies of Walter Rauschenbusch, John A. Ryan and Reinhold Niebuhr* (Louisville, KY: John Knox Press, 1992).

11. Quoted in Miller, *How Shall They Hear Without a Preacher?*, 356.

12. On the idea that realists and pacifists in mainline circles were far more similar than is often understood, see David A. Hollinger, *After Cloven Tongues of Fire: Protestant Liberalism in the Twentieth Century* (Princeton: Princeton University Press, 2013), 56–81.

13. George McGovern, interview by author, September 22, 2008, Mitchell, SD.

14. "Returning G.I.s in Garrett . . . ," *Garrett Tower*, June 1946, 5.

15. This fascination with doomsday is traced in Paul Boyer, *When Time Shall Be No More: Prophecy Belief in Modern American Culture* (Cambridge: Belknap Press of Harvard University Press, 1992). Erling Jorstad provides an earlier historical analysis in *The Politics of Doomsday: Fundamentalists of the Far Right* (New York: Abingdon, 1970). Graham's status as a Cold Warrior is detailed in Jay Douglas Learned, "Billy Graham, American Evangelicalism, and the Cold War Clash of Messianic Visions, 1945–1962" (Ph.D. diss., University of Rochester, 2012). The role of religious faith as an ally of anticommunist forces is the topic of Jonathan Herzberg, *The Spiritual-Industrial Complex: America's Religious Battle Against Communism in the Early Cold War* (Oxford: Oxford University Press, 2011).

16. Andrew Juvinall, "Prophecy: Crystal Ball or Clarion Call?," *Garrett Tower*, September 1946, 8–9.

17. "Returning G.I.s at Garrett . . . ," 5.

18. Richard E. Gibbons, "Normal Men as True Prophets," *Garrett Tower*, June 1947, 1.

19. "Social Action at Garrett," *Garrett Tower*, June 1947, 8.

20. Tom Slocum, "Student Pastor McGovern Has Cheering Section," *Chicago Tribune*, May 14, 1972.

21. Ibid.

22. Hiley H. Ward, "When Candidate McGovern Was an Illinois Pastor," *Christian Advocate*, September 14, 1972, 10–11.

23. McGovern interview, 2008.

24. "McGovern Recalled as a Young Pastor near Mundelein," *Daily Herald* (Arlington, IL), October 26, 2012.

25. Matthew 16:25, King James Version.

26. George McGovern, *Grassroots: The Autobiography of George McGovern* (New York: Random House, 1977), 38. McGovern displayed a lifelong preference for this verse and its emphasis on sacrificial service to others. When Martha Hartke, the wife of Indiana's senator Vance Hartke, asked her husband's colleagues to submit their favorite Bible verse, McGovern chose this one. See George McGovern, letter to Martha Hartke, July 28, 1975, GMCP, box 502, folder "Personal, H, 1975."

27. Robert Sam Anson, *McGovern: A Biography* (New York: Holt, Rinehart, and Winston, 1972), 54–55. Anson's claims are supported by his interview with Bob Pennington.

28. Lester Kinsolving, "Minister in the White House? The (Nearly) Rev. McGovern," *Washington Daily News*, June 16, 1972.

29. Slocum, "Student Pastor McGovern Has Cheering Section."

30. George McGovern, telephone interview by author, July 28, 2009.

31. Ward, "When Candidate McGovern Was an Illinois Pastor," 10.

32. McGovern interview, 2008.

33. Anson, *McGovern*, 61.

34. Overviews of Billington's career appear in Martin Ridge, "Ray Allen Billington, Western Historian and American Exceptionalist," *Pacific Historical Review* 56 (November 1987): 495–511; and "Frederick Jackson Turner, Ray Allen Billington, and American Frontier History," *Western Historical Quarterly* 1 (January 1970): 5–20. See also Patricia Nelson Limerick, "Persistent Traits and the Persistent Historian: The American Frontier and Ray Allen

Billington," in *Writing Western History: Essays on Major Western Historians,* ed. Richard Etulain (Albuquerque: University of New Mexico Press, 1991), 277–310.

35. Billington's nuanced defense of Turner's work is demonstrated in his books *The Far Western Frontier* (New York: Harper, 1956); and *Westward Expansion: A History of the American Frontier* (New York: Macmillan, 1949).

36. See Leften Stavrianos, Loretta Kreider Andrews, George I. Blanksten, Roger F. Hackett, Ella C. Leppert, Paul L. Murphy, and Lacey Baldwin Smith, *A Global History of Man* (Boston: Allyn and Bacon, 1966). For a postmortem assessment, see Kevin Reilly, "Remembering Leften Stavrianos, 1913–2004," *World History Connected,* http://world-historyconnected.press.illinois.edu/. On his significance in the field of world history, see Gilbert Allardyce, "Toward World History: American Historians and the Coming of the World History Course" *Journal of World History* 1 (Spring 1990): 23–76.

37. McGovern interview, 2009.

38. McGovern, *Grassroots,* 40.

39. See Peter Rand, *China Hands: The Adventures and Ordeals of the American Journalists Who Joined Forces with the Great Chinese Revolution* (New York: Simon and Schuster, 1995); Paul Gordon Lauren, ed., *The China Hands' Legacy: Ethics and Diplomacy* (Boulder, CO: Westview, 1987); and Robert P. Newman, *Owen Lattimore and the "Loss" of China* (Berkeley: University of California Press, 1992).

40. In his autobiography, McGovern lists the books that influenced this line of thought. They include E. H. Carr, *The Soviet Impact on the Western World* (New York: Macmillan, 1947); Leland Stowe, *While Time Remains* (New York: Knopf, 1946); Edgar Snow, *Red Star over China* (New York: Random House, 1938, 1944); Howard K. Smith, *The State of Europe* (New York: Knopf, 1949); John King Fairbank, *The United States and China* (Cambridge: Harvard University Press, 1948); Edwin Reischauer, *The United States and Japan* (Cambridge: Harvard University Press, 1950); Theodore White, *Thunder out of China* (New York: Sloane Associates, 1946); Frederick Schuman, *International Politics: The Destiny of the Western State System* (New York: McGraw-Hill, 1948); and Owen Lattimore, *The Situation in Asia* (Boston: Little, Brown, 1949).

41. McGovern, *Grassroots,* 42.

42. McGovern interview, 2009.

43. An archetypical example was Thomas A. Bailey, *America Faces Russia: Russian-American Relations from Early Times to Our Day* (Ithaca, NY: Cornell University Press, 1950).

44. Arthur Link's more critical early assessments include *Wilson: The Road to the White House* (Princeton: Princeton University Press, 1947); and *Woodrow Wilson and the Progressive Era, 1910–1917* (New York: Harper and Row, 1954). Both argued that Wilson was a reluctant progressive and stressed his southern conservatism.

45. For an account of Link's career, see John Milton Cooper Jr., "Arthur S. Link," in *Clio's Favorites: Leading Historians of the United States, 1945–2000,* ed. Robert Rutland (Columbia: University of Missouri Press, 2000), 111–25.

46. Henry A. Wallace has been the subject of a complex, often polemic, historiography since the early years of the Cold War. Early critical assessments often portrayed him as a dupe of international communism; for example, see David A. Shannon, *The Decline of American Communism* (New York: Harcourt, Brace, and World, 1959). These views are counterbalanced by Wallace apologists, who argue that he foresaw the conflicts of interest bred by Cold War militarism. See, for instance, Karl Schmidt, *Henry A. Wallace: Quixotic Crusade, 1948* (Syracuse, NY: Syracuse University Press, 1960); and Curtis MacDougall, *Gideon's Army* (New York: Marzani and Munsell, 1965). A similar rehabilitation of Wallace, this time positioning him against a belligerent Truman administration, appears in Norman Markowitz, *The Rise and Fall of the People's Century: Henry A. Wallace and American Liberalism, 1941–1948* (New York: Free Press, 1973). Wallace became a useful foil for Cold War liberals, as evidenced by Arthur Schlesinger Jr., "Who Was Henry A. Wallace? The Story of a Perplexing and Indomitably Naïve Public Servant" *Los Angeles Times,* March

12, 2000. For a generally favorable biography that tries to account for his idealism, see Graham White and John Maze, *Henry A. Wallace and His Search for a New World Order* (Chapel Hill: University of North Carolina Press, 1995). For a sympathetic account by his fellow Iowans, see John C. Culver and John Hyde, *American Dreamer: The Life and Times of Henry A. Wallace* (New York: Norton, 2000).

47. Anson, *McGovern*, 58.

48. McGovern interview, 2008.

49. For a discussion of Wallace's grandfather, a social gospel practitioner also named Henry Wallace, see Culver and Hyde, *American Dreamer*, 5–41.

50. Henry A. Wallace, "Judaism and Americanism," *Menorah Journal*, July–September 1940, 127.

51. George McGovern, "The American Way," *Mitchell Daily Republic*, September 22, 1948.

52. Although Anson makes these claims in *McGovern*, 60–62, he does not list his sources.

53. Questions about the nature and magnitude of McGovern's support followed him throughout his career. For an exploration of this matter during 1972, see "How Radical Is McGovern?," *Newsweek*, June 19, 1972. Despite souring on Wallace at the Philadelphia convention, McGovern was still writing editorials on his behalf as late as September 1948.

54. Thomas J. Knock, *The Rise of a Prairie Statesman: The Life and Times of George McGovern* (Princeton: Princeton University Press, 2016), 121.

55. Ted Van Dyk, *Heroes, Hacks, and Fools: Memoirs from the Political Inside* (Seattle: University of Washington Press, 2007), 132.

56. John Hyde, "Interview with George McGovern," *Iowa Public Television*, May 3, 2003, www.iptv.org.

57. George McGovern, interview by Jon Lauck and John E. Miller, November 25, 2003, Mitchell, SD. I am grateful for their permission to quote from this interview.

58. Robert Sam Anson, "Just Plain George," *Harper's Magazine*, November 1972, 77.

59. Mark L. Kleinman, *A World of Hope, A World of Fear: Henry A. Wallace, Reinhold Niebuhr, and American Liberalism* (Columbus: Ohio University Press, 2000), 71. For more on Niebuhr's influence on postwar social movements, see David Chappell, *A Stone of Hope: Prophetic Religion and the Death of Jim Crow* (Chapel Hill: University of North Carolina Press, 2004), 26–36.

60. This view is famously outlined in Niebuhr's magnum opus, *Moral Man and Immoral Society: A Study in Ethics and Politics* (New York: Scribner, 1932).

61. McGovern interview, 2008.

62. This longstanding desire to purge liberalism of socialist influence was the impetus behind Arthur Schlesinger Jr., *The Vital Center* (Boston: Houghton Mifflin, 1949).

63. See Eyal Naveh, "The Legacy: Non-Utopian Discourse after Niebuhr," in *Reinhold Niebuhr and Non-Utopian Liberalism* (Portland, OR: Sussex Academy Press, 2002), 160–81. Jimmy Carter's affinity for Niebuhr is outlined in Randall Balmer, *Redeemer: The Life of Jimmy Carter* (New York: Basic Books, 2014), 33–37.

64. George McGovern, "The Colorado Coal Strike, 1913–1914" (Ph.D. diss., Northwestern University, 1953), 123, 398.

65. Anson, *McGovern*, 65–66.

66. Hilburn's tenure as president is covered in Violet Miller Goering, "Dakota Wesleyan University, 1885–1960" (M.A. thesis, University of South Dakota, 1970), 136–43.

67. Jonathan Ellis, "Part 2: See McGovern's FBI Files," *Sioux Falls Argus Leader*, July 26, 2015.

68. George McGovern, letter to Arthur Link, July 9, 1951, ALC, box 14, folder "McGovern, Senator George, 1950–1960."

3. Brother George—A Politician as Churchman

1. Richard John Neuhaus, *The Naked Public Square: Religion and Democracy in America* (Grand Rapids: Eerdmans, 1984).

2. For a sensationalist and alarmist discussion of this cooperation, see Jeff Sharlet's two books: *The Family: The Secret Fundamentalism at the Heart of American Power* (New York: Harper Perennial, 2009); and *C Street: The Fundamentalist Threat to American Democracy* (Boston: Little, Brown, 2010).

3. Richard Dougherty, *Goodbye, Mr. Christian: A Personal Account of McGovern's Rise and Fall* (New York: Doubleday, 1973), 208.

4. Adlai Stevenson, "Speech Accepting the Democratic Presidential Nomination," Democratic National Convention, Chicago, July 26, 1952, *American Rhetoric,* www.american-rhetoric.com. The Bible verse is Micah 6:8, King James Version.

5. The historical significance of Stevenson's speech is detailed in Scott Farris, *Almost President: The Men Who Lost the Race but Changed the Nation* (Guilford, CT: Lyons, 2012), 149–74. Farris notes that it attracted intellectuals by virtue of its high-mindedness and erudition but cost the party many working-class votes.

6. "Remarks of Senator George McGovern," GMCP, box 749, folder "November 30, 1971, Tape Transcripts, Cassette No. 71-8, Remarks of Senator George McGovern, Bloomington, IL, November 30, 1971."

7. McGovern's unsuccessful attempt to collect memories of Stevenson is cataloged in GMCP, box 477.

8. Robert Sam Anson, *McGovern: A Biography* (New York: Holt, Rinehart, and Winston, 1972), 69.

9. On Benson's unpopularity among corn-belt farmers, see Edward L. Schapsmeier and Frederick H. Schapsmeier, "Eisenhower and Ezra Taft Benson: Farm Policy in the 1950s," *Agricultural History* 44 (October 1970): 369–78.

10. Jon K. Lauck, *Prairie Republic: The Political Culture of Dakota Territory, 1879–1889* (Norman: University of Oklahoma Press, 2010), 178.

11. The descriptor *Judeo-Christian* is not ancient but caught on in the postwar years as a way of asserting a common American religiosity. See Kevin Kruse, *One Nation Under God: How Corporate American Invented Christian America* (New York: Basic Books, 2015).

12. "Christian Citizenship Responsibilities," October 25, 1964, GMCD, box 11, folder "Christian Citizenship Responsibilities."

13. Bruce Miroff, *The Liberals' Moment: The McGovern Insurgency and the Identity Crisis of the Democratic Party* (Lawrence: University of Kansas Press, 2007), 34.

14. Thomas J. Knock, *The Rise of a Prairie Statesman: The Life and Times of George McGovern* (Princeton: Princeton University Press, 2016), 167–68.

15. George McGovern, remarks in the US House of Representatives, *Congressional Record,* January 29, 1959, 1288.

16. On McGovern's use of this strategy, see Jon K. Lauck, "George McGovern and the Farmer: South Dakota Politics, 1953–1962," *South Dakota History* 32 (Winter 2002): 331–53.

17. George McGovern, remarks in the US House, *Congressional Record,* February 23, 1959, app. A1335.

18. George McGovern, "McGovern Says U.S. Has Great Weapon in Surplus Food," *Huron (SD) Plainsman,* November 20, 1957.

19. Anson, *McGovern,* 95.

20. George McGovern, letter to Arthur Link, November 18, 1960, ALC, box 47, folder "McGovern, George S."

21. For a colorful account of a fact-finding and goodwill trip to Latin America with McGovern, see Arthur Schlesinger Jr., *A Thousand Days: John F. Kennedy in the White House* (Boston: Houghton Mifflin, 1965), 165–85. See also Thomas J. Knock, "Feeding the World and Thwarting the Communists: George McGovern and Food for Peace," in *Architects of the American Century: Individuals and Institutions in Twentieth-Century U.S. Foreign Policymaking,* ed. David F. Schmitz and T. Christopher Jespersen (Chicago: Imprint, 1999), 98–120.

22. See George McGovern, *War Against Want: America's Food For Peace Program* (New York:

Walker, 1964); George McGovern, ed., *Agricultural Thought in the Twentieth Century* (Indianapolis: Bobbs-Merrill, 1967); and George McGovern, *The Third Freedom: Ending Hunger in Our Time* (New York: Simon and Schuster, 2001). On the religious dimensions of the struggle against food shortages, see George McGovern, Bob Dole, and Donald E. Messer, *Ending Hunger Now: A Challenge to Persons of Faith* (Minneapolis: Fortress, 2005).

23. Knock, *Rise of a Prairie Statesman*, 272.

24. Knock, "Feeding the World," 109.

25. Lillian Stewart, letter to George McGovern, February 27, 1961, GMCP, box 474, folder "Congrats: FFP."

26. George McGovern, letter to Lillian Stewart, April 15, 1961, ibid.

27. George McGovern, letter to Leland Case, July 17, 1961, GMCP, box 463, folder "Public Relations."

28. John F. Wood, letter to James W. Symington, July 7, 1961, ibid.

29. George McGovern, transcription of comments, October 5, 1969, GMCP, box 699, folder "Worldwide Communion Sunday, Interview for Publicity, Evanston, IL, October, 1969."

30. Theodore Palmquist, letter to George McGovern, January 13, 1961, GMCP, box 474, folder "Congrats: FFP."

31. Cameron Hall, letter to George McGovern, February 1961, GMCP, box 475, folder "Invitations, Feb. 1961."

32. Dulles's relationship with the NCC became more difficult as the organization turned to the left and began critiquing Eisenhower's heavy-handed foreign policy. See Charles F. Edmunson, "The Lord and John Foster Dulles," *Nation*, September 13, 1958, 131–33.

33. Ross Douthat, *Bad Religion: How We Became a Nation of Heretics* (New York: Free Press, 2012), 21.

34. Robert McAfee Brown, *Reflections over the Long Haul: A Memoir* (Louisville, KY: John Knox Press, 2005), 236.

35. This leftward turn is discussed in Henry J. Pratt, *The Liberalization of American Protestantism: A Case Study in Complex Organization* (Detroit: Wayne State University Press, 1972), 127–266.

36. John Adams, *Heart of the Whirlwind* (New York: Harper and Row, 1976), ix.

37. On the churches' efforts on behalf of civil rights, both as marchers and as lobbyists, see James F. Findlay Jr., *Church People in the Struggle: The National Council of Churches and the Black Freedom Movement* (New York: Oxford University Press, 1993).

38. "The Time Is Now to Heal Our Racial Brokenness," *Interchurch News*, June–July 1963, 6.

39. Brown, *Reflections over the Long Haul*, 100.

40. Carter Dalton Lyon, "Easter in Jackson, Mississippi, 1964," *Methodist History* 49 (January 2011): 99–115.

41. Findlay, *Church People in the Struggle*, 56.

42. These developments are traced, with measured criticism about their propriety and efficacy, in James L. Adams, *The Growing Church Lobby in Washington* (Grand Rapids, MI: Eerdmans, 1970). For contemporary accounts, see Robert W. Spike, *The Freedom Revolution and the Churches* (New York: Association Press, 1965); and Harvey Cox, "The 'New Breed' in American Churches: Sources of Social Activism in American Religion," in *Religion in America,* ed. Robert Bellah and William C. McLaughlin (Boston: Beacon, 1968).

43. Garry Wills, *Bare Ruined Choirs* (New York: Doubleday, 1971), 146–48.

44. See Luke Ebersole, *Church Lobbying in the Nation's Capital* (New York: Macmillan, 1951). By the 1950s, sixteen denominations had opened church offices, and their activities were coordinated through the Joint Washington Staff of Church Legislative Representatives. Presciently, Ebersole observed that "church lobbyists promote the causes in which groups of church leaders are interested rather than the views of church members in general" (100).

45. Adams, *Growing Church Lobby,* 210.

46. Quoted ibid., 24.

47. James K. Mathews, *A Global Odyssey: The Autobiography of James K. Mathews* (Nashville, TN: Abingdon, 2000), 291.

48. Adams, *Growing Church Lobby,* 210.

49. George McGovern, "The Christian in Politics: The New American," *Theology Today* 26 (September 1969): 410.

50. Quoted in George McGovern, "The Politics of Hunger," in *Congress and Conscience,* ed. John B. Anderson (New York: Lippincott, 1970), 55. The Bible quotes are, respectively, Matthew 25:41–45 and Isaiah 58:6–8, King James Version.

51. Ibid., 56.

52. John W. Meister, "Report from Uppsala," *Theology Today* 24 (October 1968): 286.

53. *Uppsala Speaks: Section Reports of the Fourth Assembly of the World Council of Churches, 1968* (Geneva: Friendship Press, 1968), 52.

54. M. M. Thomas, "Issues Concerning the Life and Work of the Church in a Revolutionary World," in *Unity of Mankind: Speeches from the Fourth Assembly of the World Council of Churches,* ed. Albert H. van den Heuvel (Geneva: World Council of Churches, 1969), 98.

55. Ibid., 80. King had been scheduled to be the opening speaker at Uppsala but was assassinated in April 1968.

56. George McGovern, telephone interview by author, July 28, 2009.

57. George McGovern, "Opening Statement by Senator George McGovern, Press Conference, World Council of Churches Fourth Assembly, Uppsala, Sweden, July 11, 1968," GMCP, box 693, folder "World Council of Churches Press Conference, Statement, July 11, 1968."

58. George McGovern, "Senator McGovern Reports," GMCP, box 477, folder "1968."

59. For a full account of the WCC's efforts to eradicate racism, particularly in South Africa, see Claude E. Welch Jr., "Mobilizing Morality: The World Council of Churches and Its Program to Combat Racism," *Human Rights Quarterly* 23 (November 2001): 863–910.

60. "Schedule, 1969," GMCP, box 502, folder "Schedules, 1969." Tambo had been invited to replace the keynote speaker, Eduardo Mondlane of Mozambique, who was assassinated in February 1969.

61. Quoted in Welch, "Mobilizing Morality," 876.

62. Quoted ibid., 878.

63. A. J. van der Bent, ed., *Breaking Down the Walls: World Council of Churches' Statements and Actions on Racism, 1948–1985* (Geneva: World Council of Churches Programme to Combat Racism, 1986), 36–37.

64. George McGovern, letter to J. Brooke Mosley, April 8, 1970, GMCP, box 492, folder "Personal correspondence: M, 1970."

4. Pastors, Public Men, and Peacemakers

1. James Armstrong, "Ernest Fremont Tittle and Courage" (speech), April 4, 1972, George Eberhardt Audio Collection; University Archives, Drew University Library, Madison, NJ.

2. For more on Coffin's career and influence, see Jessica Mitford, *The Trial of Dr. Spock, the Rev. William Sloane Coffin Jr., Michael Ferber, Mitchell Goodman, and Marcus Raskin* (New York: Knopf, 1969); William J. Carl, "Old Testament Prophecy and the Question of Prophetic Preaching: A Perspective on Ecclesial Protest to the Vietnam War and the Participation of William Sloane Coffin, Jr." (Ph.D. diss., University of Pittsburgh, 1977); Steven Paul Loy, "Find Something Worth Doing: The Preaching of William Sloane Coffin, Jr., 1977–1987: The Hermeneutics of Socially Responsible Homiletics" (Ph.D. diss., New Mexico State University, 2003); and Warren Goldstein, *William Sloane Coffin, Jr.: A Holy Impatience* (New Haven: Yale University Press, 2004). On the Berrigans, see William Van Etten Casey and Philip Nobile, *The Berrigans* (New York: Praeger, 1971); Jack Nelson and Ronald J. Ostrow, *The F.B.I. and the Berrigans: The Making of a Conspiracy* (New York: Coward, McCann, and Geoghegan, 1972); Stephen Halpert and Tom Murray, *Witness of*

the Berrigans (Garden City, NY: Doubleday, 1972); Anne Klejment, *As in a Vast School without Walls: Race in the Social Thought of the Berrigans* (Notre Dame, IN: University of Notre Dame Press, 1981); and Murray Polner and Jim O'Grady, *Disarmed and Dangerous: The Radical Lives of Daniel and Philip Berrigan* (Boulder, CO: Westview, 1998).

3. James Armstrong, *The Journey That Men Make* (Nashville, TN: Abingdon, 1969), 107. The italics are his.

4. The case for personalism in King's philosophies of social action is documented in Ervin Smith, "The Role of Personalism in the Development of the Social Ethics of Martin Luther King Jr." (Ph.D. diss., Northwestern University, 1976); Clayborne Carson, "Martin Luther King, Jr.: The Crozer Seminary Years," *Journal of Blacks in Higher Education* 16 (Summer 1997): 123–28; Warren E. Steinkraus, "Martin Luther King's Personalism and Nonviolence," *Journal of Ideas* 34 (January–March 1973): 97–111; Rufus Burrow Jr., *God and Human Dignity: The Personalism, Theology, and Ethics of Martin Luther King Jr.* (Notre Dame, IN: University of Notre Dame Press, 2006); and Kenneth L. Smith and Ira G. Zepp, *Search for the Beloved Community: The Thinking of Martin Luther King Jr.* (Valley Forge, PA: Judson, 1974).

5. James Armstrong, *The Public Servant and the Pastor* (Nashville, TN: Tidings, 1972), 84.

6. On the facts and fictions of the Smathers-Pepper primary campaign, see Hugh Douglas Price, "The Negro and Florida Politics, 1944–1954," *Journal of Politics* 17 (May 1955): 192–220; James C. Clark, "Claude Pepper and the Seeds of His 1950 Defeat, 1944–1948," *Florida Historical Quarterly* 74 (Summer 1995): 1–22; Brian Crispell, *Testing the Limits: George Armistead Smathers and Cold War America* (Athens: University of Georgia Press, 1999); Jonathan W. Bell, "Conceptualizing Southern Liberalism: Ideology and the Pepper-Smathers 1950 Primary in Florida," *Journal of American Studies* 37 (April 2003): 17–45; and Tracy Danese, *Claude Pepper and Ed Ball: Politics, Purpose, and Power* (Gainesville: University of Florida Press, 2000).

7. James Armstrong, interview by author, Casselberry, FL, February 5, 2009.

8. For a brief informal history of Broadway Methodist, see Paul Lahr, *This Is Broadway: 1873–1987* (Indianapolis: Broadway Methodist Church, 1987).

9. For contemporary observations and studies on this exodus to the suburbs, see Gibson Winter, *The Suburban Captivity of the Churches* (New York: Macmillan, 1962); Peter L. Berger, *The Noise of Solemn Assemblies* (New York: Doubleday, 1961); Pierre Burton, *The Comfortable Pew* (Toronto: McClelland and Stewart, 1965); and Harvey Cox, *The Secular City* (New York: Macmillan, 1965).

10. Robert Gildea, "The Church That Refuses to Die," *Together*, October 1967, 51.

11. Armstrong interview, 2009.

12. Gildea, "The Church That Refuses to Die," 51.

13. Armstrong, *The Public Servant and the Pastor*, 54.

14. The National Citizens' Committee for Community Relations had the difficult job of following up on the civil rights legislation of the mid-1960s. Its work is covered in Bertram J. Levine, *Resolving Racial Conflict: The Community Relations Service and Civil Rights, 1964–1989* (Columbia: University of Missouri Press, 2005).

15. James Armstrong, *Telling Truth: The Foolishness of Preaching in the Real World* (Waco, TX: Word Books, 1977), 101.

16. Armstrong, *The Public Servant and the Pastor*, 43. The italics are his.

17. On the history of the Board of Christian Social Concern and its ties to prophetic social witness, see Steven Tipton, *Public Pulpits: Methodists and Mainline Churches in the Moral Argument of Public Life* (Chicago: University of Chicago Press, 2007), 69–103. The board was also known for publishing strong critiques of militarism. For example, see Peter Davies, *The Truth about Kent State: A Challenge to the American Conscience and the Methodist Board of Church and Society* (New York: Farrar, Straus, 1973).

18. James Armstrong, *Feet of Clay on Solid Ground* (Charleston, SC: BookSurge, 2002), 58.

19. Armstrong interview, 2009.

20. James Armstrong, letter to George McGovern, October 26, 1971, GMCP, box 1117, folder "Armstrong–1971."
21. James Armstrong, "The Senate Race in Indiana," GMCP, box 493, folder "Personal: A–1970."
22. Armstrong interview, 2009.
23. James Armstrong, telephone interview by author, January 21, 2010.
24. Armstrong interview, 2009.
25. George McGovern, foreword, in *The Urgent Now*, by James Armstrong (Nashville, TN: Abingdon, 1970), 9.
26. Charles P. Henderson, "The [Social] Gospel According to 1. Richard Nixon, 2. George McGovern," *Commonweal*, September 29, 1972, 522.
27. George McGovern, letter to James Armstrong, October 14, 1970, AJA.
28. My information about the team's findings is from Mary Herschberger, *Traveling to Vietnam: American Peace Activists and the War* (Syracuse, NY: Syracuse University Press, 1998), 158.
29. Armstrong, *The Urgent Now*, 91.
30. Harvey Cox, telephone interview by author, June 17, 2015.
31. Armstrong, *The Urgent Now*, 98.
32. Armstrong, *Telling Truth*, 97.
33. Armstrong, *The Public Servant and the Preacher*, 16–17.
34. James Armstrong, "Is 'Peace' a Dirty Word?," *Engage*, June 1, 1970, 6–7.
35. Armstrong, *The Urgent Now*, 98.
36. Armstrong, *Mission: Middle America* (Nashville: Abingdon, 1971), 49.
37. The entire speech appears in George McGovern, *A Time for War, a Time for Peace* (New York: Random House, 1968), 48–60. McGovern's early reservations about Vietnam are documented in Thomas J. Knock, *The Rise of a Prairie Statesman: The Life and Times of George McGovern* (Princeton: Princeton University Press, 2016), 286–305.
38. McGovern discusses Fulbright's efforts to persuade him to vote for the Gulf of Tonkin Resolution in Robert Sam Anson, *McGovern: A Biography* (New York: Holt, Rinehart, and Winston, 1972), 152–54.
39. George McGovern, *Grassroots: The Autobiography of George McGovern* (New York: Random House, 1977), 104.
40. Quoted in Robert Mann, *A Grand Delusion: America's Descent into Vietnam* (New York: Basic Books, 2001), 368.
41. McGovern was particularly influenced by three of Bernard Fall's books: *Vietnam Witness, 1953–1966* (New York: Praeger, 1966); *The Two Viet-Nams: A Political and Military Analysis* (New York: Praeger, 1967); and *Hell Is a Very Small Place: The Siege of Dien Bien Phu* (Philadelphia: Lippincott, 1967).
42. George McGovern, "The Historian as Policy Analyst," *Public Historian* 11 (Spring 1989): 42.
43. McGovern, *Grassroots*, 104.
44. Ibid., 107.
45. George McGovern, "America in Vietnam," in *Vietnam: Four American Perspectives*, ed. Patrick J. Hearden (West Lafayette, IN: Purdue University Press, 1990), 24.
46. Quoted in Knock, *The Rise of a Prairie Statesman*, 351.
47. "Alternatives to Vietnam," *Christian Century*, March 10, 1965, 292.
48. Quoted in Jill K. Gill, *Embattled Ecumenism: The National Council of Churches, the Vietnam War, and the Trials of the Protestant Left* (DeKalb: Northern Illinois University Press, 2011), 100.
49. "Churches: Speaking Out on Foreign Policy" *Time*, July 30, 1965, 74.
50. "Goldwater? No!," *Christian Century*, July 1, 1964, 851.
51. Robert McAfee Brown, *Reflections over the Long Haul: A Memoir* (Louisville, KY: John Knox Press, 2005), 152.

52. The evolution of McGovern's opposition to the war is charted in Daryl Webb, "Crusade: George McGovern's Opposition to the Vietnam War," *South Dakota History* 28 (Fall 1998): 161–90.

53. Anson, *McGovern*, 165.

54. For more about white church leaders' tendency to borrow prophetic language from the black community, see Michael B. Friedland, *Lift Up Your Voice Like a Trumpet: White Clergy and the Civil Rights and Antiwar Movements, 1954–1973* (Chapel Hill: University of North Carolina Press, 1998).

55. Clergy and Laity Concerned about Vietnam (CALCAV), *In the Name of America* (Annandale, VA: Turnpike, 1968), 1–15.

56. See Tipton, *Public Pulpits*, 106–22.

57. Quoted in A. James Reichley, *Faith in Politics* (Washington, DC: Brookings Institute Press, 2002), 264.

58. Richard Lemon, *The Troubled American* (New York: Simon and Schuster, 1970), 59.

59. James L. Adams, *The Growing Church Lobby in Washington* (Grand Rapids, MI: Eerdmans, 1970), 208–9.

60. *Presbyterian Panel*, June 1974, 32–33.

61. John Wesley Lord, "After Vietnam, What?," *Together*, December 1972, 22.

62. Tom Wells, *The War Within: America's Battle over Vietnam* (Los Angeles: University of California Press, 1993), 228.

63. See Jack Newfield, *RFK: A Memoir* (New York: Nation Books, 2003), 186–88.

64. McGovern, *Grassroots*, 118.

65. Quoted in Gill, *Embattled Ecumenism*, 246.

66. William Sloane Coffin Jr., *Once to Every Man: A Memoir* (New York: Atheneum, 1977), 221, 4.

67. Michael Berkey, "M-Day: People and Peace and How," *[Boston College] Heights*, October 21, 1969, 4.

68. For an excellent contemporary consideration of the Moratorium and the Mobilization, see Francine Du Plessix Gray, "The Moratorium and the New Mobe," *New Yorker*, January 3, 1970, 32–34.

69. Melvin Small, *Johnson, Nixon, and the Doves* (New Brunswick, NJ: Rutgers University Press, 1988), 184.

70. This lineage is traced in Leilah Danielson, *American Gandhi: A. J. Muste and the History of Radicalism in the Twentieth Century* (Philadelphia: University of Pennsylvania Press, 2014).

71. Goldstein, *William Sloane Coffin, Jr.*, 251.

72. David N. Hollander and Carol R. Sternhall, "Boston: 100,000 Rally," *Harvard Crimson*, October 16, 1969, www.thecrimson.com.

73. Anson, *McGovern*, 170, 172.

74. William Sloane Coffin Jr., letter to George McGovern, March 10, 1969, GMCP, box 493, folder "McGovern, Personal, 1969."

75. Richard Nixon, "Address to the Nation on the War in Vietnam," speech, Washington, DC, November 3, 1969, www.nixonlibrary.gov.

76. Quoted in "How to Roast a Marshmallow," *Time*, May 17, 1970, 20.

77. On conceptualizing Nixon's Orthogonians as a metaphor for his career, see Rick Perlstein, *Nixonland: The Rise of a President and the Fracturing of America* (New York: Scribner, 2008).

78. Stephen Rose, "Eugene Carson Blake: A Welcome Home Interview," *Christian Century*, October 18, 1972, 1036–39.

79. "News from the Fellowship of Reconciliation," June 10, 1970, GMCP, box 705, folder "FOR Religious Press Conference on SE Asia and Thieu Government."

80. On Hatfield's role in promoting himself as the most prominent evangelical in American politics, see Robert Eells and Bartell Nyberg, *Lonely Walk: The Life of Senator Mark Hatfield* (Chappaqua, NY: Christian Herald Books, 1979); and Lon Fendall, *Stand Alone or Come*

Home: Mark Hatfield as an Evangelical and a Progressive (Newberg, OR: Barclay, 2008). On Hatfield's own musings about how his faith led him into a cautiously dovish version of Republicanism, see the following publications: "Can a Christian Be a Politician?," *HIS* 28 (October 1967): 1–5; *Conflict and Conscience* (Waco, TX: Word Books, 1971); *Between a Rock and a Hard Place* (Waco, TX: Word Books, 1976); and *Against the Grain: Reflections of a Rebel Republican* (Ashland, OR: White Cloud, 2001).

81. Wesley Granberg-Michaelson, *Unexpected Destinations: An Evangelical Pilgrimage to World Christianity* (Grand Rapids, MI: Eerdmans, 2011), 69.
82. Quoted in Mann, *A Grand Delusion,* 667.
83. George McGovern, speech before the US Senate, *Congressional Record,* September 1, 1970.
84. Quoted in Mann, *A Grand Delusion,* 667.
85. Armstrong, *Mission: Middle America,* 47.
86. Armstrong, *The Urgent Now,* 26.
87. George McGovern, "Vietnam Today: CALCAV," GMCP, box 696, folder "Vietnam Today: CALCAV, Washington DC, February 3, 1972."

5. Calling America to Come Home

1. See Rick Perlstein, *Before the Storm: Barry Goldwater and the Unmaking of the American Consensus* (New York: Hill and Wang, 2001).
2. Lowell Feld and Nate Wilcox, *Netroots Rising: How a Citizen Army of Bloggers and Online Activists Is Changing American Politics* (Westport, CT: Greenwood, 2008), 11–28.
3. I borrow the term *resident aliens* from Stanley Hauerwas and William H. Willimon, *Resident Aliens: Life in the Christian Colony* (Nashville, TN: Abingdon, 1990).
4. Gordon Weil, telephone interview by author, April 29, 2009.
5. Gary Dorrien, "Social Salvation: The Social Gospel as Theology and Economics," in *The Social Gospel Today,* ed. Christopher H. Evans (Louisville, KY: Westminster John Knox Press, 2001), 101.
6. Quoted in George McGovern, *The Essential America: Our Founders and the Liberal Tradition* (New York: Simon and Schuster, 2004), 69.
7. On the concept of anxiety as a guiding force in 1970s America, see Thomas Borstelmann, *The 1970s: A New Global History* (Princeton: Princeton University Press, 2011); Philip Jenkins, *Decade of Nightmares: The End of the Sixties and the Making of Eighties America* (New York: Oxford University Press, 2008); and Dominic Sandbrook, *Mad as Hell: The Crisis of the 1970s and the Rise of the Populist Right* (New York: Anchor, 2012).
8. For comprehensive accounts of the McGovern-Fraser Commission, see Bruce Miroff, *The Liberals' Moment: The McGovern Insurgency and the Identity Crisis of the Democratic Party* (Lawrence: University of Kansas Press, 2007), 19–23; and Byron Shafer, *Quiet Revolution: The Struggle for the Democratic Party and the Shaping of Post-Reform Politics* (New York: Russell Sage Foundation, 1983). Shafer calls the shift in delegate selection a "quiet revolution" of deep significance to American electoral politics (94). See also Denis G. Sullivan, Jeffrey Pressman, Benjamin I. Page, and John J. Lyons, *The Politics of Representation: The Democratic Convention, 1972* (New York: St. Martin's Press, 1974); and Austin Ranney, *Curing the Mischiefs of Faction: Party Reform in America* (Berkeley: University of California Press, 1975).
9. On McGovern's complicated relationship with minority movements, see Robert O. Self, *All in the Family: The Realignment of American Democracy since the 1960s* (New York: Hill and Wang, 2012), 248–75.
10. George McGovern, *Grassroots: The Autobiography of George McGovern* (New York: Random House, 1977), 154.
11. Mike Royko, "Poof Go the Democrats; Candidate with the Poofiest Hair Is Usually the Party's Nominee," *Orlando Sentinel,* October 4, 1991.

12. George McGovern, "The Announcement: A Journey Begins," *An American Journey: The Campaign Speeches of George McGovern* (New York: Random House, 1974), 6, 8, 5, 7.

13. Burton Carlson, "A Morality That Did Not Communicate," *Christian Century,* November 15, 1972, 1143–44.

14. "McGovern, Kennedy Draw Bigger Crowds, But . . . ?," *Christian Science Monitor,* September 15, 1972, 3.

15. "St. George Prepares to Face the Dragon," *Time,* July 24, 1972, 9.

16. Don Oberdorfer, "McGovern's Crusade," *Washington Post,* May 14, 1972.

17. Lloyd Shearer, "Senator George McGovern, First at the Starting Gate in the President Race," *Parade,* August 1, 1971, 16.

18. Robert Duffett, "The Gospel According to George McGovern," *Sojourners,* March 2014, http://sojo.net.

19. George McGovern, Bob Dole, and Donald E. Messer, *Ending Hunger Now: A Challenge to Persons of Faith* (Minneapolis: Augsburg Fortress, 2005), 33.

20. Miroff, *The Liberals' Moment,* 133–37.

21. Walter Rauschenbusch, *Christianity and the Social Order* (New York: Macmillan, 1907), 281.

22. Ted Van Dyk, *Heroes, Hacks, and Fools: Memoirs from the Political Inside* (Seattle: University of Washington Press, 2007), 133.

23. George McGovern, "Four Years and No Prosperity," in *An American Journey,* 162.

24. Charles P. Henderson, "The [Social] Gospel of George McGovern, Richard Nixon," *Commonweal,* September 29, 1972, 521.

25. Louis Cassels, "Of God and Man," *Terre Haute Tribune,* ESAW, box 1, folder "Clippings." Cassels's views on McGovern's faith were corroborated by my correspondence with James Armstrong.

26. George McGovern, "Christianity and Government Policies, Central Methodist Church, Atlanta, Georgia, March 14, 1971" GMCP, box 711, folder "Christianity and Government Policies, Central Methodist Church, Atlanta, Georgia, March 14, 1971."

27. George McGovern, "Political Participation: A Christian View" in *Toward a Discipline of Social Ethics: Essays in Honor of Walter George Muelder,* ed. Paul Deats (Boston: Boston University Press, 1972), 228, 230, 222.

28. George McGovern, "They, Too, Are Created in the Image of God," in *An American Journey,* 125.

29. George McGovern, "Remarks of Senator George McGovern, Keene State College, Keene, New Hampshire, January 18, 1972," GMCP, box 378, cassette 82.

30. For the story behind the Canuck letter, see Bob Woodward and Carl Bernstein, "FBI Finds Nixon Aides Sabotaged the Democrats," *Washington Post,* October 10, 1972.

31. See Jonathan Aitkin, *Charles W. Colson: A Life Redeemed* (Colorado Springs: Waterbrook, 2005), 175–81.

32. Understanding civil religion, in both its prophetic and priestly manifestations, was a key to understanding political rhetoric and its religious implications during this time. More recently, much of the intensity that surrounded the 1970s debates over civil religion has diminished. For thoughts on this idea beyond the scope of political elites, see Charles Wilson Reagan, *Judgment and Grace in Dixie: Southern Faiths from Faulkner to Elvis* (Athens: University of Georgia Press, 1995).

33. Martin Marty, "Two Kinds of Civil Religion," in *American Civil Religion,* ed. Russell E. Richey and Donald G. Jones (New York: Harper and Row, 1974), 140–53.

34. For an attempt to graft Marty's theory onto an understanding of the American presidency, see Richard Pierard and Robert D. Linder, *Civil Religion and the Presidency* (Grand Rapids, MI: Academie Books, 1988). I owe much to their assertion that "McGovern's prophetic civil religion with its accent on guilt, prodigality, and the need for America to 'come home' alienated much of the populace" (228). The historical use of the phrase "city upon a hill" is

covered in Richard M. Gamble, *In Search of the City on a Hill: The Making and Unmaking of an American Myth* (New York: Continuum / Bloomsbury Academic, 2012).

35. Robert D. Linder and Richard V. Pierard, *Twilight of the Saints: Biblical Christianity and Civil Religion in America* (Downers Grove, IL: Intervarsity Press, 1978), 21.

36. Marty, "Two Kinds of Civil Religion," 145.

37. Henderson, "The [Social] Gospel," 519.

38. Robert N. Bellah, "Civil Religion in America," *Daedalus* 96 (1967): 1–21.

39. Robert N. Bellah, "American Civil Religion in the 1970s," in Richey and Jones, *American Civil Religion*, 261.

40. See Charles P. Henderson, *The Nixon Theology* (New York: Harper and Row, 1972), 36. Henderson uses the term *folk theology* rather than *civil religion*, but the two ideas are all but identical.

41. Ibid., 39.

42. Accounts of Honor America Day appear in "Graham Deplores Distortion of Patriotism," *New York Times*, June 24, 1970; and "The Preaching and the Power," *Newsweek*, July 20, 1970, 50–55. For a study linking the event to civil religion, see Michael C. Thomas and Charles C. Flippen, "American Civil Religion: An Empirical Study," *Social Forces* 51 (December 1972): 218–25.

43. Marty, "Two Kinds of Civil Religion," 140–53.

44. Brent Gilchrist, *Cultus Americanus: Varieties of the Liberal Tradition in American Political Culture, 1600–1865* (Lanham, MD: Lexington, 2006), 47.

45. McGovern, "Christianity and Government Policies."

46. Henderson, "The [Social] Gospel," 524.

47. Weil interview, 2009.

48. In 1970, McGovern made more money delivering speeches than did any other sitting senator, with the exception of his most immediate rival for the 1972 nomination, Edmund Muskie.

49. George McGovern, remarks, GMCP, box 699, folder "Stanford University Memorial Church, Vietnam / Hunger Moratorium, Stanford CA, October 5, 1969." The hymn was written by Edward Rowland Sill, who was influenced by the Romantic poets and inclined to view religion skeptically and scientifically. As its words suggest, he saw religion in terms of transcendental truth rather than faith. See Alfred Riggs Ferguson, *Edward Sill: The Twilight Poet* (The Hague: Martinus Nijhoff, 1955).

50. George McGovern, "Statement by George McGovern, Meeting of Grand Rapids Clergy, November 3, 1972" GMCP, box 730, folder "Statement by Senator George McGovern, Meeting of Grand Rapids Clergy, November 3, 1972."

51. McGovern, "Christianity and Government Policies."

52. Like McGovern, this hymn, written by John Haynes Holmes, was rooted in the broadly liberal theological tradition. Holmes was a Unitarian minister who also was a strong advocate for organized labor. He argued that socialism was the line of political thought that came closest to the teachings of Christ. Like McGovern, he traced much of his social ethos to the Old Testament prophets, and he vocally opposed a military conflict—in his case World War I. See Holmes's *I Speak for Myself: The Autobiography of John Haynes Holmes* (New York: Harper, 1959). See also Robert W. Lawson, "A Survey of Unitarian Pacifism during the Years of the Great War" (M.Div. thesis, Meadville Theological School, 1940); and Carl Hermann Voss, *Rabbi and Minister: The Friendship of Stephen S. Wise and John Haynes Holmes* (Cleveland: World Publishing Company, 1964).

53. Henderson, "The [Social] Gospel," 518.

54. George McGovern, "Remarks of Senator George McGovern, Berlin, New Hampshire, May 11, 1972," GMCP, box 751, folder "Remarks of Senator George McGovern, Berlin, New Hampshire, May 11, 1972."

55. Alfred F. Young, letter to George McGovern, June 27, 1972, GMCP, box 329, folder "June,

1972." Young was a noted historian of the American Revolution and the Early Republic, often studying political revolution through a labor or artisanal perspective. See his *Dissent: Explorations in the History of American Radicalism* (DeKalb: Northern Illinois University Press, 1968); *The Shoemaker and the Tea Party: Memory and the American Revolution* (Boston: Beacon, 1999); and *Liberty Tree: Ordinary People and the American Revolution* (New York: New York University Press, 2006).

56. Gary Hart, *Right from the Start: A Chronicle of the McGovern Campaign* (New York: New York Times Books, 1973), 29.

57. George McGovern, "Making the System Serve Humanity," GMCP, box 705, folder "'Making the System Serve Humanity,' Colby College, Waterville, ME, June 7, 1970."

58. George McGovern, "November 14, 1971 letter," GMCP, box 329, folder "January, 1972."

59. George McGovern, *The Essential America: Our Founders and the Liberal Tradition* (New York: Simon and Schuster, 2004), 10. For insight on the hymn, see Bernard F. Donahue, "The Political Use of Religious Symbols: A Case Study of the 1972 Presidential Campaign," *Review of Politics* 37 (January 1975): 49. Its author, William Lamartine Thompson, was a noted evangelical hymnist. Its stress on sin and on personal choice to renounce that sin reinforces its evangelical origins and explains its usefulness to McGovern.

60. "The McGoverns, NET TV Hour, July 24, 1972, Reel 113," GMCP, box 821, folder "McGovern for President Committee." According to Anthony Lewis ("The Wallace Factor," *New York Times*, October 16, 1972), Democrats for Nixon vice-chair Leo Churne accused McGovern of isolationism. For this reason, McGovern focused on reframing "come home, America" as more than a dovish foreign policy; he wanted to inspire other countries by committing to a better human rights record and more socially democratic values.

61. Walter R. Mears, *Deadlines Past: Forty Years of Presidential Campaigning: A Reporter's Story* (Kansas City, MO: McMeel, 2003), 112. O'Neill had been a solid supporter of Muskie, a fellow New England Catholic, during the 1972 primaries.

62. Van Dyk, *Heroes, Hacks, and Fools,* 136.

63. George McGovern, "The Acceptance Speech," in *An American Journey,* 23. In that volume, McGovern edited the sentence reading "from military spending so wasteful that it weakens our nation" to read "from a conflict in Indochina which maims our ideals as well as our soldiers." See George McGovern, "Address Accepting the Presidential Nomination at the Democratic National Convention in Miami Beach, Florida," July 14, 1972. *The American Presidency Project,* www.presidency.ucsb.edu.

64. Ibid. McGovern's vision of the past as expressed in this speech notably declined to critique American policies that took place before the postwar era. Tribe removal, slavery, and early twentieth-century imperialism are all missing, as is any reference to the massacre at Wounded Knee, which took place in his own home state.

65. Robert Sam Anson, *McGovern: A Biography* (New York: Holt, Rinehart, and Winston, 1972), 282.

66. Kenneth R. Libbey, "The McGovern Campaign: A Grassroots Postmortem," GMCP, box 4, folder "Eagleton."

67. Donahue, "The Political Use of Religious Symbols," 52.

68. This electoral shift is covered in Steve Gillon, *The Democrats' Dilemma: Walter F. Mondale and the Liberal Legacy* (New York: Columbia University Press, 1992); H. W. Brands, *The Strange Death of American Liberalism* (New Haven: Yale University Press, 2001); and David G. Lawrence, *The Collapse of the Democratic Presidential Majority: Realignment, Dealignment, and the Electoral Change from Franklin Roosevelt to Bill Clinton* (Boulder, CO: Westview, 1996), 47–51.

69. For early discussions of the disillusion among these voters, see Kevin Phillips, *The Emerging Republican Majority* (New Rochelle, NY: Arlington House, 1969); and Ben Wattenberg and Richard Scammon, *The Real Majority* (New York: Coward, McCann, and Geoghegan, 1970).

70. For recollections of the implications on Democratic fortunes in Illinois and among blue-collar workers more generally, see William Schneider, "An Insider's View on the Election," *Atlantic Monthly,* July 1988, 29–57.

71. Quoted in Self, *All in the Family,* 250. As Jefferson R. Cowie points out, however, labor had more representation overall at the 1972 Democratic National Convention than it did at the 1968 convention; the only difference was that there were fewer Daley men in attendance in Miami. See Jefferson R. Cowie, *Stayin' Alive: The 1970s and the Last Days of the Working Class* (New York: The New Press, 2010), 105–10.

72. Amy Sullivan, *The Party Faithful: How and Why Democrats Are Closing the God Gap* (New York: Scribner, 2008), 51.

73. McGovern's frantic, last-minute attempts to procure a suitable running mate are traced, with varying degrees of comedy, in Hart, *Right from the Start,* 238–45; McGovern, *Grassroots,* 190–202; and Gordon Weil, *The Long Shot: George McGovern Runs for President* (New York: Norton, 1973), 156–72.

74. Milton Viorst, "Did Tom Eagleton Do Anything Wrong?," *Esquire,* February 1973, 63.

75. Ibid.

76. Robert Shrum, *No Excuses: Concessions of a Serial Campaigner* (New York: Simon and Schuster, 2007), 44.

77. On Eagleton's history of mental illness, see Joshua Glasser, *The Eighteen-Day Running Mate: McGovern, Eagleton, and a Campaign in Crisis* (New Haven: Yale University Press, 2012), 59–63, 131–71.

78. Weil interview, 2009.

79. George McGovern, *Terry: My Daughter's Life and Death Struggle with Alcoholism* (New York: Villard, 1996), 96.

80. Quoted in Miroff, *The Liberals' Moment,* 92.

81. Quoted in Viorst, "Did Tom Eagleton Do Anything Wrong?," 149.

82. George McGovern, "Confidential Note on the Eagleton Affair," GMCD, box 4, folder "Eagleton."

83. "A Crisis Named Eagleton," *Newsweek,* August 7, 1972, 13.

84. Haynes Johnson, "Nixon Best on Image," *Washington Post,* September 14, 1972.

85. "The Voters: Nixon Moves Out to an Astonishing Lead," *Time,* October 2, 1972, 14, 13–14.

86. Van Dyk, *Heroes, Hacks, and Fools,* 144. Van Dyk misstated the location of the child's birth certificate, writing that it was in Terre Haute, not Fort Wayne. He also wrote that she was conceived when McGovern was in the air force, not as an undergraduate.

87. Bob Woodward and Carl Bernstein, "Leak Involving McGovern Proposed," *Washington Post,* August 2, 1973.

88. I borrow this suggestion from Christopher H. Evans, *Social Gospel Liberalism and the Ministry of Ernest Fremont Tittle: A Theology for the Middle Class* (Lewiston, NY: Mellen University Press, 1996), 15. For more on how that moral authority became compromised during the 1960s and 1970s, see Harold Quinley, *The Prophetic Clergy: Social Activism Among Protestant Ministers* (New York: Wiley, 1974); Mitchell Hall, *Because of Their Faith: CALCAV and Religious Opposition to the Vietnam War* (New York: Columbia University Press, 1990); and Douglas Jacobsen and William Vance Trollinger Jr., ed., *Reforming the Center: American Protestantism, 1990 to the Present* (Grand Rapids, MI: Eerdmans, 1998).

89. "God May Be a Democrat: But the Vote Is for Nixon," *Time,* October 30, 1972, 23.

90. David A. Gerber, "The Fate of the Righteous Style in Precinct 20: The 1972 McGovern Campaign in a Buffalo Neighborhood," *New York History* 80 (October 1999): 469.

91. Quoted in Peter N. Carroll, *It Seemed Like Nothing Happened: The Tragedy and Promise of American in the 1970s* (New York: Holt, Rinehart, and Winston, 1982), 70. As a reflection of McGovern's poor performance among labor unions during the election, owing partly to the defection of George Meany into Nixon's camp, partly to McGovern's own positions and language. He lost a staggering 54 percent of the union vote, usually a bedrock of the Democratic constituency.

92. "Toppling the Titans," *Time,* July 24, 1972, 25.
93. George McGovern, "The Concession: A Journey Ends," in *An American Journey,* 42.

6. Religious Leaders for McGovern

1. Edwin S. Gaustad, "Pulpit and Pews" in *Between the Times: The Travail of the Protestant Establishment in America, 1900–60,* ed. William R. Hutchison (New York: Cambridge University Press, 1989), 21.
2. For a succinct summary, see Jill K. Gill, "Peace Is Not the Absence of War, but the Presence of Justice: The National Council of Churches' Reaction and Response to the Vietnam War, 1965–1972" (Ph.D. diss., University of Pennsylvania, 1996), vii.
3. Ross Douthat, *Bad Religion: How We Became a Nation of Heretics* (New York: Free Press, 2012), 59.
4. James L. Adams, *The Growing Church Lobby in Washington* (Grand Rapids, MI: Eerdmans, 1970), viii, 244.
5. Robert Booth Fowler, *Unconventional Partners: Religion and Liberal Culture in the United States* (Grand Rapids, MI: Eerdmans, 1989), 89.
6. Elliot Wright, "Methodist Publishing House Ordered to Pay Taxes," *New England Churchman,* January 1972, 5.
7. James Armstrong, *The Urgent Now* (Nashville, TN: Abingdon, 1970), 129.
8. Quoted in Mitchell K. Hall, *Because of Their Faith: CALCAV and Religious Opposition to the Vietnam War* (New York: Columbia University Press, 1990), 57.
9. George W. Cornell, "Church Leaders Active in Politics," *Lakeland (FL) Ledger,* September 30, 1972.
10. James Armstrong, undated manuscript, GMCP, box 1117, folder "Armstrong, James, 1971." The document appears to have been originally published in *Texas Methodist,* November 26, 1971.
11. Virtie Stroup, "Churchmen Will Back McGovern," *Winston-Salem Journal,* November 22, 1971.
12. Sam R. Covington, "Religious Leaders Promoting McGovern's Candidacy," *Charlotte Observer,* November 12, 1971.
13. Religious Leaders for McGovern, undated press release, AJA.
14. See Mark Hulsether, *Building a Protestant Left: Christianity and Crisis Magazine, 1941–1993* (Knoxville: University of Tennessee Press, 1999), 24–48, 114–34.
15. For an argument in favor of Muskie's candor and sense of civic education, see Joel K. Goldstein, "The Ed Muskie Brand of Leadership," *Huffington Post,* March 28, 2014.
16. James Armstrong, letter to Harvey Cox, November 23, 1971, GMCP, box 1117, folder "Armstrong, James, 1971."
17. Religious Leaders for McGovern, undated press release, AJA.
18. Abraham Joshua Heschel, letter to the editor, *New York Times,* October 27, 1972.
19. Religious Leaders for McGovern, memo, June 5, 1972, GMCP, box 229, folder "Correspondence, 1971."
20. "Mary's Little Lamb's [*sic*] Make Bids for Peace," *Dayton Daily News,* July 30, 1972.
21. Religious Leaders for McGovern, "It's a Moral Issue" mailing, undated, AJA.
22. In 1960, there was an entrenched effort among Protestants to direct their flocks toward Nixon rather than the Catholic Kennedy. See Shaun Casey, *Making of a Catholic President: Kennedy vs. Nixon* (New York: Oxford University Press, 2009), 81–100.
23. Michael McIntyre, letter to James Armstrong and Joseph Glaser, December 20, 1972, AJA.
24. James Armstrong, interview by author, Casselberry, FL, February 5, 2009.
25. Randall Balmer, *Grant Us Courage: Travels along the Mainline of Protestant America* (New York: Oxford University Press, 1996), 18.
26. James Armstrong, telephone interview by author, January 21, 2010.

27. James Armstrong, "Ernest Fremont Tittle and Courage" (speech), April 4, 1972, George Eberhardt Audio Collection; University Archives, Drew University Library, Madison, NJ.
28. Armstrong, *The Urgent Now*, 119. The italics are his.
29. Georgia Harkness, letter to James Armstrong, September 21, 1971, AJA.
30. Rebekah Miles, *Georgia Harkness: The Remaking of a Liberal Theologian* (Louisville, KY: Westminster John Knox Press, 2010), 17.
31. Helen Chase [secretary of Krister Stendahl], letter to James Armstrong, September 27, 1971, AJA.
32. James E. Bell, "Filling a Need," *Christian Century*, March 21, 1971, 505.
33. This office arrangement involved a degree of irony. Initially, the churches had enthusiastically supported Shriver after Johnson had assigned him to the directorship of the Office of Economic Opportunity, which focused on combating domestic poverty. See Adams, *The Growing Church Lobby*, 44–63.
34. Rich Eychaner, telephone interview by author, May 5, 2009.
35. Dolores Moseke, telephone interview, January 19, 2010.
36. McIntyre, letter to Armstrong and Glaser.
37. James Armstrong, letter to George McGovern, October 26, 1971, GMCP, box 1117, folder "Armstrong, James, 1971."
38. Gary Hart, letter to James Armstrong, December 6, 1971, GMCP, box 1117, folder "Armstrong, 1971."
39. Harvey Cox, telephone interview by author, June 17, 2015.
40. William A. McWhirtier, "The Preacher's Son," *Life*, April 21, 1972, 60.
41. Mark Wheeler, *Celebrity Politics* (Boston: Polity, 2013), 48.
42. James Armstrong, "Clear Choice on the Issues," *Engage*, October 1972, 17.
43. Armstrong, letter to McGovern, October 26, 1971.
44. James Armstrong, letter to Jacob Kiefer, January 27, 1972, GMCP, box 1919, folder "Personal Correspondence: A, 1972."
45. Bosley was Tittle's first successor at First Methodist Church in Evanston after Tittle's death in 1949.
46. On McGovern's difficulties in persuading Jewish voters to support him, see Bruce Miroff, *The Liberals' Moment: The McGovern Insurgency and the Identity Crisis of the Democratic Party* (Lawrence: University of Kansas Press, 2007), 194–96.
47. James Armstrong, letter to Harold Bosley, June 26, 1972, GMCP, box 1919, folder "Personal Correspondence: A, 1972."
48. James Armstrong, letter to George McGovern and Eleanor McGovern, June 23, 1972, GMCP, box 1919, folder "Personal Correspondence: A, 1972."
49. Henry J. Pratt, *The Liberalization of American Protestantism: A Case Study in Complex Organization* (Detroit: Wayne University Press, 1972), 154.
50. "A Brave Man Chooses," *Christian Century*, February 24, 1971, 243.
51. James D. Fairbanks and John Francis Burke, "Religious Periodicals and Presidential Elections, 1960–1988," *Presidential Studies Quarterly* 22 (Winter 1992): 95.
52. George W. Cornell, "Religious Factors May Affect Election," *Free-Lance Star* (Fredericksburg, VA), September 30, 1972.
53. James Armstrong, addendum to a letter to George McGovern, January 5, 1972, GMCP, box 1919, folder "Personal, A, 1972."
54. George M. Ricker, "All the Church Does Is Ask for Money," *Together*, March 1972, 28.
55. For an early indication of this trend, see Allan R. Brockway, "Political Factions in the United Methodist Church," *Engage*, October 1970, 4–8.
56. Cornish Rogers, "The Methodists at Atlanta," *Christian Century*, May 17, 1972, 566.
57. Dick Johnson, "Conference and Caucus," *Engage*, March 1972, 3.
58. "Suffering Ecumenical Cats," *Christian Century*, February 11, 1970, 163.
59. Allan R. Brockway, "Political Factions in the United Methodist Church," *Engage*, October 1970, 8.

60. Albert Wildrick, "Letters," *Together*, July 1972, 46.
61. Clarence W. Hall, "Must Our Churches Finance Revolution?," *Reader's Digest*, October 1971, 1–6.
62. A. James Richey, *Religion in America Public Life* (Washington: Brookings Institute, 1985), 278.
63. Harold Quinley, *The Prophetic Clergy: Social Activism among Protestant Ministers* (New York: Wiley, 1974), 2, 8.
64. Dean M. Kelley, *Why Conservative Churches Are Growing: A Study in Sociology of Religion* (New York: Harper and Row, 1972), vii.
65. Elesha Coffman, *The Christian Century and the Rise of the Protestant Mainline* (New York: Oxford University Press, 2013), 217.
66. Michael McIntyre, "Religionists on the Campaign Trail," *Christian Century*, December 27, 1972, 1320.
67. James Armstrong, *Wilderness Voices* (Nashville, TN: Abingdon, 1974), 149.
68. Ibid., 40.

7. Evangelicals for McGovern

1. Martin Marty is widely credited as the first scholar to discuss the divisions within these two branches. See his *Righteous Empire* (New York: Dial, 1970).
2. Tony Campolo, *Can Mainline Denominations Make a Comeback?* (Valley Forge, PA: Judson, 1995), 8.
3. Randall Balmer, *Grant Us Courage: Travels along the Mainline of Protestant America* (New York: Oxford University Press, 1996), 4.
4. On this dichotomy, see Jean Miller Schmidt, *Souls or the Social Order: The Two-Party System in American Protestantism* (Brooklyn: Carlson, 1991). For an argument about blurrier lines between the mainline and evangelical camps, see Douglas Jacobsen and William Vance Trollinger Jr., *Reforming the Center: American Protestantism, 1900 to the Present* (Grand Rapids, MI: Eerdmans, 1998).
5. The authoritative text on the developments and reactions of American fundamentalism is George Marsden, *Fundamentalism and American Culture* (New York: Oxford University Press, 2006). For more recent work on the dynamism and resilience of fundamentalism, see Christopher Rios, *After the Monkey Trial: Evangelical Scientists and a New Creationism* (New York: Fordham University Press, 2014); Matthew Bowman, *The Urban Pulpit: New York City and the Fate of Liberal Evangelism* (New York: Oxford University Press, 2014); and Randall Stephens, "It Has to Come from the Hearts of the People: Fundamentalists, Race, and the 1964 Civil Rights Act," *Journal of American Studies* (June 2015): 1–27. Priscilla Pope-Levison challenges the idea that fundamentalists did not engage in social action during their split from modernism. See her *Building the Old Time Religion: Women Evangelists in the Progressive Era* (New York: New York University Press, 2015).
6. For an early history of *Christianity Today*, see Daryl Alan Porter, "*Christianity Today*: Its History and Development, 1956–1978" (M.T. thesis, Dallas Theological Seminary, 1978).
7. For evangelical and fundamentalist castigations of the NCC and the WCC, see Billy James Hargis, *The National Council of Churches Indicts Itself on Fifty Counts of Treason Against God and Country* (Tulsa, OK: Christian Crusade, 1964); American Council of Christian Churches, Laymen's Commission, *How Red Is the National Council of Churches?* (Madison, WI: American Council of Christian Laymen, 1996); Edgar Bundy, *Collectivism in the Churches: A Documented Account of the Political Activities of the Federal, National, and World Council of Churches* (Wheaton, IL: Church League of America, 1958); James DeForest Murch, *The Protestant Revolt: Road to Freedom for American Churches* (Arlington, VA: Crestwood, 1967); G. Russell Evans, *Apathy, Apostasy and Apostles: A Study of the History and Activity of the National Council of Churches of Christ of the USA with Sidelights on its Ally, the World Council of Churches* (New York: Vintage, 1973); and K. L. Billingsley, *From*

Mainline to Sideline: The Social Witness of the National Council of Churches (Lanham, MD: University Press of America, 1990).

8. These wealthy backers included the oil mogul J. Howard Pew. On his role in funding *Christianity Today,* see Michael Joseph McVicar, *Christian Reconstruction: R. J. Rushdoony and American Religious Conservatism* (Chapel Hill: University of North Carolina Press, 2015), 113–23. On the role of corporatism in modern evangelism, see Kevin Kruse, *One Nation under God: How Corporate America Invented Christian America* (New York: Basic Books, 2015); Sarah Hammond, "God's Business Men: Entrepreneurial Evangelicals in Depression and War" (Ph.D. diss., Yale University, 2010); and Timothy Gloege, *Guaranteed Pure: The Moody Bible Institute, Business, and the Making of Modern Evangelicalism* (Chapel Hill: University of North Carolina Press, 2015).

9. For a prominent example of this line of Graham's thought, see "Here Is Text of Graham's Saturday Night Sermon," *Charlotte Observer,* September 28, 1958.

10. On the degree to which both the United States and the Soviet Union viewed themselves as messianic nations (and on Graham's role in American messianism), see Jay Douglas Learned, "Billy Graham, American Evangelicalism, and the Cold War Clash of Messianic Visions, 1945–1962" (Ph.D. diss., University of Rochester, 2012).

11. Quoted in Michael Long, *Billy Graham and the Beloved Community* (New York: Palgrave, 2006), 21.

12. Steven P. Miller, *Billy Graham and the Rise of the Republican South* (Philadelphia: University of Pennsylvania Press, 2009), 3.

13. John C. Cooper, "The Revival of the Conservative Spirit in America," *Christianity Today,* October 9, 1964, 7.

14. Michael Harrington, *The Other America: Poverty in the United States* (New York: Macmillan, 1962); and Harry M. Caudill, *Night Comes to the Cumberlands: A Biography of a Depressed Area* (Boston: Little, Brown, 1963).

15. Judy Alexander, "The Other Side," *Other Side,* July–August 1972, 46.

16. Fred Alexander, "Evangelism," *Other Side,* March–April 1972, 3.

17. I owe this insight to David Swartz, "Left Behind: The Evangelical Left and the Limits of Evangelical Politics, 1965–1988" (Ph.D. diss., Notre Dame University, 2008), 29. He argues that attempts to collect disparate denominational and theological traditions under a common banner of evangelicalism were only marginally successful and were often overstated in triumphalist evangelical narratives.

18. Richard Mouw, *The Smell of Sawdust: What Evangelicals Can Learn from Their Fundamentalist Heritage* (Grand Rapids, MI: Zondervan, 2000), 36.

19. Richard Pierard, telephone interview by author, January 13, 2009.

20. Boyd T. Reese Jr. notes a bifurcation in the dissident evangelical magazines of the early 1970s, between the merely liberal (such as the *Reformed Journal*) and the truly radical (such as *Post-American,* later known as *Sojourners*). See his "Resistance and Hope: The Interplay of Theological Synthesis, Biblical Interpretation, Politics Analysis and Praxis in the Christian Radicalism of *Sojourners* Magazine" (Ph.D. diss., Temple University, 1990).

21. Lester DeKoster, "Man and State in the Teaching of Calvin," *Reformed Journal,* April 1965, 27. DeKoster's later work reconsidered his generally positive view of the welfare state in favor of a stronger defense of free enterprise. See Lester DeKoster and Gerard Berghoef, *Liberation Theology: The Church's Future Shock* (Grand Rapids, MI: Christian's Library, 1984)

22. Richard Mouw, telephone interview by author, December 18, 2008. Michael G. Long's *Billy Graham and the Beloved Community* (New York: Palgrave Macmillan, 2006) is sympathetic toward the titular community but offers measured criticism of Graham, characterizing his professions of friendship with King after the latter's death as largely self-serving revisionism.

23. Richard Mouw, "The Vietnam Moratorium, 1969," *Reformed Journal,* February 1970, 8.

24. Jim Wallis, *Revive Us Again: A Sojourner's Story* (Nashville, TN: Abingdon, 1983), 73.

25. John Alexander, "The Old Testament in Today's Society," *Other Side,* May–June 1970, 3.

26. Arthur Gish, *The New Left and Christian Radicalism* (Grand Rapids, MI: Eerdmans, 1970), 111.

27. Lewis Smedes, "Peace and Moratorium," *Reformed Journal,* December 1969, 3.

28. "Culture and Counterculture," *Christianity Today,* April 28, 1972, 25.

29. "Billy Graham: On Calley," *New York Times,* April 9, 1971.

30. Joe Roos, "American Civil Religion," *Post-American,* Spring 1972, 9.

31. Jim Wallis, *The Great Awakening: Reviving Faith and Politics in a Post-Religious Right America* (New York: HarperOne, 2008), 53.

32. Wallis, *Revive Us Again,* 57.

33. Jason Bivins groups the *Post-American* community with that of the radical antiwar Berrigan brothers and the home-schooling movement on the grounds that each is opposed to a bureaucratic and administrative state. All three, he maintains, used systematic critiques to prioritize the local community. The correlation between the *Post-American/Sojourners* group and EFM, however, forces some reconsideration of the compromises they were willing to make with American liberalism under optimal conditions and in support of leaders such as McGovern, who generally shared their aims. See Bivins's *The Fracture of Good Order: Christian Antiliberalism and the Challenge to American Politics* (Chapel Hill: University of North Carolina Press, 2003).

34. Jim Wallis, "Post-American Christianity," *Post-American,* Fall 1971, 2.

35. Jim Wallis, "Airwar!," *Post-American,* Spring 1972, 4.

36. Jim Wallis, "Evangelicals in Babylon," *Post-American,* Summer 1972, 8.

37. Accounts of Honor America Day appeared in "Graham Deplores Distortion of Patriotism," *New York Times,* June 24, 1970; and "The Preaching and the Power," *Newsweek,* July 20, 1970, 53. For a contemporary study linking the event to civil religion, see Michael C. Thomas and Charles C. Flippen, "American Civil Religion: An Empirical Study," *Social Forces* 51 (December 1972): 218–25.

38. See Martin Van Eldren, "Explo '72 and Campus Crusade," *Reformed Journal,* July–August 1972, 16; and Wallis, *Revive Us Again,* 83.

39. Roos, "American Civil Religion," 9.

40. Richard Pierard, *The Unequal Yoke: Evangelical Christianity and Political Conservatism* (New York: Lippincott, 1970), 52.

41. Edwin Walhout, "The Pattern of God's Acts," *Reformed Journal,* February 1973, 6.

42. Wesley Pippert, *Memo for 1976: Some Political Options* (Downers Grove, IL: InterVarsity, 1974): 59.

43. There is a substantive body of feminist critiques against the language of the Old Testament prophets. They argue that the same prophets who inspired EFM tended to viciously castigate rich women while doing comparatively little to champion poor and needy ones. For example, see Julia M. O'Brien, *Challenging Prophetic Metaphor: Theology and Ideology in the Prophets* (Louisville, KY: Westminster John Knox Press, 2008).

44. R. Laird Harris, "The Message of the Prophets Today," *Other Side,* May–June 1970, 16.

45. Nicholas Wolterstorff, telephone interview by author, May 5, 2009.

46. John Alexander, "Prophets and Politicians: Some Biblical Guidelines," *Other Side,* September–October 1972, 3.

47. David O. Moberg, *The Great Reversal: Evangelicalism versus Social Concern* (Philadelphia: Lippincott, 1972), 40.

48. Jim Wallis, "The Issue of 1972," *Post-American,* Fall 1972, 3.

49. Richard Pierard, letter to W. T. Miller, November 15, 1972, ESAW, box 1, folder 6.

50. Moberg, *The Great Reversal,* 38.

51. Wallis, "The Issue of 1972," 3.

52. H. H. Claassen, "Shift to Civil Crises Needed," *Wheaton Record,* October 20, 1972, 6.

53. Richard Pierard, "Is Richard Nixon Still a Conservative?," *Other Side,* September–October 1972, 42.

54. David O. Moberg, telephone interview by author, January 29, 2009.

55. Hatfield's chief aide during this time, Wes Granberg-Michaelson, shared his evangelical faith and was an early subscriber to *Post-American.* In a telephone interview (May 23, 2009), Granberg-Michaelson discussed bringing *Post-American* to Hatfield's attention during its first year of publication. The senator was elated to learn that other Christians opposed the war for scriptural reasons and soon became a contributor and an editor. Ironically, his involvement gave the deeply anti-establishment magazine a strong ally in Washington, DC.

56. Mark O. Hatfield, "Remarks at the National Prayer Breakfast," *Christian Century,* February 1, 1973, 221.

57. Pippert, *Memo for 1976,* 14.

58. Nick Wolterstorff, "McGovern at Wheaton," *Reformed Journal,* November 1972, 4.

59. Wolterstorff interview, 2009.

60. Wolterstorff, "McGovern at Wheaton," 4.

61. "The Evangelical Vote," *Newsweek,* October 30, 1972, 93.

62. Pierard interview, 2009. Pierard wrote many years later that both McGovern and Nixon had used civil religion. However, a crucial distinction was that "Nixon's message was one of comfort and national affirmation, while McGovern challenged people to recognize they had sinned and were in need of redemption." See Richard Pierard and Robert Linder, *Civil Religion and the Presidency* (Grand Rapids, MI: Academie Books, 1988), 228.

63. See Ronald Sider, "Karlstadt's Orlamunde Theology: A Theology of Regeneration," *Mennonite Quarterly Review* (July–October 1971): 352–76.

64. For an argument that Sider's theology was a radical rather than a reformist or liberal development in the history of Christian theology, see Jeffrey McClain Jones, "Ronald Sider and Radical Evangelical Political Theology" (Ph.D. diss., Northwestern University, 1990). Sider provides a view of his own theological background in the most intensely personal of his books, *Good News and Good Works: A Theology for the Whole Gospel* (Grand Rapids, MI: Baker, 1993), 18–26.

65. Ronald J. Sider, interview by author, Wynnewood, PA, March 24, 2009.

66. For a summary of this movement, see Richard Quebedeaux, *The Worldly Evangelicals* (San Francisco: Harper and Row, 1978), 96–97.

67. See Tom Skinner and Fred Basher, *At Last I'm Free to Live: The True Story of Tom Skinner* (Seattle: Life Messengers, 1968.)

68. Walden Howard, circular letter, ESAW, box 1, folder 2.

69. Sider interview, 2009.

70. Stephen Monsma, telephone interview by author, January 14, 2009.

71. William Harper, telephone interview by author, January 9, 2009.

72. Pierard interview, 2009.

73. Jim Wallis, telephone interview by author, July 14, 2015.

74. Quoted in "Honoring Billy Graham," *Charlotte News,* October 19, 1971.

75. Quoted in "*Christianity Today* Editor Sees Most Evangelicals Backing Nixon," *Religious News Service,* October 17, 1972.

76. Howard, circular letter.

77. "The Evangelical Vote," 93.

78. Richard Pierard, letter to W. T. Miller, November 17, 1972, ESAW, box 1, folder 2.

79. Mouw interview, 2008.

80. For more on these feminist and gay groups, see Bruce Miroff, *The Democrats' Dilemma: The McGovern Insurgency and the Identity Crisis of the Democratic Party* (Lawrence: University of Kansas Press, 2007), 202–18. Ronald Alheim formed Gay Citizens for McGovern, the first group of gay citizens to openly endorse a presidential candidate, and the National Women's Political Caucus also gave McGovern a good deal of support.

81. Howard, circular letter.

82. James Daane, "On the Stoning of Prophets," *Reformed Journal,* February 1972, 5.

83. Alexander, "Prophets and Politicians," 56.

84. W. T. Miller, letter to Evangelicals for McGovern, November 8, 1972, ESAW, box 1, folder 2.

85. Lynne Burrier, letter to Walden Howard, October 31, 1972, ESAP.

86. Henry W. Coray, letter to Evangelicals for McGovern, October 21, 1972, ESAP.

87. Albert J. Menendez, *Evangelicals at the Ballot Box* (Amherst, NY: Prometheus, 1996), 126.

88. E. M., "The Monkey Show and Billy," *U.S. Farm News* 20, no. 8 (1972): 4.

89. "Born to Be President," *Associated Press,* November 3, 1972.

90. Harold Ockenga, "McGovern vs. Nixon," *Hamilton-Wenham (MA) Chronicle,* November 2, 1972.

91. Richard Pierard, "Is Evangelism Awakening from Its Social Slumber?," April 13, 1973, 24, Calvin College Archives, Grand Rapids, MI, box 474, folder 3.

92. Daane, "On the Stoning of Prophets," 3.

93. Richard Mouw, "Evangelicals and Political Activism," *Christian Century,* December 27, 1972, 1316.

94. Ronald J. Sider, circular letter, November 14, 1972, ESAW, box 1, folder 5.

95. Quoted in Joel Fetzer and Gretchen S. Carnes, "Dr. Ron Sider, Mennonite Environmentalist on the Evangelical Left," in *Religious Leaders and Faith-Based Politics: Ten Profiles,* ed. Jo Renee Formicola and Hubert Morken (Lanham, MD: Rowman and Littlefield, 2001), 160.

96. Clark Pinnock, "Election Reflections," *Post-American,* January–February 1973, 2.

8. The Christian Left's Failure to Launch

1. Gordon Weil, telephone interview by author, April 29, 2009.

2. [Wes Michaelson], "George McGovern and the Evangelical Constituency," GMCP, box 329, folder "1972."

3. Jim Wallis, "The George McGovern I Remember," *Huffington Post,* October 26, 2012, www.huffingtonpost.com.

4. Martin J. Medhurst, "McGovern at Wheaton: A Quest for Redemption," *Communication Quarterly* 25 (Autumn 1977): 32–39.

5. James Armstrong, email message, March 29, 2011. While Armstrong and McGovern were visiting together, Armstrong relayed one of my questions to the senator and forwarded me his response.

6. Wesley Granberg-Michaelson, *Unexpected Destinations: An Evangelical Pilgrimage to World Christianity* (Grand Rapids, MI: Eerdmans, 2011), 75.

7. Randall Balmer, *Thy Kingdom Come: Thy Kingdom Come: How the Religious Right Distorts Faith and Threatens America* (New York: Basic Books, 2006), xiii.

8. Ronald Sider, interview by author, Wynnewood, PA, March 24, 2009.

9. David Malone, "The Race for the White House," *ReCollections,* October 29, 2008, http://recollections.liblog.wheaton.edu.

10. Duncan Spencer, "McGovern Preaches, Goes to Daley Lunch," *Evening Star and Daily News* (Washington, DC), October 12, 1972.

11. John Holum, telephone interview by author, April 9, 2010.

12. Wesley Granberg-Michaelson, telephone interview by author, May 23, 2009.

13. Holum interview, 2010.

14. Wesley Pippert, telephone interview by author, April 6, 2009.

15. Richard Dougherty, *Goodbye, Mr. Christian: A Personal Account of McGovern's Rise and Fall* (New York: Doubleday, 1973), 204–8.

16. David Moberg, telephone interview by author, January 29, 2009.

17. Sider interview, 2009; Richard Mouw, telephone interview by author, December 18, 2008. Sider and Wallis were familiar with one another's work long before this meeting.

18. Granberg-Michaelson interview, 2009.

19. Jim Wallis, telephone interview by author, July 14, 2015.

20. Wesley Pippert, "U.P.I. Writing, Not Transmitted," WPP, box IVB2, folder "McGovern, Religious."

21. Donald W. Dayton was aware of these changes and would articulate them four years later in *Discovering an Evangelical Heritage* (New York: Harper and Row, 1976). Also see Timothy L. Smith, *Revivalism and Social Reform: American Protestantism on the Eve of Civil War* (New York: Harper and Row, 1957); and David Moberg, *The Great Reversal: Evangelicalism vs. Social Concern* (Philadelphia: Lippincott, 1972), which emphasize the historic capacity of evangelical Christianity to reinforce spiritual faith with the creation of a more perfect society unburdened by endemic social problems.

22. Wallis, "The George McGovern I Remember."

23. Tom Skinner's best-known book, *How Black Is the Gospel?* (Philadelphia: Lippincott, 1970), skewers affluent, suburban-friendly practices in American Christianity.

24. Tom Skinner, introduction, in George McGovern, "Sources of Our Strength," speech, Wheaton College, October 13, 1972, WCA, CD-29.

25. Wallis interview, 2015.

26. Pippert, "U.P.I. Writing, Not Transmitted."

27. McGovern's mispronunciation was brought to my attention during the Mouw interview, 2008. Audio recordings of the speech confirm Mouw's recollection.

28. McGovern, "Sources of Our Strength."

29. Ibid.

30. Arthur Holmes, "Evangelicals, Morality and Politics," *Reformed Journal,* November 1972, 3. By "ghosts of the theological past," the author likely meant the fundamentalist-modernist controversies of the early 1900s.

31. McGovern, "Sources of Our Strength."

32. H. Richard Niebuhr, *The Kingdom of God in America* (New York: Harper and Row, 1937), 193.

33. Spencer, "McGovern Preaches, Goes to Daley Lunch."

34. Balmer, *Thy Kingdom Come,* xxv.

35. Wallis interview, 2015.

36. See George McGovern, *An American Journey: The Presidential Campaign Speeches of George McGovern* (New York: Random House, 1974), 205–12.

37. Pippert interview, 2009.

38. Spencer, 1972.

39. Sider interview, 2009.

40. Michael McIntyre, "Religionists on the Campaign Trail," *Christian Century,* December 27, 1972, 1319.

41. Richard Quebedeaux, *The Young Evangelicals: Revolution in Orthodoxy* (New York: Harper and Row, 1974), 5.

42. Richard G. Hutcheson, *Mainline Churches and the Evangelicals: A Challenging Crisis* (Atlanta: John Knox Press, 1984), 26.

43. See James Smylie, "Church Growth and Decline in Historical Perspective," in *Understanding Church Growth and Decline, 1950–1978,* ed. Dean Hoge and David Roozen, (New York: Pilgrim, 1979), 76–82. For arguments that the social gospel was particularly well suited to the hegemony of the middle class, see Christopher H. Evans, *Social Gospel Liberalism and the Ministry of Ernest F. Tittle* (Lewiston, NY: Mellen University Press, 1996); and *The Kingdom Is Always but Coming: A Life of Walter Rauschenbusch* (Grand Rapids, MI: Eerdmans, 2004).

44. Martin Marty, *Righteous Empire* (New York: Dial, 1970), 246.

45. Reinhold Niebuhr, "Editorial Notes," *Christianity and Crisis,* March 5, 1956, 8–9. For a much later assessment of Graham, one that castigates his association with Nixon, see Niebuhr's "The King's Chapel and the King's Court," *Christianity and Crisis,* August 4, 1969, 211–13.

46. John Opie Jr., "The Modernity of Fundamentalism," *Christian Century*, May 12, 1965, 610.

47. Bernard Eugene Meland, "Modern Protestantism: Aimless or Resurgent?," *Christian Century*, December 4, 1963, 1494.

48. Stephen Monsma, telephone interview by author, January 14, 2009.

49. Marlin Van Eldren, "Evangelicals and Liberals: Is There Common Ground?," *Christianity and Crisis*, July 8, 1974, 154.

50. Monsma interview, 2009.

51. David Moberg, letter to Ronald Sider, August 20, 1973, ESAW, box 1, folder 2.

52. Richard Mouw, *Political Evangelism* (Grand Rapids, MI: Eerdmans, 1973), 8.

53. Ronald Sider, letter to David Moberg et al., March 19, 1973, ESAW, box 1, folder 11.

54. Ibid.

55. Mouw interview, 2008.

56. Ronald Sider, "Spirituality and Social Concern," *Other Side*, September–October 1973, 9.

57. Jim Wallis, *The Great Awakening: Seven Ways to Change the World* (New York: HarperOne, 2009), 15.

58. David R. Swartz, *Moral Minority: The Evangelical Left in an Age of Conservatism* (Philadelphia: University of Pennsylvania Press, 2012), 170–84; Robert Booth Fowler, *A New Engagement: Evangelical Political Thought, 1966–1976* (Grand Rapids, MI: Eerdmans, 1982), 95–101.

59. Sider, letter to Moberg et al., March 19, 1973.

60. Ronald Sider, "A National Congress on Biblical Faith and Social Concern," ESAW, box 1, folder 8.

61. John Yoder, "The Biblical Mandate," November 23, 1973, ESAW, box 2, folder 1.

62. Sider, letter to Moberg et al., March 19, 1973. Interestingly, this warning was at odds with his earlier prediction that theological liberalism was in irreparable decline.

63. Sider, "A National Congress."

64. Handwritten note, undated, ESAW, box 2, folder 1.

65. Although the YMCA had strong evangelical roots, its work in the cities during the twentieth century was chiefly a manifestation of the social gospel. See Charles Howard Hopkins, *History of the Y.M.C.A. in North America* (New York: Association Press, 1951); Mayer M. Zald and Patricia Denton, "From Evangelism to General Service: The Transformation of the YMCA," *Administrative Science Quarterly* 8 (September 1963): 213–33; and Nina Mjagkij and Margaret Spratt, *Men and Women Adrift: The Y.M.C.A. and the Y.W.C.A. in the City* (New York: New York University Press, 1997). For a compelling account of the organization's activities overseas (and an example of a "Pacific crossing" of the social gospel), see Jun Xing, *Baptized in the Fire of Revolution: The Social Gospel and the YMCA in China, 1919–1937* (Cranbury, NJ: Associated University Presses, 1996).

66. Mouw interview, 2008.

67. Sider, "A National Congress."

68. Draft of "Our Situation," ESAW, box 2, folder 8.

69. Richard Pierard, editorial comments, ibid.

70. Nancy Hardesty, editorial comments, ibid.

71. "Worship: Evangelicals and Social Concern, Thanksgiving Workshop, November 25, 1973," ESAW, box 2, folder 1.

72. Ronald Sider, ed., *The Chicago Declaration* (Carol Stream, IL: Creation House, 1974).

73. Jim Wallis, "Putting Flesh on Words: A Report on the Calvin Conference on Christianity and Politics," *Post-American*, May 1974, 23.

74. Paul Jewett, "Why I Won't Sign," *Reformed Journal*, May–June 1974, 8–9.

75. Wesley Pippert, "Ten Years Late," *Christianity Today*, January 18, 1974, 26.

76. "Evangelicals on Justice," *Christianity Today*, December 21, 1972, 38.

77. Roy Larsen, "Evangelicals Do U-Turn, Take on Social Problems," *Chicago Sun-Times*, December 1, 1973. See also Alma Kaufman, "Evangelicals Get Cue on Social Concerns," *Cleveland Plain Dealer*, December 1, 1973.

78. See Joel Carpenter, "Compassionate Evangelicalism," *Christianity Today,* December 2003, 40–43; and Amy Sullivan, *The Party Faithful: How and Why Democrats Are Closing the God Gap* (New York: Scribner, 2008), 14–15.

79. Michael McIntyre, "Selected Themes in Preparation for an Evaluation of the Bishop's Call for Peace and the Self Development of Peoples" (D.Min. thesis, Wesley Theological Seminary, 1978), 76.

80. James Robert Ross, "Evangelicals and Social Concern: A Report on the Chicago Thanksgiving Workshop," *Christian Standard,* February 3, 1974.

9. Becoming Sojourners

1. Jim Wallis, *Revive Us Again: A Sojourner's Story* (Nashville, TN: Abingdon, 1983), 109.

2. Jim Wallis, "Sojourners," *Sojourners,* October 1975, 3.

3. James Armstrong, *Wilderness Voices* (Nashville, TN: Abingdon, 1974), 149.

4. For an argument that the decade's reputation as a depressing quagmire ignored more subterranean dynamism, see Peter Carroll, *It Seemed Like Nothing Happened: The Tragedy and Promise of America in the 1970s* (New York: Holt, Rinehart, and Winston, 1982). On the decade's growing conservatism, see Bruce J. Schulman and Julian E. Zelizer, eds., *Rightward Bound: Making America Conservative in the 1970s* (Cambridge: Harvard University Press, 2008). On the interplay of electoral politics and growing working-class rage, see Jefferson Cowie, *Stayin' Alive: The 1970s and the Last Days of the American Working Class* (New York: New Press, 2010); and Rick Perlstein, *Nixonland: The Rise of a President and the Fracturing of America* (New York: Scribner, 2008). On cynicism and a loss of faith in prevailing 1970s cultural and political institutions, see David Frum, *How We Got Here: The 1970s, the Decade That Brought You Modern Life—for Better or Worse* (New York: Basic Books, 2000). On the decade as a dystopia, see Philip Jenkins, *Decade of Nightmares: The End of the Sixties and the Making of Eighties America* (New York: Oxford University Press, 2006). For more a more optimistic view, see Edward Berkowitz, *Something Happened: A Political and Cultural Overview of the 1970s* (New York: Columbia University Press, 2006); and Robert O. Self, *All in the Family: The Realignment of American Democracy since the 1960s* (New York: Hill and Wang, 2012).

5. Tom Wolfe, "The Me Decade and the Third Great Awakening," *New York,* August 23, 1976, 26–40.

6. See Donald Critchlow, *Phyllis Schlafly and Grassroots Conservatism: One Woman's Crusade* (Princeton: Princeton University Press, 2005); and Adam Winkler, *Gunfight: The Battle over the Right to Bear Arms in America* (New York: Norton, 2011), 45–94.

7. *Network,* directed by Sidney Lumet (1976; Burbank, CA: Warner Home Video 2000, DVD).

8. George McGovern, "American Politics: A Personal View," in *An American Journey: The Campaign Speeches of George McGovern* (New York: Random House, 1974), 232.

9. On the nature of failure in presidential elections, see Scott Farris *Almost President: The Men Who Lost the Race but Changed the Nation* (Guilford, CT: Lyons, 2012), 1–19.

10. For a comparative exploration of the careers of Goldwater and McGovern and their long-term significance to American politics, see Jeffrey J. Volle, *The Political Legacies of Barry Goldwater and George McGovern: Shifting Party Paradigms* (New York: Palgrave Macmillan, 2010).

11. George McGovern, "A Good Friend," *Washington Post,* June 14, 1998.

12. James Wall, "Politics and Morality: A Postelection Interview with George McGovern," *Christian Century,* January 31, 1973, 122.

13. James Armstrong, interview by author, Casselberry, FL, May 5, 2009. Also see George McGovern, "Can Good News Come from Watergate?," *Christian Century,* July 4, 1973, 724–25.

14. Details of the Kissinger-McGovern meeting as well as their subsequent correspondence are in GMCD, box 5, folder "Kissinger, Henry."

15. See Richard Pierard, "Can Billy Graham Survive Richard Nixon?," *Reformed Journal,* April 19, 1974, 7–13. Also see Steven P. Miller, *Billy Graham and the Rise of the Republican South* (Philadelphia: University of Pennsylvania Press, 2009), 184–94. Miller argues that Graham passed through three stages in his response to Watergate: first, he denied its significance; then he used it to demonstrate the universality of sin; and finally he announced his negative view of Nixon's character, at one point maintaining that Christians had not prayed enough for him. In his largely favorable study of Graham's political activities ("Modern Mordecai: Billy Graham in the Political Arena, 1948–1980" [Ph.D. diss., Ohio University, 1999]), even Eric Paddon criticizes Graham's reaction to Watergate (262–68).

16. George McGovern, telephone interview by author, July 28, 2009.

17. See Jon K. Lauck, *Daschle vs. Thune: Anatomy of a High-Plains Senate Race* (Norman: University of Oklahoma Press, 2007).

18. Quoted in Ira Shapiro, *The Last Great Senate: Courage and Statesmanship in Times of Crisis* (New York: Public Affairs, 2012), 73.

19. Henry Kimelman, letter to George McGovern, September 9, 1975, GMCD, box 4, folder "Election, 1976."

20. George McGovern, interview by author, Mitchell, SD, September 22, 2008. Also see George McGovern, *Grassroots: The Autobiography of George McGovern* (New York: Random House, 1977), 260–62.

21. See Robert Shrum, *No Excuses: Concessions of a Serial Campaigner* (New York: Simon and Schuster, 2007), 62–67. Shrum remembers that McGovern was so serious about running in 1976 that he was reluctant to free him to write speeches for Carter. When Shrum finally did join Carter's staff, he quit after one week because he felt that the candidate's moderate policies were bloodless and self-serving.

22. George McGovern, letter to James Armstrong, October 31, 1975, GMCP, box 502, folder "Personal: A, 1975."

23. McGovern did not reveal his vote until after Ford's death, during an interview with Larry King. See "Farewell to President Ford," *CNN Larry King Live,* January 2, 2007, http://transcripts.cnn.com.

24. McGovern, "Can Good News Come from Watergate?," 724.

25. Quoted in "The New Right: The Politics of Negativism in South Dakota" (memo), 1, 6, GMCD, box 6, folder "The New Right."

26. Life Amendment Political Action Committee, pamphlets, GMCD, box 6, folder "The New Right."

27. "From the Office of McGovern: Abdnor/NCPAC Association Charged—Complaint on Possible Violation of Federal Election Laws Filed with Federal Election Commission," GMCD, box 6, folder "Dolan, John."

28. Americans for Life, "Stop the Baby Killers," GMCD, box 6, folder "Life Amendment PAC."

29. Life Amendment Political Action Committee, "Devils Incarnate," GMCD, box 6, folder "Life Amendment PAC."

30. Life Amendment Political Action Committee, "Why I as a Christian Cannot Vote for McGovern," GMCD, box 6, folder "Life Amendment PAC."

31. Chuck Lane, "Gone but Not Forgotten: Good Soldiers," *Harvard Crimson,* October 22, 1981.

32. Stephen F. Hayward, *The Age of Reagan: The Fall of the Liberal Order* (New York: Prima, 2001), 713.

33. George McGovern, letter to Leonard Nemmers, December 18, 1980, GMCD, box 6, folder "Nemmers Letter."

34. Ira Shapiro, "The Year the Senate Fell," *New York Times,* January 7, 2010.

35. Quoted in James Armstrong, *Telling Truth: The Foolishness of Preaching in the Real World* (Waco, TX: Word Life Books, 1977), 111–12.

36. Only one work has seriously considered the churches' role in mediating the conflict: Jill K. Gill, "Preventing a Second Massacre at Wounded Knee, 1973: United Methodists Mediate for Peace," *Methodist History* 93 (October 2004): 45–56. For an evangelical, and critical, perspective of the events, see Barne Doyle, "Bury My Tithe at Wounded Knee," *Christianity Today,* June 8, 1973, 40–41.

37. See John P. Adams, *At the Heart of the Whirlwind* (New York: Harper and Row, 1976); and his "Wounded Knee, 1973: A Journal," *American Report,* June 18, 1973, 9–11. For the perspective of an AIM member who dealt frequently with the NCC officials, see Dennis Banks, "Consciousness Raising," *Engage,* January 1975, 37–39.

38. "The Church: Reasserting Its Interest in the Indians," *Harvard Crimson,* April 11, 1973.

39. Rolland Dewing, *Wounded Knee: The Meaning and Significance of the Second Incident* (New York: Irvington, 1985), 149.

40. Armstrong interview, 2009.

41. After passing a resolution that simply called for better education for Native Americans and a reconsideration of tribal treaties, the Episcopal Church was deluged by parishioners' criticisms. See Dewing, *Wounded Knee,* 149.

42. Adams, *At the Heart of the Whirlwind,* 131.

43. Quoted in Dewing, *Wounded Knee,* 56.

44. James Armstrong, "Dear Friends," *Sturgis Tribune,* April 18, 1973.

45. Russell Dilley, "Standoff at Wounded Knee," *Christian Century,* May 9, 1973, 527–28.

46. Rolland Dewing, "South Dakota Newspaper Coverage of the 1973 Occupation of Wounded Knee," *South Dakota History* 12 (Spring 1982): 54. Dewing's work is a crucial window into how the white citizens of South Dakota interpreted the Wounded Knee hostilities. For a journalistic view of the television coverage, see Neil Hickey, "Was the Truth Buried at Wounded Knee?: An Inquest into a Political Confrontation in Which Television Was the Primary Weapon," *TV Guide,* December 1, 1973, 7–8, 10, 12.

47. G. Richard Hutcheson, *Mainline Churches and the Evangelicals: A Challenging Crisis* (Atlanta: John Knox Press, 1984), 144.

48. James Armstrong, *From the Underside: Evangelism from a Third World Vantage Point* (Maryknoll, NY: Orbis, 1981), 65–66, 69.

49. James Armstrong, "A Conversation with Castro," *Christian Century,* August 31, 1977, 743.

50. Michael Disend, "Have You Whipped Your Child Today?," *Penthouse,* February 13, 1983, 59–64, 182–87. On the Moral Majority's efforts to discredit Armstrong and defeat Bayh, see Richard Pierard and James L. Wright, "No Hoosier Hospitality for Humanism: The Moral Majority in Indiana," in *New Christian Politics,* ed. David G. Bromley and Anson Shupe (Macon, GA: Mercer University Press, 1984), 195–212.

51. James Armstrong, "Election Aftermath," *Christian Century,* December 5, 1980, 1182.

52. Ibid.

53. Armstrong interview, 2009.

54. Rael Jean Isaac, "Do You Know Where Your Church Funds Are Going?," *Reader's Digest,* January 1983, 124. On the conservatism of *Reader's Digest,* see J. P. Sharpe, *Condensing the Cold War: Reader's Digest and American Identity* (Minneapolis: University of Minnesota Press, 2000).

55. Armstrong interview, 2009.

56. "The Gospel According to Whom?," *60 Minutes,* January 23, 1983, transcript courtesy of the CBS News Archives.

57. Charles Austin, "National Council of Churches Disavows Charges of Extremism," *New York Times News Service,* November 22, 1982.

58. "60 Minutes Disputed," *Christian Century,* February 2, 1983, 88.

59. James Wall, "The True Shame of IRD as Informant," *Christian Century,* February 2, 1983, 139. For a more recent mainline defense, see Stephen Swecker, ed., *Hardball on Holy*

Ground: The Religious Right vs. the Mainline for the Church's Soul (North Berwick, ME: Boston Wesleyan Association, 2005).

60. "Armstrong Urges Action," *Christian Century,* March 16, 1983, 240.

61. "Are Churches Too Political?," *Firing Line,* September 24, 1982, transcript courtesy of Stanford University.

62. James Armstrong, *Feet of Clay on Solid Ground* (Charleston, SC: BookSurge, 2002), 1–7. He chose to open his autobiography with the biggest public mistake of his career.

63. "Armstrong Resigns," *Christian Century,* November 30, 1983, 1104.

64. *Newsweek,* October 25, 1976.

65. Jim Wallis, *The Call to Conversion* (San Francisco: Harper and Row, 1981), 7. He was probably oblivious to any gay overtones in his "closet" metaphor.

66. See Robert Linder and Richard Pierard, *Politics: A Case for Christian Action* (Downers Grove, IL: Intervarsity, 1973); Paul B. Henry, *Politics for Evangelicals* (Valley Forge, PA: Judson, 1974); Richard Mouw, *Political Evangelism* (Grand Rapids, MI: Eerdmans, 1973); Ronald Sider, *Rich Christians in an Age of Hunger: A Biblical Study* (Downers Grove, IL: Intervarsity, 1977); John Yoder, *The Politics of Jesus: Vicit Agnus Noster* (Grand Rapids, MI: Eerdmans, 1972); and Jim Wallis, *Agenda for a Biblical People* (San Francisco: Harper and Row, 1976).

67. Brantley Gasaway, *Progressive Evangelicals and the Pursuit of Social Justice* (Chapel Hill: University of North Carolina Press, 2014), 53–74.

68. Doris Longacre, *More-with-Less Cookbook* (Scottdale, PA: Herald, 1976). On the cookbook's relevance in the larger evangelical movement, see David Swartz, *Moral Minority: The Evangelical Left in an Age of Conservatism* (Philadelphia: University of Pennsylvania Press, 2012), 160–67.

69. Cheryl Forbes, "Doing the Declaration," *Christianity Today,* December 20, 1974, 28–29.

70. Pamela D. H. Cochran, *Evangelical Feminism: A History* (New York: New York University Press, 2005), 11–32.

71. "Chicago Crisis," *Christianity Today,* October 10, 1975, 69.

72. For overviews of evangelical conservatism, see William Martin, *With God on Our Side: The Rise of the Religious Right in America* (New York: Broadway Books, 1996); and Daniel K. Williams, *God's Own Party: The Making of the Christian Right* (New York: Oxford University Press, 2010). For a study showing that evangelicals rarely addressed abortion prior to *Roe v. Wade,* see Randall Balmer, *Thy Kingdom Come: How the Religious Right Distorts the Faith and Threatens America: An Evangelical's Lament* (New York: Basic Books, 2006). For more conventional histories that trace Christian politics through the Moral Majority and the Christian Coalition, see Erling Jorstad, *The Politics of Moralism: The New Christian Right in American Life* (Minneapolis: Augsburg, 1981); and Clyde Wilcox, *Onward Christian Soldiers: The Religious Right in American Politics* (Boulder, CO: Westview, 1996). For studies of the rise of the religious Right as a social force, see Michael Lienchsch, *Redeeming America: Piety and Politics in the New Christian Right* (Chapel Hill: University of North Carolina Press, 1993); and D. Michael Lindsay, *Faith in the Halls of Power: How Evangelicals Joined the American Elite* (New York: Oxford University Press, 2007). On the role of geography, see Darren Dochuk, *From Bible Belt to Sun Belt: Grassroots Politics and the Rise of Evangelical Conservatism* (New York: Norton, 2011). On the rise of conservatism in general and insights into its religious dynamics, see Jerome Himmelstein, *To the Right: The Transformation of American Conservatism* (Los Angeles: University of California Press, 1990); and Godfrey Hodgson, *The World Turned Right Side Up: A History of the Conservative Ascendancy in America* (Boston: Houghton Mifflin, 1996). Although all of these works trace conservative Christian activism, they limit the role played by the many evangelicals who did not agree with the militarism and free-market ethos that dominated that view.

73. Wallis, *Agenda for a Biblical People,* 72.

74. Richard Pierard, editorial, *Sojourners,* January 1981, 39.

75. Jim Wallis, "Coming Together on the Sanctity of Life," *Sojourners,* November 1980, 4.
76. Ronald Sider, *Completely Pro-Life: Building a Consistent Stance* (Downers Grove, IL: Inter-Varsity, 1987).
77. With the important exception of John Alexander and a few other members of the floundering *The Other Side* magazine, twentieth-century progressive evangelicals rarely endorsed same-sex relationships. Alexander's opinions on the matter severely curtailed evangelical support of his magazine. See Gasaway, *Progressive Evangelicals,* 163–99.
78. Richard Quebedeaux, *The Worldly Evangelicals* (San Francisco: Harper and Row, 1978), 136.
79. Jim Rice, "Peace Pentecost," *Sojourners,* May 1982, 3.
80. Michael Leahy, "What Might Have Been: In Which George McGovern, the Senior Member of a Rare and Burdened Tribe, Reveals Just How Long It Takes to Get Over Losing the Presidency," *Washington Post,* February 20, 2005.

Conclusion

1. "Opening Remarks by George McGovern at 1/29 Forum in Dubuque," GMCD, box 4, folder "Election, 1984."
2. Quoted in Barbara J. Keys, *Reclaiming American Virtue: The Human Rights Revolution of the 1970s* (Cambridge: Harvard University Press, 2014), 72.
3. Jim Wallis, telephone interview by author, July 14, 2015.
4. Michelle Bortstein, "At United Methodist Building, a Meeting of Prayer and Politics," *Washington Post,* July 22, 2011.
5. Matthew 16:25, King James Version.
6. Donald Miller, *Blue Like Jazz: Nonreligious Thoughts on Christian Spirituality,* (Nashville: T. Nelson, 2003).
7. Tobin Grant, "InterVarsity Backs #BlackLivesMatter at Urbana 15," *Religion News Service Online,* December 29, 2015, http://religionnews.com.
8. Rachel Held Evans, "7 Ways to Welcome Young People to the Mainline," *Rachel Held Evans,* May 7, 2015, http://rachelheldevans.com.
9. Diana Butler Bass, "Can Christianity Be Saved? A Response to Ross Douthat," *Huffington Post,* July 15, 2012, www.huffingtonpost.com.
10. "Here We Stand: An Evangelical Declaration on Marriage," *Christianity Today,* June 6, 2015, www.christianitytoday.com.
11. Wallis interview, 2015.
12. George McGovern, Robert Dole, and Donald E. Messer, *Ending Hunger Now: A Challenge to Persons of Faith* (Minneapolis: Augsburg Fortress, 2005), 27–33.
13. "2008: Dole and McGovern," *World Food Prize,* www.worldfoodprize.org.
14. George McGovern, *Terry: My Daughter's Life-and-Death Struggle with Alcoholism* (New York: Villard, 1996).
15. Cal Thomas and Ed Dobson, *Blinded by Might: Why the Religious Right Can't Save America* (Grand Rapids, MI: Zondervan, 2009), 209.

Index

MARK A. LEMPKE grew up in the Adirondack foothills of upstate New York. He attended Houghton College for his bachelor's degree and completed a PhD in history at the State University of New York at Buffalo. Currently, he teaches at the University at Buffalo's campus in Singapore, located at the Singapore Institute of Management. When home in the United States, he and his wife, Heather, live in Rochester, New York.